The Cooperative State

The Case for Employee Ownership on a National Scale

By Tom Winters

2022 Edition

Introduction

The average person will spend over 90,000 hours of their life at work. Most of us will accept that going to work is simply a part of life, a necessary activity we must all take part in to get the things we need and want. Some of us will be lucky enough to enjoy our profession and others will dread it, yearning instead for their 'dream job'. We are brought up to respect the hierarchies of the workplace. We are accountable to our bosses, who are accountable to their bosses and so on. If we challenge those hierarchies, or under-perform in our roles and responsibilities, we can expect not to remain in our roles for very long. On the other hand, if we work hard and display loyalty, we should, in time, expect to receive promotions and pay rises. Employment is not for everyone though. Some of us may instead start our own business, and if successful, employ our own members of staff. This too takes hard work and dedication, but the added risk can lead to higher rewards. Many of us will go about our daily lives with unquestioning allegiance to these basic principles of work and reward, for none of us, it is argued, can expect something for nothing.

This all may sound sensible enough, but underneath these apparently just and common sense principles lies a series of contradictions and unstable fault-lines. In a market economy, we can be forgiven for believing that we get paid a wage which is related to the amount of money we create for our employers and the level of effort and loyalty we display. The first purpose of this work is to dispel this myth and to proclaim that there is a discrepancy between work and reward in the conventional workplace. Put simply, what we are paid is often less than what we should rightfully receive. The second purpose of this work is to identify how our working lives could be readjusted, so that work does equal reward. The third purpose of this study is to unravel how this readjustment can be brought about, to make these propositions a reality. A society where work equals reward is certainly a more just and fair place to live, this study will propose what sort of society this would look like. In a nutshell, we could call this type of society an 'economic democracy'.

Introducing... Democracy

Those of us fortunate enough to live in a democratic country enjoy certain qualities of political life not present under dictatorship. These include the ability to change governments through elections, our ability to a fair voicing of our opinions and a transparent means of governing where information is public and scrutinised freely. The fight for political democracy is largely over, in the Western world at least, but the fight for economic democracy has barely just begun. When we enter the workplace, we enter a state within a state. The democratic rights given to us by political democracy are not replicated in this environment – one in which we will spend so much of our lives. Walking through the front door of a typical employer is the economic equivalent of walking through the passport gate of a foreign dictatorial country. Some even go as far as to call Western capitalist firms "islands of fascism in a sea of democracy" (George, 2007:535). Although the 'dictator' of the company may be a benevolent one, who does offer transparency and freedom of speech, these are nothing more than privileges, they are not rights, like they under political democracy. An employee does not gain these rights again until their shift is over. As Karl Polanyi (1944) might say, our (undemocratic) economic structures are disembedded from the rest of (our democratic) society. This reality has persisted and gone by relatively unchallenged. This research is a direct challenge. Through the medium of political economy, it will be suggested that economic democracy can be brought about to complement our political democracy. It will, however, not happen naturally. Political democracy was actively opposed by those who had something to lose from it, the same will be the case for promoting economic democracy too.

Only a 'cooperative state' has the ability to establish a meaningful and universal economic democracy. We can define the term 'cooperative state' as a government which is actively seeking to make all companies employee-owned. A desired outcome such as this will not come about by itself, it must be promoted, nourished and sustained. With that being said, a cooperative state can only come about through the processes of political democracy – it must be deliberately chosen by the electorate. This work has a purpose of assisting those who wish to bring about economic democracy through the means of political democracy, by constructing a solid argument in favour of worker ownership of all private companies.

Defining Capitalism

Before moving on to define what we mean by economic democracy and worker ownership, we should first take a moment to ask ourselves what type of economic system we currently tolerate. An economic system is more or less made up of two sub-systems, a mode of production (how goods and services are made) and a mode of distribution (how those goods and services reach the end user). The mode of distribution which most economies across the globe follow today is the 'free market' model, where the forces of supply and demand largely determine what is sold to who and at what price. This is in contrast to central planning, where the state decides who gets what and at what price. The mode of production most economies have embraced is capitalism. Under this system, those with money (capitalists) invest their savings into a business which produces and sells commodities in order to make a return on the capitalist's investment. This is in contrast to other modes of production, such as (traditional) socialism, where the state produces goods and services. By combining these two modes, we can identify the type of economic system a particular country has embraced. For most countries today, that economic system can be called 'free market capitalism'.

The term 'capitalism' is a rather peculiar one to apply, as it implies our economy revolves around capital – money applied to create more money. Although this may indeed be true, the accessibility of capital for ordinary people remains rather limited. Surely it would only make sense to define our economic system as 'capitalist' if the majority of people have access to capital. For vast swathes of people in both developed and developing countries, this is simply not the case. Capital is more likely to be found within small groups of people: corporations, hedge-funds, wealthy families (dynasties), etc. The form of capitalism we currently experience is more akin to 'monopoly capitalism', as capital is largely reserved for a monopolistic elite. If true capitalism (or whatever we wish to call it) is to be unearthed, it must enable the majority of citizens to gain access to capital and to apply it in a practical and sustainable way. Although calling our existing economic system 'capitalism' would be somewhat unrepresentative, as it is known by this name more commonly, we will refer to this system as 'conventional capitalism' for the remainder of this study. Unsurprisingly, the de-coupling of work and reward has a lot to do with the unequal ownership of capital, and thankfully, the debate surrounding capital ownership is slowly beginning to open up.

> And we need to create a balanced economy that supports long-term sustainable growth and a fairer society. That requires us to rethink what companies are for, asking not simply about the wealth they produce, but how they create value and for whom.
>
> Lampel et al (2010:3)

> Unequal patterns of capital ownership act as a fundamental driver of inequality. Ownership of capital confers the right both to the receipt of income and to a say in the use of the economic asset. How companies are owned consequently has a powerful bearing on the distribution of power and reward within the economy and society.
>
> Lawrence and Mason, (2017:4)

> Many of the most severe problems afflicting our economy today stem from failures of private sector ownership ... Excessive profit-chasing, failures of accountability, low levels of employee engagement have damaged many British businesses, and undermined their capacity to deliver value to customers and high quality jobs to their employees.
>
> Davies (2011:3)

Although ownership of capital could be distributed more fairly, without a fundamental change in the mode of production, this is never likely to occur. Indeed, this has never even been observed historically. The idea of the UK as a 'shareholding democracy', as once promoted by Margaret Thatcher's government, is all but dead. This dream needs to be revived. Capital as a concept is starting to take new forms. Housing is now seen more as an investment than somewhere to live. The concept of a 'home owning democracy' promoted in the UK during the 1980s (also by Thatcher) artificially redistributed the UK's housing stock. This benefited many at the time, giving the working masses an opportunity to own an asset that inevitably increased in value over time. For many, this provided access to capital that came not from the mode of production, but from a scarce resource – housing. However, as this scare resource became scarcer, more and more workers see the prospect of owning their own home, and thus capital, as little more than a pipedream. Instead, the housing stock is slowly being accumulated by wealthy landlords who increase their own capital at the expense of those who now have little prospect of owning any capital at all.

As with company ownership and more recently home ownership, capital left to its own devices is naturally destined to be concentrated to a smaller and smaller group of people. This process does not breed confidence in the reigning economic system, indeed it is more likely to unsettle it. As one British MP put it, "why would you support capitalism if you have no prospect of owning any capital?"

By rewriting the rules of the game, capital can be more evenly spread on a sustainable basis. Tackling ownership of companies is a good place to start, as our workplace is somewhere we spend so much of our time and which determines our quality of life. The ownership of other potentially profitable assets (such as housing) is important, but what is of most importance is the work we perform and reward we gain. Ending the discrepancy between work and reward is therefore the best place to start on our journey to a more egalitarian and just society.

The purpose of this work is not to argue in favour of capitalist ownership of the companies that make up our economy, but instead to argue in favour of worker-owned firms. The concepts of worker ownership and capitalist ownership are very different. Where capitalist ownership seeks to maximise total profit for the investors who have invested in the firm, worker ownership seeks to maximise the incomes of those who work in the firm. As will be argued, worker-owned firms have the potential to be more productive, innovative and socially just than capitalist firms, state owned firms, or any other type of business model we are currently aware of. The reason for this is simple, when a worker owns a piece of the company they work for, they earn a slice of the profits that company makes. That incentive ensures the worker, along with their colleagues, maximise the effort they apply into their work, in an attempt to maximise their income. This incentive does not exist in other types of firms.

Worker ownership on its own will not guarantee better worker engagement and participation. As such, workers should be able to control and manage the company they work for in a democratic fashion – what we could call 'economic democracy'. Under this arrangement, the individual worker is still accountable to their boss, but their boss is also now accountable to the workers. This interdependent relationship reduces the levels of fear and anxiety many workers in capitalist firms experience on a daily basis. It removes any militaristic style of management and replaces it with democratic accountability, transparency and freedom of speech in the workplace. Those 90,000 hours of our lives we spend at work should be spent somewhere where we have an element of control, where we are partners in a common endeavour rather than disposable pawns who must obey the whims of our appointed superiors. Worker management it would seem is clearly as important as worker ownership.

When workers own a share of the company they work for, they own capital. They own something which generates an income from what they have invested into the firm, their hard work and effort. Unlike other attempts to spread wealth creating assets among the population, worker-owned firms must remain worker-owned, they cannot sell off shares of their firm. This ensures that an even spread of capital ownership can be sustained, avoiding the accumulating effect that has plagued our existing system so many times before. An economy where all workers own a share of the company they work for, and where capital is spread more evenly, should be called 'capitalism', or 'true capitalism'. As we have already noted, however, quite ironically our current economic model has been given this label rather undeservedly. Rather than referring to this proposed model as a capitalist economy, or capitalist mode of production, we will instead refer to it as a cooperative economy, or cooperative mode of production. The free market will remain to be the mode of distribution for this type of economy. Although the free market system entails many of its own contradictions and limitations, this topic is not of our concern. What we are most interested in for this study, is the world of work and its relation to reward.

One commonly known type of worker-owned firm is the 'worker cooperative' model. A cooperative can be defined as "an autonomous association of persons united voluntarily to meet their common economic, social, and cultural needs and aspirations through a jointly-owned and democratically-controlled enterprise." (International Co-operative Alliance[1]). Although there are different types of cooperative, this work will argue that worker cooperatives are the best type of cooperative. However, worker cooperatives are not the only type of worker-owned firms. Employee-owned trusts are another type, which are quite distinct from worker cooperatives. Both models have their own advantages and disadvantages, as we shall explore. With that said, it is important to make clear at this stage that we will use the terms 'worker-owned' and 'employee-owned' interchangeably throughout the remainder of this research. It is also important to mention at this stage, that the 'cooperative economy' model we will be proposing does not give preference to worker cooperatives or any other specific type of worker-owned firm.

The Structure of this Study

The question for this research is not whether worker ownership can work – we know this to be true already – the question is whether it should be 'universalised', i.e. whether it should be demanded of all businesses. The focus will be more upon whether a cooperative economy can work, whether it is desirable over the conventional capitalist model and whether this new system can be implemented and sustained.

Part I explores why a new system is sought to begin with, by delving a little deeper into the disconnect between work and reward. This is where the concept of the 'dual-contradiction' comes in. The theory of the dual-contradiction demonstrates two of conventional capitalisms' greatest flaws, both of which are interlinked. Chapter 1 examines how workers are paid a lot less than the value of the goods or services they are producing. The two primary opposing theories of value (labour theory and marginalist theory of value) are used to show how this dynamic works from either perspective. Chapter 2 builds on this economic injustice, by revealing the lack of incentive most workers of capitalist firms have to maximise the effort they apply to their work. Both of these factors make up the dual-contradiction. We are using the word 'contradiction' here in the Hegelian sense, "when two seemingly opposed forces are simultaneously present within a particular situation" (Harvey, 2014:1). What makes this concept contradictory, is that the end result of the dual-contradiction (economic injustice and lack of worker incentive) prevents firms from reaching their maximum profitability, when the very purpose of the firm is to maximise total profits, for the benefit of the shareholders. Worker ownership, as Chapter 3 will divulge, largely eliminates the dual-contradiction, allowing profits to be maximised for the shareholders. The only caveat being, that those shareholders have to be the firm's workers. If any other group takes ownership of the firm other than the workers, the dual-contradiction will re-emerge.

Part II of this study puts a spotlight on the concepts of worker ownership and worker management, Chapters 4 and 5 respectively. This will demonstrate to the reader the different forms of ownership workers can take, and how different styles of worker management can have different effects. This will also be an opportunity to highlight some of the best practises these types of firms can take to maximise their potential.

Part III examines the economics of worker ownership, and how they differ from conventional capitalist firms in various markets. Two of these markets are inputs; labour (Chapter 6) and capital (Chapter 7). The third market is output (Chapter 8). These chapters reveal how switching the firms priority from maximising total profit to maximising income per head can change the demand and supply for each of these components. This work will refrain where possible in using complicated equations and graphs. It has been put together to be 'user friendly' to those not otherwise acquainted to economic theory, and its current unhealthy obsession with mathematics.

Part IV brings everything together to form a national framework. This explores the macroeconomic differences between a capitalist economy and a cooperative economy. By this stage, it will be no surprise to the reader that the cooperative economy appears to be the more socially just and economically efficient system. Chapter 9 examines the differences on a national level, with Chapter 10 examining the international ramifications.

With the economic frameworks in mind, Part V serves to move the discussion forward to arguably the most important part – the transition from a capitalist economy to a cooperative economy. Chapter 11 will be possibly the most interesting from the point of view of the sceptic, as it is titled 'Why Now?'. This chapter gives a brief overview of the history of worker ownership and the most relevant parts of the history of the cooperative movement. It reveals how the environment needed for worker-owned firms to flourish has never truly been present. Most of the experiments of the past failed as a result. It also explains how the transition from one form of economic model to another takes place, highlighting the necessary 'preconditions' each type of model needs before it can emerge. Chapter 12 is a brief manifesto on the main reforms a cooperative state should seek to bring about, reforms that will pave the way to a cooperative economy. Chapter 13 ends this study by exploring how a cooperative state should come to power and how it should manage the process of transition. Every country and economy is different, but laying down the general principles is important if we are to discuss a realistic means of bringing about change.

---

[1] See https://www.ica.coop/en/whats-co-op/co-operative-identity-values-principles

Chapter 1: Work & Value

In a state which is desirous of being saved from the greatest of all plagues - not faction, but rather distraction - here should exist among the citizens neither extreme poverty, nor, again, excess of wealth, for both are productive of both these evils. Now the legislator should determine what is to be the limit of poverty or wealth.

Plato, 327 B.C.

Plato's observation of extreme poverty and excess of wealth in Ancient Greece is unfortunately one that could be also be observed in most developed countries today. The prospect of confronting inequality - one of the greatest challenges of our time - is daunting and perhaps somewhat obscure compared to the many other issues humanity must confront. For too long inequality has been left undisturbed, both today and in the days of the ancient Greeks.

The focus of this chapter is to locate the first element of the dual-contradiction of conventional capitalism - economic inequality. By doing so we must frame what we think of economic inequality, where it comes from, how it sustains itself. Do all forms of economic inequality have a common link? Are there types of economic inequality which are desirable? Thankfully, a lot of the hard work has already been done and acknowledged. The largest stumbling block for economists to form a consensus on the origins of inequality in the workplace is found in the way we understand 'value'. This will therefore be our first concern.

The theory of value has been largely dominated by two schools of thought: the labour/supply-side theorists, and the subjective/demand-side theorists. Although a great deal of time could be saved by simply picking one theory and running with it for the remainder of the study, we must instead subject ourselves to the often dispiriting noises of classical economic theory if we are to form an argument in which both schools of thought can (more or less) find satisfactory. Once this has been achieved, we will be able to locate one of the primary sources of economic inequality, and will be better equipped to understand how our hypothetical legislator (the cooperative state) will 'determine what is to be the limit of poverty or wealth' as Plato puts it.

<h1 style="text-align:center">How do we Define Value?</h1>

Our very subsistence (ability to survive) is determined by the production and consumption of goods and services, this has been true throughout the story of humanity. Capitalism however, is concerned with the goods and services that are used for exchange – those we call 'commodities'. Although not everything we produce or consume is a commodity (we may produce and/or consume something just for ourselves, and not for exchange), the majority of goods and services in modern capitalist economies can be described as commodities. If we do not consume the commodity ourselves we can exchange commodities for money and exchange that money for the commodities we do need and want.

Quite comically, many often confidently claim that 'money makes the world go round', but what is money's use if not to purchase commodities, either now or at a later date? Commodities are purchased for what we call 'utility' – the satisfaction from consuming a particular human need or want over another. We gain satisfaction from fulfilling our basic human needs, such as eating and drinking, and from the things we like to do, like playing sports, watching films, etc. A specific commodity may not give you satisfaction *per se*, but may enable us to achieve satisfaction via other means. For example, a tennis racket gives us no utility on its own, only combined with a tennis ball, a tennis court and a willing partner can the satisfaction of the racket be realised.

The decisions over which commodities we purchase are usually based on rational calculations on the things we most need and the things we most want. Most of us try to budget our income and our expenditure, prioritising the things we need first and using what is left over to purchase the things we want, or save it to purchase something in future. The decisions we make are not always rational, but we can assume they tend to be for most of the time. If we are to determine why some people have more or less of these commodities than others, we must decode the value of commodities. Value is thus an essential concept to understand if we are to gather whether something has any worth and by what amount.

Before moving onto the two schools of thought on the theory of value, we must first recognise that a commodity may in fact hold different types/forms of value, rather than just one. In Marx's (1867) *Capital* three types of value are explored; use value, exchange value and social value[2], of which I will give three basic definitions:

1. Use Value: this is the utility (satisfaction) of consuming a commodity – eating an apple, watching a film, wearing a coat, etc. All commodities must have a use value or the commodity will not be needed/wanted and thus will not be

exchangable, voiding it as a commodity. Use value is also rather difficult to measure as we cannot initially put a number on how much satisfaction we gain or enable from something, more on this later.

2.   Exchange Value: how much of one commodity we value against another. This is usually represented numerically, for example 1 cow is equal to 2 sheep, or 1 car is equal to 1 gold bar, or if we recognise money as a commodity[3], 1 loaf of bread is equal to £1. Exchange value is often represented by what we call 'price'. Again, a commodity must have an exchange value or it cannot be exchanged, voiding it as a commodity.

3.   Social Value: how much time and effort has been spent producing the commodity. If the average time to produce a specific quantity of wood is 1 hour, the wood will have a social value of 1 hour. If the lumberjack then sells the wood to a carpenter, who spends 2 hours producing a table from that wood, then the total value of the table will be 3 hours (as 3 hours of human work has been expended in total). Social value is also found in commodities that are not necessarily produced but are instead procured: mining diamonds, picking apples, etc. If something is abundant and requires little if any human work to procure, such as air, it holds no social value.

Labour Theory of Value

Although three types of value are mentioned above, most economists try to reveal a commodity's 'true value', or more specifically, the main factor which gives it worthiness. The traditional labour theory of value implies that the true value of a commodity is the amount of work and effort expended upon/within the commodity – the social value. The origins of this theory are contested, but is mostly widely considered to derive from the Scottish political economist Adam Smith (1776) in his *Wealth of Nations*.

> The value of any commodity, therefore, to the person who possesses it, and who means not to use or consume it himself, but to exchange it for other commodities, is equal to the quantity of labour which it enables him to purchase or command. Labour, therefore, is the real measure of the exchangeable value of all commodities.
>
> Smith (1776:28)

Although David Ricardo (1817) later expanded on Smith's theory in his work *Principles of Political Economy and Taxation*, it was Karl Marx who took up the baton for the labour theorists. In *Capital*, Marx implies that the true source of value is social value, or, the socially necessary labour time that is expended on producing a commodity. The main difference between Marx's approach and the approach of Smith and Ricardo was the concept of 'socially necessary' labour time. If the average (socially necessary) time to produce a table is 2 hours, but a more idle carpenter takes 5 hours, the table of the lazy carpenter does not hold more value – it holds the average/standard rate of value (2 hours worth rather than 5). Although it is social value that represents the real worth of commodities, according to labour theorities, a commodity needs to hold a use value and exchange value if it is to be in demand and exchanged, encompassing all three types/forms of value.

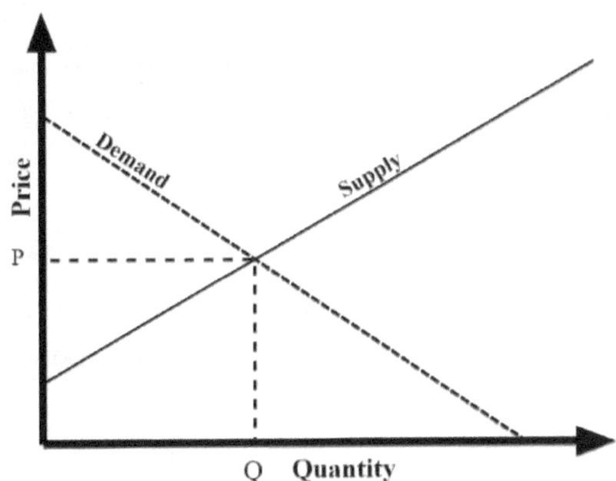

Figure 1

Regarding the typical supply and demand curve, as seen in Figure 1, this approach would accept that the demand (use value) for a commodity can increase and decrease as peoples wants and needs change over time. The supply of commodities can also alter as they become scarcer or more easier to produce/procure compared to other commodities, and thus the exchange value will alter to reflect this. When supply and demand reach equilibrium (a balance), how do we know a certain commodity is worth a certain price? If a commodity is not undersupplied or oversupplied, or overpriced or underpriced, why does a commodity cost a particular equilibrium price? In this situation, the Marxian approach would imply that the amount of time used to produce the commodity is the ultimate source of pricing. This is what we can call a supply-side theory of value, as value is derived from the supply of producing/procuring a commodity.

Although this theory of value may be useful in the case of the carpenter explained earlier, its applicability and usefulness begins to diminish (if not vanish) when production becomes more complex. If a machine or tool is used to produce a commodity, it too has social value, as it too has once been produced and exchanged. A machine can only be used to produce a certain amount of commodities before it wears out, so for every commodity it produces, a portion of its own value is transferred to the commodity it is producing. It therefore becomes more difficult to link price and social value when a commodity is comprised of various inputs and assembled by various machines which are also comprised of various inputs, to the extent where little if any human labour is expended in the production process. Under these circumstances the concept of social value still holds true, but becomes a lot more difficult to observe and calculate, and even less so when identifying why some commodities are priced the way they are. There is also the question of whether supply and demand actually meet equilibrium at a particular point. If there are constant changes in a commodity's use value and exchange value, then social value becomes difficult to observe in this case also.

Subjective Theory of Value

By contrast, the subjective theory of value implies that the true value of a good is not inherent within the commodity but is instead determined by the individual consumer, and how much use value they place within it. Perception is the more pivotal factor, making this a demand rather than supply theory of value. This theory was developed most extensively by three economists, Jevons, Menger and Walras, and remains the most prominent theory regarding value within current economic thinking. This theory of value can be summed up in the following quote: "Value is thus the importance that individual goods or quantities of goods attain for us because we are conscious of being dependent on command of them for the satisfaction of our needs." (Menger, 1871:115). Our individual utility gained from the commodity is the measure of value. Mainstream (neoclassical) economists use marginal utility theory and indifference analysis to uncover the differences in people preferences for one commodity over another, and to reveal the subsequent price that people are willing to pay. The price should reveal the true value of that commodity.

At this point we must separate the term 'utility' into two terms, 'total utility' and 'marginal utility'. Total utility is the utility gained from consuming the total amount of a particular commodity. For example, eating two is likely to give us more total utility than eating one. Having £200 is likely to give us more total utility than £20. This is an interesting concept, but total utility actually tells us very little. Marginal utility however, is how much utility was gained from consuming the last unit of a particular commodity, rather than all of those units combined. The use value of a particular commodity is not universal for each and every unit at each and every time. A marginalist version of use value is therefore determined by the quantity of the commodity purchased and consumed, rather than the individual commodity itself. For example, the first apple eaten by a hungry person holds a high use value, whilst the tenth apple eaten by the same individual holds less use value (unless they command an unusually large appetite!). This is known as the theory of diminishing utility – the more of something you consume, eventually, the less utility you will gain from it, and thus the less value it holds. A commodity like beer being another good example. The more alcohol you drink the more utility you are likely to gain from it, however there comes a point when an additional pint of beer starts to decrease utility, until eventually you reach a position which is worse than where you started. Marginal utility therefore helps us to put each commodity into a particular context.

> If an inhabitant of a virgin forest has several hundred thousand trees at his disposal while he needs only some twenty a year for the full provision of his requirements for timber, he will not consider himself injured in any way, in the satisfaction of his needs, if a forest fire destroys a thousand or so of the trees, provided he is still in a position to satisfy his needs as completely as before with the rest. In such circumstances, therefore, the satisfaction of none of his needs depends upon his command of any single tree, and for this reason a tree also has no value to him.
>
> But suppose there are also in the forest ten wild fruit trees whose fruit is consumed by the same individual. Suppose too, that the amount of fruit available to him is not larger than his requirements. Certainly then, not a single one of these fruit trees can be burned in the fire without causing him to suffer hunger as a result, or without at least causing him to be unable to satisfy his need for fruit as completely as before. For this reason each one of the fruit trees has value to him.
>
> Menger (1871:117)

Menger's (1871) example demonstrates the difference in value of one commodity compared to multiples of the same commodity. Marginal utility theory is not the only method for analysing value, indifference curve analysis can also be applied. This method is slightly more complex without delving into graphs and tables, so we will keep it brief. Put simply, indifference analysis helps us to measure how much of one commodity an individual is likely to choose over another and at what cost. As 'utility' is a rather immeasurable concept, indifference analysis helps to better quantify value[4].

This approach is used to determine how we value each unit of a commodity against each unit of another commodity, and which mixture of the two we would most prefer acknowledging that we only have a set budget. This type of analysis attempts to combine both use value with exchange value, as it measures both the utility gained from one product over another and the rate of which we are likely to exchange one commodity over another. There is one thing notably missing however. Unlike the Marxian theory which includes all three value concepts, the marginal theory of value does not include the use of social value. Social value in the marginalist approach is simply a theoretical construct that bears no tangible truth in reality. As a consequence, although the marginal theory may better explain the price of a commodity in complex economies, it leaves out the human element of producing the commodity, and views everything in the eyes of the marketplace and how much each commodity is worth according to each individual's preferences.

The debate over which theory best explains the true source of value remains up to the reader. One could argue that there is no 'true source' of value. Whichever approach is subscribed, the theory of the source of inequality, which we will shortly uncover, can encompass either or both theories of value. To understand how inequality is derived, the discussion must move on to the relationship between value and work.

Theory of Surplus Value

The theory of surplus value builds upon Marx's work in *Capital*, which applies the labour theory of value to reveal how inequality emerges within the process of work and labour. At this point it is important to differentiate between what we mean by work and labour. 'Work' is simply the process of applying effort to get something done, be it building a fence, filling a tax return, picking apples, etc. 'Labour' however, is the exchange of work for another commodity, usually money – working for a company in exchange for a wage for example. 'Labour power' is the ability to conduct the exchange of labour for money – being physically and mentally fit to perform the tasks required. There is no point selling your labour if you cannot perform the tasks set. What employees actually sell is not their labour but their labour power, their capability to perform work. In most modern capitalist economies, the majority of people sell their labour-power to a company in return for wages, or in the case of the self-employed, sell their labour-power to a variety of companies, individual clients or other economic actors. It would not be controversial to assume that only a small minority of people can sustain themselves without being a part of the labour process. Most of us need a job to sustain ourselves.

Using the Labour Theory

Using a basic Marxian example, we can identify how inequality is bred within the labour process. Take again the example of a carpenter, who this time is unable to obtain the means of producing their own tables, and instead enters the labour market looking for a company who does have the means to produce tables. The carpenter can only sell their labour-power if they have the means to sustain themselves: enough food, water and other life necessities. Rather than the company directly giving the carpenter the necessities of life, they will pay them a wage in the form (usually) of money, which is equal to the life necessities required.

Under this example, we assume that the combined value of all the things required for the carpenter to sustain themselves for one day (their daily wage) has the same exchange value and social value as one table. If the carpenter is employed, and produces one table in exchange for one day's ability to work, equality has been reached. That would be a fair exchange. A fair day's work for a fair day's pay. The carpenter's employer will, however, have earned no profit, as the cost of production equals the price sold[5]. As such, the capitalist will wish to obtain more than the one table per day the carpenter is producing. If the worker only produces as much value as they earn (or less so), there is no incentive for the capitalist to hire them. The employer has an incentive to exploit the worker. Therefore, the employer instead would prefer two tables to be made each day rather than just the one – this is where inequality develops. Under these circumstances the carpenter is producing two tables a day in exchange for a daily wage which is worth only 1 table. The difference between what the worker makes and what they receive is called the 'surplus value'. Although the carpenter has accepted to exchange their labour-power in exchange for the ability to perform labour (and to remain alive more generally), what they inevitably produce is worth more than their daily subsistence. This is essentially unpaid surplus labour, which produces for the capitalist a surplus value, which translates into profits.

> Our capitalist has two objectives: in the first place, he wants to produce a use-value which has exchange-value, i.e. an article destined to be sold, a commodity; and secondly he wants to produce a commodity greater in value than the sum of the values of the commodities used to produce it, namely the

means of production and the labour-power he purchased with his good money on the open market. His aim is to produce not only a use-value, but a commodity; not only use-value, but [social] value; not only [social] value, but also surplus-value.

Marx (1867:293, bracket and comment added)

Further on in *Capital,* Marx carefully and methodically sets out how the capitalist will always strive to squeeze more and more surplus value out of the worker. The capitalist cannot pay the worker less than what is required for subsistence, otherwise the worker will be physically and mentally unable to perform the tasks the next day. And the capitalist has no interest in paying the worker more than what is absolutely necessary, because of the incentive to exploit. The capitalist's interest lies in increasing the very thing that allowed surplus value to be produced in the first place, that being 'capital' – money used solely to produce a profit. With this profit, it too can be used as further capital, to produce more surplus value, more profit, more capital and so the process of accumulation continues. In his usual mystical and ghoulish manner, Marx states that:

As a capitalist, he is only capital personified. His soul is the soul of capital. But capital has one sole driving force, the drive to valorize itself, to create surplus-value, to make its constant part, the means of production, absorb the greatest possible amount of surplus labour. Capital is dead labour which, vampire-like, lives only by sucking living labour, and lives the more, the more labour it sucks.

Marx (1867:342)

In all other markets apart from the labour market, Marx accepts that generally, commodities are exchanged for their true value. Supply and demand reach equilibrium, and prices reflect the commodities true value – social value. Supply and demand must balance eventually due to the process of exchange. If a seller tries to overprice their commodity to the buyer, the buyer will eventually work out that the price offered does not match the true value of the commodity and will seek an alternative seller. The same works in reverse, if the commodity is underpriced the seller will soon work this out and readjust the price to reflect its true value.

It is true that commodities may be sold at prices which diverge from their values, but this divergence appears as an infringement of the laws governing

the exchange of commodities. In its pure form, the exchange of commodities
is an exchange of equivalents, and thus it is not a method of increasing value.

Marx (1867:261)

Where there are multiple buyers and sellers, this is how 'equilibrium' between supply and demand is found. When equilibrium is reached, profits from production can only come from surplus labour. For example, if every buyer and seller was currently at equilibrium in supply and demand, and were receiving no profit, the sellers of all commodities may decide to increase the price of their commodities, by say ten per cent in order to gain a profit. However, this 'profit' would be cancelled out, as the profits earned by the sellers would now be spent on commodities which are now more expensive by the same amount of ten per cent – an inflationary effect. Supply and demand would readjust. Therefore, it is argued that only surplus value can create profits in the production process when equilibrium has been reached between supply and demand[6]. The commodity of labour-power would appear to be the only commodity which is consistently undervalued when exchanged. As Albert Einstein (1949:3) confidently states; "It is important to understand that even in theory the payment of the worker is not determined by the value of his product."

But is this simple Marxian process true of all employees and employers? In *Democracy at Work*, Richard Wolff (2012) extends and applies Marx's theory to the modern context. In many companies today employees are not directly involved in the production of goods and services, but instead enable others to do so. These so called 'enablers' are responsible for advertising, human resources, accounting, and a whole host of other responsibilities which are pivotal to the enterprise but which on the surface appear to produce no social value. For simplicity, we will assume that these roles do add social value to the commodity, especially as these enabling features are represented in the final price of the commodity. A commodity can only be a commodity if it can be exchanged. Marketing, accounting, etc. are all a part of the production process for the final commodity, which is then put onto the open market ready for exchange.

Adding these enabling features into the final value of the commodity thus makes sense, if indeed it is possible. It is worth noting here that more and more of the 'enabling' components of production are becoming 'universalised'. Paul Mason's *PostCapitalism* highlights how more and more information is becoming zero-cost. The rise of Wikipedia, Wikileaks, illegal sites like Pirate Bay, Putlocker and the like, are spurring information and other services away from conventional market processes and towards a sharing non-market economy. A sort of 'digital commons' is emerging, with free platforms slowly egging their way into the production process. Knowledge is becoming universalised, free at the point of use with the ability to freely contribute towards that knowledge. How can we realistically derive the social value of a commodity when it encompasses so much zero-cost inputs?

> Second, Marx argued, knowledge-driven capitalism cannot support a price mechanism whereby the value of something is dictated by the value of the inputs needed to produce it. It is impossible to properly value inputs when they come in the form of social knowledge.
>
> Mason (2015:136)

Perhaps Mason is referring to the following quote in Marx's *Grundrisse* (*The Fragment on Machines*):

> As soon as labour in the direct form has ceased to be the great well-spring of wealth, labour time ceases and must cease to be its measure, and hence exchange value [must cease to be the measure] of use value.
>
> Marx (1857-61:637)

As we have already argued, the complexity of modern production has already tainted our ability to use the labour theory to effectively value commodities. Perhaps we are currently at a half-way-house between the labour-intensive capitalism of the past and Marx's hypothesised knowledge-intensive capitalism. It's not just the concept of value that's under strain, the concept of labour-power is also being challenged. In Guy Standing's (2011) *Precariat*, Standing explains how more and more work is being undertaken which is not a part of the normal labour process. For example, housework is considered work, but is only considered labour if it is undertaken by a maid who cleans in exchange for money. If the housework is instead undertaken by a family member, it still remains work, but not labour – there is no economic exchange taking place.

There is also more un-remunerated work that workers are doing for their employment in what is meant to be their free time. Work commitments start to interfere with all aspects of life, from answering emails and taking calls out of hours, to those on zero-hour contracts traveling to their workplace just to ascertain whether they are needed for work that day. The more unpaid/zero-cost labour and commodities that emerge, the more difficult it becomes to use the labour theory of value as a means of understanding commodity exchange.

Although these new processes are beginning to take shape, it is still safe to assume that the majority of people will rely on the labour process as a means of maintaining subsistence. It is also safe to say that labourers are still the most essential components of production. The theory of surplus value thus remains as relevant as it ever has been. As such, the 'theft' of surplus value from the worker to the capitalist is still alive and well, but operating in a modern context.

Using the Marginal Theory

Even if one rejects the labour theory of value, a modified theory of surplus value can still be identified using the subjective theory of value. For the most part, neoclassical economists reject the relevance of the theory of surplus value. Within this spectrum, all markets (including the labour market) must be in, or in the process of reaching, equilibrium. This is the same as the example of the buyer and seller mentioned earlier – a commodity should not be under or over valued in the long run. Regarding the labour market, the employer has demand for an additional worker, which a worker subsequently supplies at a rate of mutual agreement. Marginalism helps us to understand why a firm would need an additional labourer. 'Marginal product' is the amount of output produced and (more importantly) revenue gained by employing one additional worker. Like the examples of apples and beer used earlier, the company will keep hiring workers until they reach a point where hiring or firing any more workers will actually decrease their revenue rather than increase it. Put simply, a company will only hire a worker if their marginal product is greater than the wages that worker is paid.

Wages are determined by the supply and demand of workers with particular skill sets. The worker is paid exactly what their work is worth in the economic marketplace, regardless of whether they are directly producing a commodity or enabling its production. If there is more demand than supply for a particular type of worker (a professional footballer for example), then the price paid to the worker will be higher. If there is more supply than demand, the employer will offer a lower than average wage, they may even attempt to offer a wage which is below the value of subsistence, assuming no minimum/living wage has been legislated.

The same incentive, however, for the capitalist to gain more from the worker than what they pay the worker is still present, otherwise there would be no incentive in employing that worker. Basic microeconomic theory indicates how firms must earn a normal rate[7] of profit if they are to supply the goods demanded. So although the worker is being paid what their work is worth, the worker could be earning more still – a surplus value – if they were also entitled to a share of the profits. This profit could be earned by the worker whilst still producing, and consequently selling, commodities at a price that reaches equilibrium in that respective commodity's market. It is a rate of profit that can sustain itself, *ceteris paribus* (everything else being equal).

The only reason why a worker cannot earn that profit is because they do not have a right to a share of those profits. One can only have the right to a share of the profits if one owns a piece of the company, what we call 'owning the means of production'. The reason that most workers cannot own the means of production is because they cannot afford to do so, because they are only earning a market-rate wage to meet their subsistence. Although starting a business is simple enough, to grow it to the extent where the business owner can cover the cost of their own subsistence, or the subsistence of any employees, requires a significantly large means of production. Obtaining the means of production, for most people, is only affordable if they can earn an income above what is required for their subsistence. However, this is difficult to achieve without first owning a piece of the means of production or deriving a large quantity of wealth from another non-labour related source. As a result of this situation, owning the means of production is typically left to a minority of wealthy 'investors' who expect at least a normal rate of profit from their investments. What emerges is a generally paradoxical scenario. If employees were earning more than the wage rate, they themselves may be able to obtain the means of production. But for the vast majority, this is simply inconceivable. Smith (1776) observes this in his own time, stating:

> It sometimes happens, indeed, that a single independent workman has stock sufficient both to purchase the materials of his work, and to maintain himself till it be completed. He is both master and workman, and enjoys the whole produce of his own labour, or the whole value which it adds to the materials upon which it is bestowed. It includes what are usually two distinct revenues, belonging to two distinct persons, the profits of stock, and the wages of labour. Such cases, however, are not very frequent, and in every part of Europe, twenty workmen serve under a master for one that is independent; and the wages of labour are everywhere understood to be, what they usually are, when the labourer is one person, and the owner of the stock which employs him another.

Smith (1776:56)

A Marxian theorist may also argue that due to an intentional excess of labour supply relative to demand (what we call 'unemployment'), wage rates are kept below equilibrium, and as workers are forced to work - where capitalists are not forced to employ[8] - the worker can only accept the wage rate on offer. An exchange (of labour for money) is not an exchange, if one party is forced into it. The same would be the case for exchanging other life necessities. If, for example, one party is in desperate need of water, whilst the other controls the only means of obtaining water, surely this can never be a fair exchange. They cannot act in a rational manner whilst they are deprived of the basic necessities of life. If there is more demand than supply (as Marx argues there always is in the labour market), the buyer of water cannot fairly negotiate with the water seller - there is a disequilibrium in bargaining power. The water buyer is forced to accept the price offered, the labourer is forced to accept the wage offered[9]. Under these circumstances, there can never be a true equilibrium wage rate in the labour market. Whether or not we regard the labour market to be in equilibrium or not, we can still nonetheless accept that most workers could be sustainably earning more than what they are currently paid by their employers if they were able to receive a share of the profits. Although identifying the theory of surplus value within the subjectivist theory of value is more complicated and perhaps more controversial, it nonetheless remains a solid theory that can be easily understood and identified in economic reality.

Inequality Under Capitalism

Until now, we have yet to even define economic inequality, nor explain its wider implications upon wider society. More generally we can define economic inequality to be the difference in economic well-being between various groups within a particular geographical area. Economic inequality can also be divided into two distinct categories; income inequality and wealth inequality. The latter is a stock value, the differences in total wealth owned at a particular time, whilst income inequality deals with the differences between flows of wealth - either from labour (wages, bonuses, etc.) or from capital (dividends, rents, etc.). What is of more concern, is how economic inequality sustains itself - how certain groups are consistently better or worse off compared to others. The theory of surplus value begins to shed light on that matter. In his ground breaking work *Capital in the Twenty-First Century*, Thomas Piketty (2014:19) states early on that "Inequality is not necessarily bad in itself: the key question is to decide whether it is justified, whether there are reasons for it". Absolute equality is neither practical nor desirable. Some form of inequality needs to exist. One important factor when considering the theory of surplus value is that under conventional capitalism, work does not necessarily equal reward. Using the labour theory of value, the labourer is creating more (social) value than they receive in exchange for that work. For the workers, there is more work than reward. Under the subjective theory of value, although the worker is earning what they are worth, the market rate for their labour power, they could be earning more. Instead, the profits are distributed to those who may not necessarily work, but do receive reward – usually capitalist shareholders/investors. For many investor-owners, there is more reward than work[10]. Using both theories of value, work does not equal reward in the process of production. What has become more apparent in recent times, is that for larger corporations, ownership and control are becoming dispersed. When the ownership of a company is held by a single individual or a small group of shareholders, ownership roughly translates to control. When ownership has been diluted across potentially thousands of shareholders, as in the case of large public limited corporations, shareholders individually hold little power in the decision-making processes of the firm. This is also translated into profits.

> If capital was owned equally throughout the income distribution, the increasing returns to capital – and the appreciation of assets – would not cause rising inequality. However, different individuals and households hold different assets and liabilities, which generate differing rates of return and increase in value at differing rates. In particular, the biggest force driving wealth inequality in the UK since 2010 has been high equity returns and their sharp rise in value. This is because ownership of equity is disproportionately concentrated; the 10 per cent wealthiest UK households directly own an estimated 77 per cent of all stocks and 64 per cent of bonds. By contrast, less wealthy households typically own little to no stocks and bonds. If the value of equity continues to rise more than other assets and labour income, and generates greater returns, it is likely to increase wealth inequality by increasing net wealth among those at the top of the distribution.

Roberts and Lawrence (2017:19-20)

Inequality has undoubtedly increased more recently. CEOs and fund managers are able to pay themselves exorbitant salaries and justify it on the grounds of incentivising higher performance. There has been little evidence to conclude that increasing rates of pay at these levels beyond already high levels will necessarily create a higher revenue for the company. Although these individuals do not own the means of production, they do in many respects, control the means of production. As Atkinson (2015:107) states, "Top earners have caught up with, or overtaken, those living off capital income. Rentiers clipping their dividend coupons have been replaced by hedge fund managers, CEOs, and footballers". Along with high salaries and bonuses, such individuals can also be rewarded with shares of the firm, thus cementing their position the firm even more.

We are increasingly seeing an overlap, where those on the highest salaries are also those who earn the most from capital income. This makes the straightforward conflict between worker and capitalist, as presented by Marx, much more complex. A resurrected Marx may describe such CEOs and fund managers as capitalists in disguise, functioning in the costume of a worker. However we may wish to describe this new trend, it goes without saying that owning the means of production is still the best means of obtaining the surplus value created by the workforce. Although such surplus value can be earned without ownership, having the ability to control the means of production (owned by others) can, in the vast majority of respects, lead to similar if not the exact same outcomes as owning of the means of production outright.

As soon as an individual can obtain and/or control the means of production, the surplus value process can begin, and that individual can cement their position of wealth. The proceeds of profit can be poured into non-productive forms of investment, such as property and land, the shares of other companies, government debt, antiquities, patents, and so on. Gaining wealth from non-value creating activities such as these is known as rent-seeking, which, as some have argued[11], is becoming more and more common in conventional capitalist economies.

It goes without saying that economic inequality can be developed through rent-seeking and outside the productive process and the process of surplus value. Potential solutions to dealing with inequality stemmed only from rent-seeking will be discussed in Chapter 12. In many cases, however, these two sources of inequality are often combined. A lucky individual may suddenly find a great deal of wealth in their own property and land, or perhaps a new invention or something more creative and artistic. However, the surplus value process will still be involved in some way or another. An individual whose land suddenly becomes valuable may sell it to a company to build a factory, or sell it to an individual whose wealth from the surplus value process has allowed them to purchase that land for their own purposes. An inventive individual will require the surplus value process to make their patented commodity a reality. Although economic inequality is not always derived from the production process, it will always be linked to it in some way, either at the forefront or maliciously lurking in the background. The type of inequality that can not be justified (to use Piketty's earlier statement) is the disequilibrium between work and reward. Although luck plays too greater part in determining our overall well-being, it must be our aim to recouple work with reward and strengthen equality of opportunity.

> "Our democratic societies rest on a meritocratic worldview, or at any rate a meritocratic hope, by which I mean a belief in a society in which inequality is based more on merit and effort than on kinship and rents. This belief and this hope play a very crucial role in modern society, for a simple reason: in a democratic society, the professed equality of rights of all citizens contrasts sharply with the very real inequality of living conditions, and in order to overcome this contradiction is vital to make sure that social inequalities derive from rational and universal principles rather than arbitrary contingencies. Inequalities must therefore be useful to all, at least in the realm of discourse and as far as possible in reality as well."
>
> Piketty (2012:422)

The Challenge of Our Time

When equality of opportunity is not reached, and when work does not equal reward, rather unsavoury patterns begin to emerge. Another ground breaking piece of research was Richard Wilkinson and Kate Pickett's (2009) *Spirit Level*, published prior to the 2007/08 crash. Within it, they argue that rising levels of inequality within advanced countries hold a strong correlation with factors included in the Index of Health and Social Problems. Such factors include worsening rates of physical health, mental health, drug abuse, educational performance, imprisonment, obesity, social mobility, trust and community life, violence, teenage pregnancies, and child well-being. Increased public spending to solve these issues is not enough – it is the cause of these factors which must be addressed – as Wilkinson and Pickett (2009:33) state: "The best way of responding to the harm done by high levels of inequality would be to reduce inequality itself". The *Spirit Level* also notes how for the most advanced economies increasing growth rates have no significant impact on reducing inequality and its consequential results compared to developing countries. "Economic growth, for so long the great engine of progress, has, in the rich countries, largely finished its work" (2009:5). Indeed, rather than economic growth being used to reduce inequality, reduced inequality will likely lead to more growth, for good or for bad. Regardless of whether the current spell of 'secular stagnation' in the advanced economies is here to stay, solutions to resolve inequality must be suitable for both growing and stagnant economies. Piketty's (2012) research highlights how inequality can both widen and narrow significantly in a relatively short space of time. Recent studies[12] suggest that 25 to 30 per cent of the UK population are living on an inadequate income.

> Households in the bottom 10% of the population [as of 2015-2016] have on average a disposable (or net) income of £9,644 (this includes wages and cash benefits, and is after direct taxes like income tax and council tax, but not indirect taxes like VAT).
>
> In 2012, the top 1% had an average income of £253,927 and the top 0.1% had an average income of £919,882.
>
> The Equality Trust[13]

It's not just labour income which is becoming more unequal, wealth inequality is also on the rise. As capital ownership is not currently an option for most working people, other forms of wealth generation have come forward. The most obvious asset that comes to mind is housing. Although home ownership and the rise in property values has helped to give some an additional spout of wealth, the prospect of home ownership is becoming more out of reach for younger generations. Home ownership is slowly starting to replicate the inaccessibility of capital more generally, giving rentier capitalists an opportunity to move in and thus increasing inequality further.

> Worryingly, while wealth inequality fell for much of the 20th century, it is now rising again, and is set to rise further. Between 2010-2012 and 2012-2014, over half of the increase in personal wealth went to the top 10 per cent of households. A political focus on income inequality alone has masked the true extent of inequality in the UK.
>
> Roberts and Lawrence (2017:2)

These levels of income inequality are simply intolerable, and are much higher than most other developed countries. Resolving such grotesque levels of inequality is neither utopian nor impractical – indeed it may be the only way to save capitalism from its long-term irrationalities. Dealing with the types of inequality that polarise work with reward must be resolved, indeed it is one of the primary aims of this research.

[2] In *Capital* the terms; use value, exchange value and value are used, yet to avoid confusion the third term will be referred to as social value for the remainder of this book, as is also found in Harvey's (2014) *Seventeen Contradictions*.

[3] Is money a commodity? It certainly has an exchange value, as money is the primary use of exchange in developed capitalist economies. Money has a use value as it is an easier form of exchanging than bartering for example. The social value of money however, is more controversial. Although money made from gold may have a social value, money which is simply worth the paper its written on (fiat money) holds little if any social value, and has been a constant source of unease, particular in Marxian economics.

[4] Using multiple indifference curves and budget lines when the price of one of the goods alters (with income and the price of the other good remaining constant) will uncover multiple optimum consumption points to form a price-consumption curve. As we now know the demand of that good when the price alters, a demand curve can be drawn (the other good, whose price remains constant, has to now be refined to represent 'all other goods'/what is not spent on the original good).

[5] Under the labour theory of value, the final value/cost of the commodity should equal the total value of all the factors of production.

[6] Profit could be made if the buyer/seller can be consistently fooled to overpay/undersell the commodity, but this is unlikely to take place for the majority of the time. Monopolies are another unique exception, where a lack of competition can enable the seller to consistently overprice their product.

[7] A 'normal rate of profit' is the minimum level of profit needed for a company to remain competitive in the market, from the perspective of the investor. It is usually considered to be a cost of the firm. Abnormal profits make the firm more competitive, whilst a loss makes the firm less competitive.

[8] A capitalist could invest their money in other endeavours, such as property speculation, where they are not required to employ.

[9] The word 'forced' is perhaps a little heavy, as this would imply something akin to slavery, which is obviously not the case. In addition, most capitalist economies also have forms of social security such as unemployment benefit which can relieve the initial pressure to find work. In these situations people are not forced to work but are heavily influenced to do so. Either way, people are heavily influenced, if not ' subtlety forced', to work for someone if they are to maintain their subsistence in most cases.

[10] There are cases, as discussed in Chapter 3, where the investor-owners also face a great injustice.

[11] See Stiglitz (2012)

[12] Joseph Rowntree Foundation (2017), https://www.jrf.org.uk/press/just-about-managing-four-million-more-living-britain

[13] The Equality Trust, https://www.equalitytrust.org.uk/scale-economic-inequality-uk. Data taken from the ONS and the World Top Incomes Database respectively.

Chapter 2: Work & Incentive

Quite intuitively, if there is no economic, social, or personal incentive for any individual to do work, it will not get done. Therefore, a society must provide incentives for the work necessary for its own maintenance.

Dalkir, 2005:310

If there is one thing that capitalism's advocates should have learnt from the fall of communism, it's that incentives are an essential component of economic development, not just for those at the top, but for all those who stimulate economic activity. The second element of the dual-contradiction of capitalism deals with incentives – or more specifically, a lack of them. Incentives are a foundational function of economics. Incentives give us the willingness to pursue short term and long term gains, they give markets and economic exchange a purpose and relevance. Without incentives, there is no driving force behind the change and sporadic shifts we witness across societies and economies. Indeed, it seems almost impossible to imagine a world in which individual and collective self-interest does not spur the process of history. The purpose of incentive theory in this chapter is to uncover how conventional capitalist enterprises distribute incentives throughout its structure, to reveal where they are overly abundant and where they are insufficient.

Defining 'Incentive'

Although we are primarily interested in economic incentives, it is nonetheless essential to define the term 'incentive' more generally. In Dalkir's (2005) work *Knowledge Management in Theory and Practice* one can find a useful introduction to basic incentive theory. Within it, she defines the term incentive as: "A reward for a specific behavior, designed to encourage that behavior; also called inducement. In economics, an incentive is anything that provides a motive for a particular course of action—that counts as a reason for preferring one choice to the alternatives".

Individual self-interest is a pivotal foundation of most microeconomic theories, marginalism especially. Each and every one of us seeks to maximise our utility/satisfaction. Within economics our needs and wants are usually met by consuming goods and services. This assumption must hold for both the labour theory and subjective theory of value to hold. The reason we produce, distribute and consume goods and services is because we have an incentive to do so – because we value more of one thing over another, whether that be a commodity, free-time, or fulfilling a variety of other desires and wishes. As we mentioned at the beginning of Chapter 1, although not everything we want or need is a commodity (an exchangeable good or service), in a capitalist economy commodities do take centre stage.

The term 'incentive' on its own is still too general. Callahan (2004) and Dalkir (2005) can assist us further by identifying three general types of incentive that we witness within economic relations. They go as follows:

- Remunerative incentives (or financial incentives) are said to exist where an agent can expect some form of material reward—especially money— in exchange for acting in a particular way.

- Coercive incentives are said to exist where a person can expect that the failure to act in a particular way will result in physical force being used against him or her (or her loved ones) by others in the community—for example, by punishment, imprisonment, firing, or confiscating or destroying their possessions.

- Moral incentives are said to exist where a particular choice is widely regarded as the right thing to do, or as particularly admirable, or where the failure to act in a certain way is condemned as indecent. A person acting on a moral incentive can expect a sense of self-esteem and approval or even admiration from her community; a person acting against a moral incentive can expect a sense of guilt and condemnation, or even ostracism, from the community.

(Dalkir, 2005:309)

Put simply, remunerative incentives are concerned with what is gained, coercive incentives are concerned with what is lost, and moral incentives are concerned with what is right/just. Each and every individual will value certain types of incentive over another in various situations. None of us are wired the same way, we all interpret decisions and behaviours differently. For example, some may find that the financial incentive to produce and distribute prohibited recreational drugs far outweighs the moral incentives (the possible impact the drugs may have on users and their families) and the coercive incentives (the likelihood of being caught breaking the law). Incentives are also time sensitive. There may be a short term incentive to spend money but a long term incentive to save it – again, different individuals will act differently based on their situation and on their ability to act rationally, or at least to be perceived to do so. Moral incentives are based largely on the social situation one finds themselves in.

> Social behavior, in particular in small groups, is more complex, and norms of behavior culturally inculcated play a large role in shaping societies. However, it would be foolish not to recognize the role of private incentives in motivating behavior in addition to these cultural phenomena.
>
> Laffont and Martimort (2001:12).

Coercive incentives are often related and interlinked with moral incentives, often in the most extreme cases (as with the example of the drug dealer), yet many others are not. As the tale of *Robin Hood* shows us, there may be a moral incentive to take from the rich and give to the poor, but there is certainly a coercive incentive not to do so. The fictional character is also commonly known for taking none of this stolen wealth for himself, omitting any potential remunerative incentive. Indeed we could ponder for much time the various hypothetical examples which include various mixtures of these incentives – we must, however, move onto the theory of the capitalist firm and how incentives are structured within them.

The Principal-Agent Dilemma

As stated in the previous chapter, although not all of us are required to work for an enterprise to earn enough to maintain subsistence, it can generally be assumed that most of us have/are/will. Although a self-employed individual may not work for a particular firm, they may exchange their labour-power with various companies and individual clients. What is essential nonetheless is that an exchange takes place between two parties – what we can call a 'principal' and an 'agent'. Under the classical example, an agent is someone who is given a task to perform on the behalf of the principal. For example a large multinational corporation could be the principal, whilst an individual worker for that company is the agent. Another example could be a resident being the principal, whilst a self-employed labourer, tasked to erect a wall in the resident's garden, is the agent. It is in the self-interest of the principal (an incentive) that the task delegated to the agent is carried out specifically to the principle's specifications. In return, the principal offers something in exchange, usually a payment of money, to give the agent as an incentive to perform the task. The two parties negotiate to form a contract or an informal agreement. Like all negotiated agreements, both parties accept that the deal reached will not be the best possible outcome for either side. The resident would like a wall built for free, whilst the labourer would like to receive payment without building the wall, or to build the wall for a very high payment. These polar opposites must meet somewhere in the middle. Concessions must be made and an agreement must be reached, as the incentive to reach a deal outweighs the consequences of not.

Although the two parties both have an 'incentive' for the task to be performed, this may not necessarily be a remunerative incentive. To use the earlier example, if the resident fails have a wall erected in their garden, they may run the risk of having their house flooded – a coercive incentive. Similarly, if the self-employed labourer requires the money exchanged for performing the task in order to maintain their own subsistence, they too have a coercive incentive to accept the task. The 'principal-agent dilemma' arises when the contract/agreement of the two parties is breached and an inequality emerges. This typically emerges when the agent has an incentive to diverge from the contract, usually if the principal is unbeknown of the agent's actions.

Under these circumstances, the agent has private knowledge on how to cheat the unsuspecting principal, and the principal has 'imperfect information' regarding the agent's intent and subsequent actions. "Delegation of a task to an agent who has different objectives than the principal who delegates this task is problematic when information about the agent is imperfect. This is the essence of incentive questions." (Laffont and Martimort, 2001:12). Our self-employed wall builder may overprice the resident once the job is complete, on the pretence that more materials needed to be used when they in fact were not. The labourer may do a shoddy job, using cheaper materials or not upholding to the principal's specifications but knowing the principal is unlikely to find out and will be paid the original price. Both examples demonstrate the principal-agent dilemma in action. An employee (the agent) of a large corporation (the principal) holds similar incentives to cheat, for example by doing as little work as possible, again knowing that management are unlikely to find out. All of this involves risk, and the practice of diverging from the agreement creates a 'moral hazard', one party taking a risk at the expense of the other. Situations such as these always have and always will continue to bedevil the principal of any transaction. Nothing is likely to change this reality.

Under a labour theory of value analysis, a great battle between the capitalist and the worker emerges. Using Marx's analysis, the exchange of labour for life necessities is an unequal one, as the capitalist will work tirelessly until the worker produces more value for them than the value of what that worker is consequently paid. In retaliation, the worker may strive to utilise as little effort as possible, or break the contract/agreement in another way to their own reward. As the worker bares the greater risk of losing their job, the capitalist will always hold the upper hand. Under this scenario the capitalist corporation (the principal) has a remunerative incentive to exploit the labourer (the agent), the labourer has a coercive incentive to follow the guidelines of the company as strictly as possible. Whereas the company can simply find another labourer to produce further profits, the labourer requires employment if they are to maintain their own subsistence, and may not be able to find another job if fired. Political economists as early as Smith recognised that the bargaining power between the masters and the workmen was far from equal, noting the consequences if neither individual master nor individual workman come to an agreement.

> In all such disputes the masters can hold out much longer. A landlord, a farmer, a master manufacturer, a merchant, though they did not employ a single workman, could generally live a year or two upon the stocks which they have already acquired. Many workmen could not subsist a week, few could subsist a month, and scarce any a year without employment. In the long run the workman may be as necessary to his master as his master is to him; but the necessity is not so immediate.
>
> Smith (1776:56-7)

In the short run, as in Smith's time as our own, the main incentive for the principal is remunerative, whilst the main incentive for the agent it is coercive. With this being said, the agent will still attempt to cheat the principal if they can, but to what extent? In the vast majority of cases, it is not what the agent takes from the principal, but what they do not give. Jaroslav Vanek, an economist who will feature repeatedly throughout this work, sheds further light on the matter. Due to the agent-principal dilemma, workers in a capitalist company will strive to find what Vanek (1970) calls a 'minimal acceptable effort limit' (MAEL). This theory has been illustrated in Figure 2. Imagine that the amount of effort our imaginary 'worker X' applies can be drawn as a vertical column. The top line of the column shows what the firm expects from the worker, the expected level of effort (ELE). As the firm wants to maximise the amount of value the worker creates/enables, the top line also represents what the firm believes is the maximum amount of effort that worker can apply.

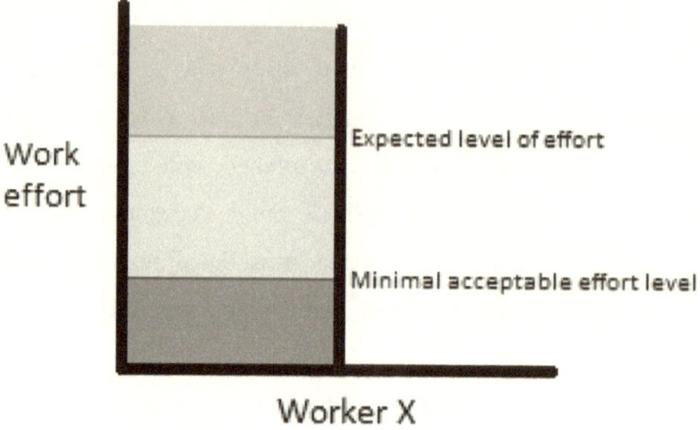

Figure 2

If the worker is applying effort in the upper zone, above the ELE line, they are applying more work than the firm expects. If they are in the middle zone, below the ELE line, they are applying less effort than the firm expects. If worker X applies too little effort, going below the bottom line, they will be sacked. As such, they must ensure they apply at least the minimal acceptable effort level, to be at or just above the MAEL line.

The MAEL will always be below what the expected level of effort the capitalist demands. It is important to re-emphasise that it is in the self-interest of the principal that the task delegated to the agent is carried out specifically to the principal's specifications. If the agent can perform that task with a lesser degree of effort but not to an extent that they will lose their job, they have located the minimal acceptable effort limit. Although there is a coercive incentive for the worker to retain their job, there is a remunerative incentive to locate the minimal acceptable limit of effort. Usually, this is not a case of employees intentionally deciding to apply less effort than usual, but is usually a subconscious acceptance that they needn't work any harder than what they need to. A worker will try their hardest not to drop below this boundary, or they will lose their job and the means to maintain subsistence. On the other hand, a worker will not move above the boundary as there is often no initial remunerative, moral or coercive incentive to do so – they get paid the same amount regardless. This understanding is not a particularly new phenomenon. John Stuart Mill explains the intricate relationship between capitalist and labourer in his *Principles of Political Economy*, and makes the following remarks:

But the civilizing and improving influences of association, and the efficiency and economy of production on a large scale, may be obtained without dividing the producers into two parties with hostile interests and feelings, the many who do the work being mere servants under the command of the one who supplies the funds, and having no interest of their own in the enterprise except to earn their wages with as little labour as possible.

Mill, (1848:198)

As greater utility/satisfaction can be gained from applying less effort, and as there is no incentive for the agent to apply more effort, there is thus a remunerative incentive for the agent to locate the MAEL. The MAEL for a particular worker is never static, it is likely to adjust to changing situations and circumstances. If a work-shy worker suddenly realises their work is being more carefully monitored, the MAEL is likely to increase up our imaginary scale – there is less opportunity to shirk, as shown in Figure 3. If the regional manager is visiting the premises and plans to spend an hour or so inspecting the business, the collective MAEL is likely to increase for that short amount of time, until the regional manager eventually leaves and things return to business at usual.

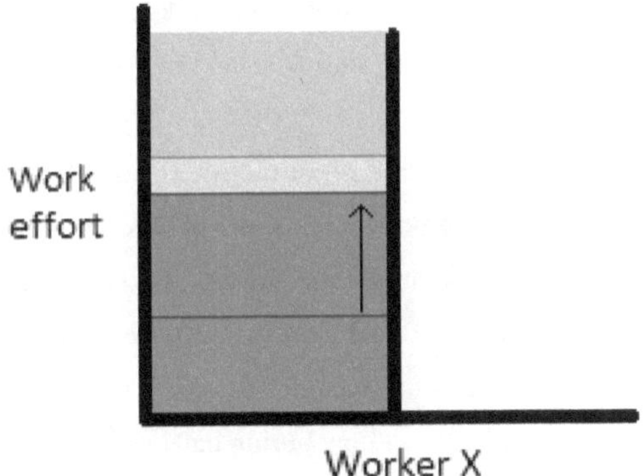

Figure 3

The same process happens in reverse. If your superior is away for the week, you may suddenly find the workplace becomes less strenuous and more relaxed and informal. One may start to take more liberties, to apply less effort, to be less productive or more wasteful. The MAEL decreases down the scale, as there is more scope for shirking, as shown in Figure 4.

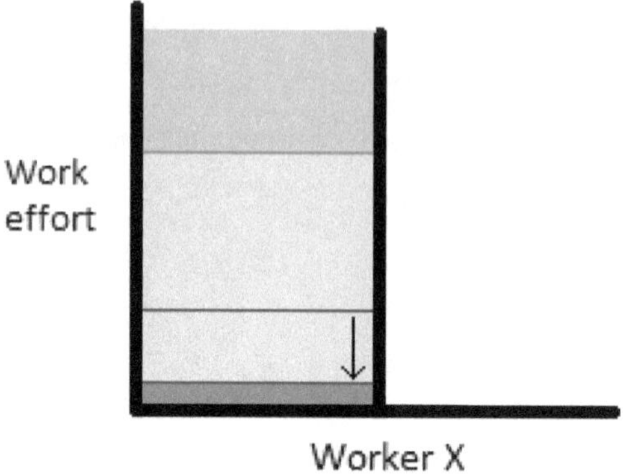

Figure 4

We must also remember that due to the agent-principal dilemma, the worker maybe in the middle or bottom zones without the employer initially knowing, they could be under the impression that the worker is instead working at or around the top ELE line. The worker will themselves interpret what the MAEL is and what risks they can take. If the employer realises that the worker has worked below the minimal level (in the bottom zone), the worker will be fired. If the employer realises that the worker is instead in the middle zone, they will not sack the worker, but will likely take steps in future to raise the MAEL or find other ways to increase effort applied.

Most working people will be able to think of a time where something like this has taken place. There are is an abundance of humorous accounts of workers who have found their MAEL to be lower than the norm. For example the story of the employee who simply stopped attending work on Fridays, preferring instead to do a 4 day week, without any other employee or superior taking notice. Another story includes that of a secretary who spent a large portion of her working day writing a book on how boring her job was. These examples demonstrate how incentives influence our actions at work.

Only if there is some form of alternative remunerative, moral or coercive incentive will the minimal acceptable effort limit of the worker reach the expected effort limit desired by the principal. As Vanek notes below, a fixed income at subsistence level is by no means a route to resolving this.

[I]t is a well known biological fact that near subsistence one is generally able to supply only very small effort, if any, and that with increasing income beyond subsistence one can, and one generally does, increase effort considerably.

Vanek (1970:252)

Coercive Incentives Under Capitalism

One way to bring up the MAEL back to the desired level, or perhaps even beyond it, is to intensify coercive incentives. To recall, the agent must have private knowledge as to how to cheat the principal and the means to get away with it, and consequently the principal must have imperfect information regarding the agent's private knowledge and the consequential actions the agent may take. The principal, in this case a capitalist enterprise, must mitigate this information gap. However, doing so comes at a financial cost. Our hypothetical company can use coercive incentives in two methods. The first is reactionary, to actively seek out employees who are working below the expected level of effort. The second is preventative, by making it more difficult for employees to cheat in the first place.

In reality both are used. For example a new work monitoring system has the dual effect of preventing a worker to shirk, as it becomes more risky for the worker to do so, whilst also allowing the firm to pro-actively uncover shirkers allowing for some form of penalty to take place. Some policies are only preventative, by filtering access to online material such as social media on company computers for example. This prevents the worker from cheating the firm but the firm is unlikely to know the worker ever tried to cheat to begin with. At the same time some policies are solely reactionary. A company may conduct an unannounced crackdown on a particular habit, such as exceeding the length of breaks or overusing company facilities, and may enact disciplinary measures to compensate. In this case, the agent had no prior knowledge of the actions the principal took.

Some companies may even go to extreme measures to enact coercive incentives to close the informational gap. One British example of this was Sports Direct, a UK based retailer in sporting equipment and clothing. An investigative report by *The Guardian*[14] revealed the extent to which employees were poorly treated within their Derbyshire distribution centre – locally referred to as "the gulag". Undercover reporters witnessed how employees were constantly monitored on CCTV and where they constantly received shout-outs on the tannoys to work more quickly. Employees were also prohibited from wearing a vast array of clothing products which may be mistaken for products stolen by workers on shift, all of whom are required to undertake extensive searches when entering and leaving the workplace, sometimes stripping to the last layer of clothing. Pay is docked if workers clock-in a minute late or clock-out a minute early, and are paid nothing if they work overtime. It was also reported how employees were afraid of conversing with their superiors in case of being sacked.

Sports Direct is not alone in undertaking such demeaning work standards – examples such as these are being uncovered all the time. Such efforts could reach the point where the employer is not only reducing the incentive and ability to cheat, but also risking breaking the contract themselves. The 15 minute mandatory checks and hawkish clock-in procedures taken by Sports Direct effectively resulted in employees being paid below the minimum wage[15].

Whether desirable or not, coercive incentives function as an essential component of the modern capitalist firm. The greatest weakness of the coercive incentive approach is that firms must pay considerable amounts if they are to increase the collective MAEL to the level of effort which the firm expects. Installing CCTV, employing CCTV monitors, employing foremen, installing filtering, conducting random spot checks and tests, etc. all come at a cost which the firm must bear. Indeed a bizarre situation may emerge where the firm is spending more money to prevent and catch idle employees than what the company receives in additional revenue from those very measures. This is all money which could otherwise be spent towards more productive endeavours.

There is also the human element of being under constant surveillance and at constant fear of disciplinary procedures. Such approaches might even have the effect of lowering morale and reducing the MAEL rather than increasing it. As Stiglitz (2012:114) rightfully points out: "Perceptions of unfairness affect behavior. If individuals believe that their employer is treating them unfairly, they are more likely to shirk on the job." Extreme examples are not difficult to find. The militaristic working conditions of Foxconn in China being one of those examples. They had been using coercive incentives to such an extent that suicides were becoming a considerable problem, enough of a problem to the extent where the company had to install suicide nets[16]. When this effect is analysed in less extreme circumstances, we still see a high rate of staff turnover and low productivity. Why would a worker in such working conditions wish to give their absolute best, their absolute most? The short answer is, they won't. They will work as hard as they need to and no more. Coercive incentives are thus a largely ineffective, inefficient and inhumane way of dealing with the principal-agent dilemma should it occur. Ideally, alternative forms of incentive must be applied.

Moral Incentives Under Capitalism

Locating moral incentives within capitalist firms is more difficult, especially in the case of the worker and firm and the principal-agent dilemma. We can often locate moral incentives in public and not-for-profit organisations; schools, hospitals, charities, etc. In these situations an employee may actually apply more effort than what is expected (the ELE) – with or without other remunerative and coercive incentives in place. The ability to help the sick, to teach children or to serve the public good may be enough to resolve the principal-agent dilemma in these cases. Most of this will of course be dependent on the individual, as not everyone will be willing to go above and beyond what is expected for moral justifications. However, within capitalist firms such incentives are few and far between. Working not for the public good, but instead to earn profits for a rich minority of investor-owners, is far from a moral incentive.

If the principal is a small business owner who is struggling to maintain their own subsistence, whilst the agent – in this case one of a small number of employees – is living quite comfortably, there may be a moral incentive to apply an added level of effort. Family-run businesses are also likely to inhibit this line of thinking. Alternatively, an employee may have a moral incentive to perform the tasks set for reasons other than simply earning the company a profit. An employee may genuinely believe the product they are selling on the behalf of the company could drastically improve lives. The production and sale of medicines could be a good example of this. The moral incentive of performing the task set may outweigh the remunerative incentive to apply as little effort as possible at a level of minimal acceptable work effort. Although such incentives may exist for a minority of workers in capitalist firms, it can easily be assumed that this is not the case for the majority of workers, whose MAEL (however large or small) will still be below the expected level set by the firm.

Remunerative Incentives Under Capitalism

In most cases, the most effective form of incentive is remunerative. Unlike coercive incentives, an individual has the potential to gain something rather than running the risk of having something taken away. A material gain can be tangible such as money, a new car or home, or can be intangible such as a feeling of pride, having more free time, or the ability to work in a less stressful and intense workplace. The question we must answer however, is how do we reduce the remunerative incentives for the agent to cheat and instead apply remunerative incentives which bring the level of effort applied at or beyond the expected level of effort? Put simply, how do we get employees to work harder without threatening to take something away from them? The opposite to this remunerative incentive to cheat will be referred to as a remunerative incentive to cooperate – as it is in both the interest of the principal and the agent to increase the effort applied by the agent.

Let us use an example of an apple picker to illustrate this. If the owner of an orchard (the principal) employs an apple picker (the agent) to pick apples from their trees, there may be a remunerative incentive for the apple picker to cheat. The picker may stroll around the orchard at a leisurely pace, applying little effort but being paid the same wage nonetheless. Alternatively, the picker may have an incentive to steal and stash a bag of apples away to collect after work for their own consumption. As it is difficult for the orchard owner to know of whether the picker is committing such dastardly acts (a large information gap) it would be costly to apply coercive incentives, such as installing CCTV, employing monitors, searching for stashed stolen apples, etc. Instead the orchard owner applies remunerative incentives to cooperate. If the contract between the orchard owner and the apple picker was for the picker to return at the end of the day with five bags of apples in return for a money wage (equal to their subsistence), the owner could apply a bonus for every additional bag over the expected threshold of five. If this incentive to cooperate outweighs the incentive to cheat, the apple picker's level of effort applied would exceed the expected level of effort demanded by the orchard owner. It is still feasible that the picker could both cooperate and cheat, for example retuning with over five bags, collecting the bonus, whilst still having a bag of apples stashed away somewhere for collecting post-payment. If the incentive to cooperate is truly greater than the incentive to cheat, the picker would avoid cheating, as the risk of losing the bonus scheme outweighs the gains made from cheating. In economic relations there will always be some form of incentive to cheat, this is an inevitability. The question however, should be how can we can raise the collective level of effort applied up to or beyond the level of effort expected by the principal in a sustainable, effective and humane manner? Only remunerative incentives to cooperate can effectively bring about such a process.

The use of remunerative incentives applied by capitalist firms are few in number, but are not totally uncommon within modern capitalist economies. The prospect of promotion is an obvious example, employees applying more effort in order to increase the chances of being offered a more satisfying or financially rewarding job. This is never a guaranteed path to reward, it may be years until a better position is offered, and the likelihood of being offered it over others must also be considered. Bonus schemes are also prevalent across a variety of industries. Those working in sales are often given a form of commission whenever they make a sale or sell over a particular limit. Those working in the most highly paid positions are also often eligible to bonus schemes, rewarded for improving company profitability, driving up standards, improving efficiency, developing new innovations, etc.

The issue however, is that the vast majority of workers in capitalist firms are offered little if any form of remunerative incentive. In addition, the bonuses earned will not fully add up to the surplus value being created by that worker, meaning an inequality still exists. Even in the unlikely scenario where there is no incentive to cheat and employees work at the level of expected effort, there still remains no incentive to innovate, to improve efficiency, and so on. This is particularly true of those in the lowest paid positions with little prospect of promotion. The reality is that many employees will work at the minimal acceptable effort level and will care little of the company they work for other than its ability to pay their wages. Even if some form of remunerative incentive is established, there comes a cut-off point where added bonuses and commissions are no longer cost-effective for the firm – whose primary aim after all is to maximise total profits for the company owners. This arrangement is clearly not optimal.

The question arises as to how incentives can be naturally rather than artificially induced. As will be argued in the succeeding chapter, if we are to incentivise a nation's workforce, we must totally re-evaluate the capitalist-worker relationship and form a principal-agent model where remunerative incentives take centre stage in the process of production. The current situation is simply not good enough. It incentivises lower levels of effort to be applied by the workforce, whilst leaving no incentive for the workers to innovate or improve efficiency. Conventional capitalism prides itself on being the most 'efficient' economic model. Our theory of incentives contradicts this, exposing large gaps between what a firm expects of its workforce and what is actually delivered. It also exposes an untapped ability for workers to improve their productivity and stake in the firm, if only they had the remunerative incentives to want to do so. This issue, this second pillar of the dual-contradiction, must be resolved.

---

[14]   The Guardian (2015a) *A day at 'the gulag': what it's like to work at Sports Direct's warehouse.* Available at: https://www.theguardian.com/business/2015/dec/09/sports-direct-warehouse-work-conditions

[15]   The Guardian (2015b) *Revealed: how Sports Direct effectively pays below minimum wage.* Available at: https://www.theguardian.com/business/2015/dec/09/how-sports-direct-effectively-pays-below-minimum-wage-pay

[16]   The Guardian (2017) https://www.theguardian.com/technology/2017/jun/18/foxconn-life-death-forbidden-city-longhua-suicide-apple-iphone-brian-merchant-one-device-extract

Chapter 3: Solving the Dual-Contradiction

"[C]o-operation tends ... to increase the productiveness of labour ... by placing the labourers, as a mass, in a relation to their work which would make it their principle and their interest—at present it is neither—to do the utmost, instead of the least possible, in exchange for their remuneration."

Mill, 1848:202

Moulding together the previous two chapters and the dynamics of the dual-contradiction become clearer. There is a distinct relationship between the inequality of income found within the modern capitalist firm and the lack of incentives for employees to apply more effort then what is necessary. This can be framed in two ways:

The Labour Theory

- Within the process of production the worker produces more value (a surplus value) for the capitalist than the capitalist pays the worker in exchange. As the capitalist strives to pay the worker the lowest fixed wage possible, there is no incentive for the worker to apply any more effort than is needed for them to retain their job. The employees work exceeds reward, the employers reward exceeds work.

The Subjectivist Theory

- Within the process of production the worker agrees a wage rate with the capitalist which is representative of the market rate for their role. As the worker does not own the means of production they are not earning as much as they could if they were a shareholder. As the worker's wage is hardly ever affected by the profitability of the firm there is no incentive for the worker to apply any more effort than is needed for them to retain their job. The employees work is equal reward, but the employers reward exceeds work.

The dual-contradiction = employees do not earn an initial share of the profits they help to create + employees have no initial incentive to apply more effort than what they deem necessary.

We can call this a 'contradiction' because it contradicts the notion that conventional capitalism is both the most efficient and most deserving economic model available at our disposal. As we have seen, this is far from true. The purpose of this chapter is to explore how the dual-contradiction can be solved. In order to do so, previous models, current popular suggestions and the preferred suggestion of this study will be analysed each in turn. The consequences of the dual-contradiction both as they appear historically and in contemporary times must be resolved if we are to deal with the major social ills we find in our societies. The historic sporadic shifts of economic inequality and the consequential health and social implications, the lack of employee incentive to innovate and improve efficiency, the lack of purpose and worthiness many employees feel in their jobs, and a whole host of other needless social ills all have a link, in some way or another, to the dual-contradiction. We must be in no doubt that the joint issues surrounding inequality and disincentive cannot be solved individually, both must be tackled if a sustainable and humane route to success is to emerge and take shape. We must now move on to the potential suggestions for resolving the dual-contradiction.

Redistribution

In most advanced economies redistribution of income is the most widely used tool for dealing with economic inequality. This method allows the surplus value creating process to remain uninterrupted, and only addresses the issues of inequality once the surplus value has been produced. The most common route for redistributing income is through taxation. Governments tax companies once profits have been made, they tax workers once wages are paid, they tax commodities when they are finally sold, and so on. This revenue is then used to, among other things, top-up the incomes of the poor. The government is essentially a middleman which forces one party to give up a slice of their income to another party. In addition, governments may tax wealth to deal with inequality – using land taxes, inheritance taxes, wealth taxes, etc. For as long as governments are effectively able to collect tax revenue and then allocate it efficiently, this system is workable.

There are, however, a multitude of constraints which prevent redistributive policies from solving the dual-contradiction, both concerning tax collection and public spending. We shall deal with both respectively. Regarding tax collection, if the issues surrounding inequality are to be solved, the rich must pay more tax relative to the poor. Taxing the poor to only give cash back to the poor is a purposeless, bureaucratic and costly process. A redistributive approach to solving inequality requires the rich pay more than the poor, but to what degree?

Using either labour theory or subjective theory of value, we know that the employer receives a profit that is brought about by the surplus value produced by the employees. If the inequality element of the dual-contradiction is to be resolved entirely using redistributive taxation, the entire amount of profit made from surplus value must be taxed. In reality this is impractical. Front and foremost, this would remove any remunerative incentive for the capitalist to invest in an enterprise only for their profit to be taxed away and redistributed to their workforce.

Before investors invest in a particular industry, they must have some form of expectation that what they are investing in will either be the most profitable, or the least risky, or perhaps a middle ground between the two. If these returns are to be taxed, the investors are likely to shy away from that industry and perhaps invest in an alternative venture, such as property speculation for example. Solving the dual-contradiction in its entirety cannot be achieved via redistribution alone. Governments could instead tax only a small part of a company's profits, as many currently do, but this would neither fully resolve the dual-contradiction, as workers are still not earning as much as they should/could, there is still no incentive for workers to apply more effort than what is necessary, and taxes still damage incentives for investors to at least some extent. Even in a hypothetical situation where governments attempted to tax all of a company's surplus value, in an increasingly globalised financial system, firms and investors are most likely to offshore their profits and evade/avoid government tax collectors. Unless some form of international tax regime is established, the prospect of applying above average tax rates is an unrealistic method for resolving the dual-contradiction.

The issues surrounding redistribution cover not only the collection of tax, but also how it is spent. In addition to the potential disincentives that high tax rates provide to businesses and business owners, there is also no additional incentive given to the workers. In reality, governments do not tax individual businesses, keep that money separate and redistribute that money to the same firm's employees. Social welfare is universalised. Governments collect the taxes of all firms and spend that money according to national priorities. As such, taxes are collected and are then redistributed not according to the success of the company a benefit-recipient works for, but is instead based on the claimant's individual circumstances. There is no link between the work and reward of a specific worker, they are instead judged mainly on their income, which, as we have said, tends to be a fixed rate that is not reflective of effort applied. Workers can be given income top-ups, such as working tax credits for example, but these are typically distributed at a fixed rate that is in no way determined by the success or failure of any particular firm, let alone the firm they are employed by. Consequently, there is no additional remunerative incentive for the employees to work above the MAEL. As will be explored in more depth later, effort applied by a worker is only likely to fluctuate once the amount they receive for applying that effort fluctuates. If a worker is to receive a fixed income regardless of effort applied, the dual-contradiction is still in force – often regardless of how high or low that fixed income is. Governments require vast amounts of information to determine who is 'deserving' of the welfare the state can potentially provide. Many of the poorest may be left out, whilst the richest may benefit from loopholes in the system. One potential solution to this is the introduction of a 'universal basic income', where every citizen receives enough money from government to maintain their subsistence, regardless of any other factor such as whether or not they are in employment. Although policies such as this have the potential to do a great deal of good, they nonetheless fail to deal with the fundamental foundations of the dual-contradiction, nor indeed do they intend to. Fixed incomes are unlikely to affect effort applied, and state welfare will never fully recompense workers with the surplus value they have helped to produce.

In sum, redistribution is an ineffective and unrealistic method for reducing economic inequality stemming from the process of creating surplus value, it can create disincentives for businesses, and creates no incentive for workers to maximise their effort. This does not mean that redistribution is ineffective at resolving other issues. There is certainly a role for redistribution in tackling inequality from other sources, to provide access to education, healthcare, etc. This is not a critique of redistribution generally. However, the dual-contradiction cannot be prevented using this method, only partly solved, and this is not good enough. Ideas such as Piketty's (2014) global wealth tax, along with the concept of the basic income, may be radical attempts at resolving excessive levels of economic inequality, but they do not root out the cause of the surplus value process and do little to alter workers' incentives. We will pick up on radical redistributive policies later on, but for the time being they must be disregarded as an effective way of preventing the causes of the dual-contradiction.

Basic Pre-distribution

It has become clear at this stage that the causes of the dual-contradiction must be resolved before the process of production rather than after it. That is, workers must be given guarantees to the fruits of their labour prior to the production process, not forcibly done so by government or any other outside actor. Also, incentives must be naturally derived from within the firm, as nurturing incentives through the welfare system can often be expensive, ineffective and sometimes even contradictory. Rather than redistribution, we are now concerned with pre-distribution. Preventing the dual-contradiction rather than curing it.

This section will deal firstly with basic forms of pre-distribution, asking how do we guarantee workers a greater share of the profits they help produce initially rather than after the production process through the tax system, and how do we implant some form of incentive to work above the MAEL. It will be of no surprise however, that many of these basic methods inhibit the same problems surrounding redistribution. Let us take two examples: the minimum wage, and collective bargaining. The two methods are in fact very similar, with the former being driven by government whilst the latter being driven primarily by trade unions. The main similarity is that both policies intentionally push wages up above the market value[17], in an attempt to claw back the presumed surplus value the workers are expected to produce.

Minimum wage legislation is used to ensure that employers do not pay workers below a certain threshold. If this threshold equals the amount a worker requires for them to maintain subsistence, then we refer to this as a 'living wage'. In a capitalist economy, this policy is essential as it allows for employees to be guaranteed at least enough income to maintain subsistence, whilst boosting disposable income thereby increasing demand for goods and services for firms to produce and sell. Collective bargaining on the other hand, is another mechanism designed to push up employees' wages to protect their real terms value. Trade unions are also essential in a capitalist economy to ensure that working conditions are acceptable and that workers are treated with dignity. The issue, however, comes from when wages are, in the eyes of the capitalist, unjustifiably pushed above their market value – when minimum wages are above what is needed for subsistence, and when trade unions bargain wage rates which are above the market rate for the particular profession in question. Similarly to redistribution, basic pre-distributive policies do not give the workers all of what they should/could be earning (the full surplus value) and because income is not linked to effort, there is no initial remunerative incentive to work above the minimal acceptable effort limit. These mechanisms can also distort the natural incentives for businesses. Increasing wage bills means companies must either eat away at their own profits, or push up prices potentially creating an inflationary spiral or threatening competitiveness[18]. As mentioned earlier, if investors' profits begin to diminish, they are likely to look for more profitable endeavours elsewhere, threatening the very survival of the employees' jobs altogether. Indeed, companies may prefer to decrease the size of its workforce to cut costs, increasing the amount of unemployed workers in the economy, pushing down wage rates. Although basic pre-distributive policies such as the minimum wage and trade union legislation have been essential in protecting workers from under-subsistence wages and poor working conditions, they can only go so far in dismantling the root cause of the dual-contradiction. Once again, the dual-contradiction has not been fully resolved and distortionary effects can take hold. More radical solutions must be sought.

Rather than being obliged to push up wages by government or unions, the company may unilaterally decide to increase wages in order to keep employees loyal. Note the following quote: "The combination of partial monitoring with the payment of a higher wage can be used to induce workers to choose to work hard, the threat of the loss of the better-paid job acting as an incentive not to shirk" (Atkinson, 2015:251). The point on the use of coercive incentives, monitoring specifically, and the weaknesses they bring, has already been made. The wage increase theory however, holds its own contradictions. Firstly, the coercive incentive of losing a better paid job is diminished if other employers increase their wages to match it – this is not uncommon in circumstances where specialist skills are scare. Secondly, some workers may see a moral incentive to work harder as a form of appreciation for their wage increase, but there is still no remunerative incentive to do so. They are still paid the same (now higher) wage regardless of effort applied. Lastly, there is the effect of time, the effects of the pay increase are likely to diminish over time, especially if inflation starts to eat away at the value of the workers' income, or if workers believe they are due another pay rise but are unlikely to receive one. Workers' incomes should be determined by the effort they apply, and not by the moods and whims of employers, governments or other bodies.

Extensive Pre-distribution

Unlike basic pre-distribution, extensive pre-distribution focuses not upon working with or against capitalist companies, but removing the capitalist investor-owners from the ownership and management of the firm altogether. Rather than dealing with business owners, they are instead replaced with a different type of owner. This suggestion may appear radical, revolutionary and perhaps even utopian at face value, but some of the following proposals may not appear as unrealistically grandiose as it may at first seem. The principal question is: if capitalist investors are not the best actors to own and manage the 'means of production' (enterprises), who is? There are a few suggestions which will be analysed, the first of which however has often been the most popular suggestion – the state. A political economy where the majority of firms are owned and managed by the state has traditionally been called 'socialism', although this term would appear to mean different things at different times to different people. To avoid confusion we will use the traditional definition of socialism – state ownership of the means of production.

Before moving onto the intricacies of state ownership we must first make an important distinction between two core economic process: the mode of production and the mode of distribution. If we are analysing the mode of production we are analysing how commodities are produced, by whom and, more importantly, who is collecting the profits. A socialist political economy (socialist mode of production) is when the ownership of the means of production, and thus the ability to produce commodities, is the responsibility of the state, or perhaps another layer of government such as local/regional government or perhaps even an international institution like the European Union for example. If the means of production are owned and managed by investors, as they tend to be in most advanced economies, we call this a capitalist political economy (capitalist mode of production). The 'mode of distribution' however, is different to the mode of production, as it is concerned with how commodities are distributed to consumers once they have been produced.

In a 'planned economy', governments decide how much of a particular commodity needs to be produced, and once it has been produced, then distributes the commodities to its citizens according to need. Under a 'market economy' individuals and free enterprise decide how much of a particular commodity to produce and then distributes their products into a wider marketplace where consumers typically exchange money for the commodity on sale. In most advanced capitalist economies, the free market distributes the majority of goods and services, whilst the state distributes basic public services. Throughout this research we will argue that well regulated free markets are currently the most efficient means to distribute goods and services. This may not be the case for all eternity, but we are concerned with the here and now. Consequently, we are not concerned at this stage about changing the mode of distribution, but we are concerned about changing the mode of production, or the ownership and management of the means of production to be more specific, in order to resolve the dual-contradiction.

Returning to the issue of extensive pre-distribution, a socialist ownership of the means of production would have to work within a free market framework, if we are following our above rule. An example of this could be the Chinese model, where the majority of companies are owned and managed by the state, but where such companies have to work within a domestic and international free market environment. But does this socialist model do anything to resolve the dual-contradiction? The answer is almost certainly no. In fact, from previous real world examples, the socialist model would appear to exacerbate the dual-contradiction, especially regarding incentives. In theory, socialism is a form of pre-distribution because workers are guaranteed a greater share of the surplus value they help to create prior to that surplus value being produced. However the means in which workers receive that share of the surplus value works in a similar way to the 'tax and spend' policies of redistribution explored earlier. Under socialism, as the state owns the means of production, they earn the total surplus value the workers produce rather than taxing and collecting a portion of it. So far, there is no difference between this and capitalism.

Unlike capitalism, the state promises to distribute the majority of this surplus value to all the states' citizens. This is pre-distribution using redistributive methods. Workers are guaranteed a greater share of the surplus value they produce, but what they eventually receive back from the state may not equate to how much surplus value any individual worker or firm has produced. Socialist governments collect the total amount of surplus value produced by the whole economy, and then distribute it according to political preferences rather than how much surplus value each worker produced. The government may instead decide to distribute the total surplus value according to worker income, workers age, where they live, and so on and so forth. Similarly to capitalism with redistributive welfare, socialism creates a situation where workers receive a fixed income with top-up benefits that are not related to effort applied. There is no incentive for workers to apply more effort than the **MAEL** because they are assured that they will receive the same amount of income regardless of what level of effort they apply to their work. The dual-contradiction is therefore still in force. Inequality is still in place as workers have no guarantee that the amount of surplus value they produce will be the same as what they get back from the state, and as their incomes are likely to be fixed there is no remunerative incentive to apply any more effort than what is required for them to remain employed. In capitalist companies, there is usually some form of incentive for those at the top of the hierarchy to apply more effort[19]. Company owners may in fact also be company managers. They, at least, have an incentive for the firm to be as profitable as possible. In state-owned firms, not even this form of incentive is present, as the state is the sole owner of the firm and has guaranteed to distribute the surplus value among its citizens as it sees fit. Consequently, regarding initial remunerative incentives, the choice between socialism and capitalism is inconsequential. As such, both capitalist and socialist models, in terms of the dual-contradiction, share the same structural weaknesses.

If investor or state forms of company ownership inhibit the dual-contradiction, what about consumer ownership of the means of production? The most common types of firms owned by their customers are 'consumer cooperatives'. For financial institutions owned by their customer base, these types of organisations are typically referred to as 'mutuals'. Under this model, any member of the public can purchase an equal share of the company and own a share of the profits the firm makes. Dividends are usually linked to a percentage of the total amount a consumer-owner spends at the firm. Say for example the rate of profit distributed to shareholders at a grocery consumer cooperative is five per cent. If a consumer-owner visits the store very rarely, and spends £200 in total that year, their dividend for that year would be £10. If another consumer-owner uses the store quite frequently, spending £4000 that year, their dividend will be £200. There is an incentive for the consumer-owner to purchase from the store as frequently as possible in order to maximise returns. This may also prevent the consumer-owner from shopping at rival grocery stores, of which they are not shareholders of, including competitors which may for example offer cheaper prices on certain products they may buy more frequently.

It could therefore be argued to at least some degree that consumer cooperatives are anti-competitive, as they encourage consumers to stick with one particular firm rather than encouraging them to seek more competitive prices through other firms. Consumer cooperatives may be more suited for local monopolies where there is no financial scope for competition, or possibly for public goods which the state or local authorities can or should not provide. Although incentives are present for consumer-owners, there are certainly no incentives for the workers to apply any more effort than they otherwise would in a capitalist or state owned firm. The surplus value created by the workers is received by the consumer-owners in a form of dividends which is determined by the amount of goods and services each consumer-owner has bought within a given time period. Unless every consumer is simultaneously a worker, the dual-contradiction remains in place. Indeed, similar to state owned companies, consumer cooperatives are likely to offer even less remunerative incentives than capitalist firms. As mentioned earlier, in capitalist firms, those at the top of the hierarchy are usually those who have some form of ownership of that firm – their level of effort applied is likely to be the maximum possible effort they can apply, as they are the ones to gain the most from increased profitability. In consumer owned firms, those workers at the top of the hierarchy, similarly to those at the bottom, will have no initial incentive to apply any more effort than their own MAEL.

Worker Ownership and Management

The proposals we have discussed so far – redistribution, minimum wage, collective bargaining, state ownership, consumer ownership – all have relatively attractive traits in some respects. Regardless of whether the dual-contradiction has been resolved or not, all of these proposals have an important role to play in modern capitalist economies, whether it be tackling low pay, resolving workplace disputes, improving working conditions, providing public services and so on. However, regarding the ownership of the means of production, we are beginning to see a pattern emerge: all those who own the firm but who are external of the firm – the state, customers, trade unions, etc. – all conceive some form of the dual-contradiction within the process of production. Instead we must shift the argument in favour of those who are internal of the firm – the workforce. Can worker ownership of the means of production reduce surplus value inequality and increase remunerative incentives above the MAEL? Using the theory we have applied so far, it would certainly appear so.

First of all, within a worker-owned firm, the workers receive the surplus value they have created. Therefore, there is no initial inequality within the process of production. Using the labour theory of value, the worker earns the surplus value they create once the commodity has been sold, they receive it as a form of dividend/surplus on top of their wages. The worker therefore has an incentive to apply as much effort possible, well above the MAEL of a capitalist firm, in order to maximise the profit they receive. Under the subjective theory of value, a strikingly similar picture emerges. The worker continues to earn the wage expected within the wider labour market, but as the worker is now a shareholder, they now earn an income in addition to their wage in the form of a dividend/bonus. Using both theories of value, the worker receives the surplus value they help to create.

> [W]orker-owners associated with LMFs [labour managed firms] are actually worker-entrepreneurs (labour hires capital), so that financial participation can be expected to boost productivity ... That is, worker entrepreneurs are likely to be more interested in profit and the firm's survival than ordinary employees would be.
>
> Doucouliagos (1995:73-4, bracket and comment added))

Using the theory of incentives in Chapter 2, there is a clear remunerative incentive to apply as much effort possible in order to produce as much surplus value as possible. The level of effort applied is likely to be closer to the maximum level of effort that can be applied by any one worker.

To demonstrate this on our hypothetical column of effort, Figure 5 shows how the worker of an employee-owned firm is likely to apply a level of effort within the upper zone, the space between the expected level of effort (the ELE) and the maximum level of effort the worker can apply (the MLE). To recall the discussion from the previous chapter, a worker of a capitalist firm is likely to apply a level of effort within the middle zone, between the minimum level of effort he can apply without being sacked (the MAEL) and the level of effort his employer would like (the ELE).

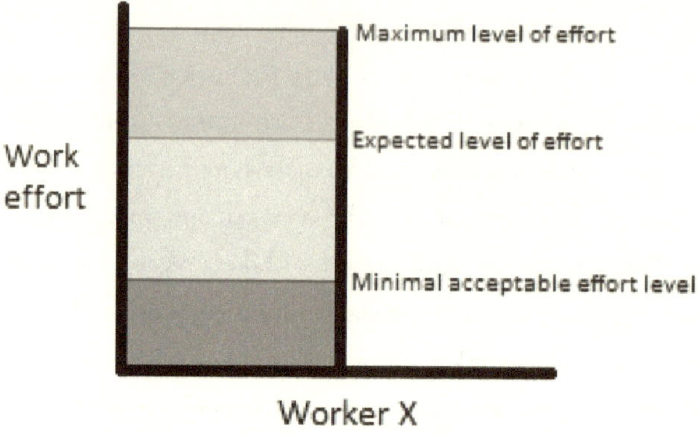

Figure 5

Using this relatively basic concept, the dual-contradiction would appear to have been solved through the use of remunerative incentives. The logic behind this theory can also be observed in reality. A 2006 study by the JOL (now the Employee Ownership Association) and Co-operatives UK found some very unsurprising discoveries. Of the 96 employee-owned companies surveyed, 91 per cent of them rated the extra commitment staff gave to the business as the greatest advantage (Burns, 2006). In addition, 81 per cent stated that staff are prepared to take on more responsibility and with 72 per cent saying that staff tend to work harder (Burns, 2006). The statistics would appear to back up the theory that worker ownership has the capacity to increase effort applied in the workplace.

When applying the theory of the principal-agent dilemma used in the preceding chapter to a worker-owned enterprise, we also find some noteworthy revelations. Under the conventional capitalist firm we find that the capitalist/company is the principal, and the employee is the agent. Under a worker-owned firm, the agent becomes the principal, and the principal becomes the agent. The agent becomes the principal as the employee is now a part-owner of the firm and they must now ensure that other worker-owners are applying as much effort as possible. On the other hand, the principal becomes the agent, meaning each worker-owner will now be accountable to all other worker-owners to ensure as much effort as possible is applied. What we essentially see is a blending of the two roles, along with a blending of both remunerative and coercive incentives. Worker-owners still have to perform the tasks allocated to them by the will of the company, but they also now have an incentive to ensure that other worker-owners are also doing so. What about the agent-principal dilemma? Will individual worker-owners attempt to cheat the company?

As each worker is also a part owner of the firm, it would only make sense to cheat the company if the individual believed they could gain more from cheating than if they did not. As cheating would usually mean damaging the profitability of the firm, this would also reduce the dividends of the cheater. Consequently, cheating starts to look a lot less appealing, as there is less to gain from cheating and a higher likelihood of being caught. As we saw in Chapter 2, under capitalism there can often be a large information gap between the capitalist and the worker. A worker can cheat the capitalist, and for as long as this does not affect the prospects of the remaining workers. Once the cheating has been revealed to the other workers, but not the capitalist, those workers have no incentive to inform the capitalist of the cheater, indeed they may even start to participate in the cheating. Under worker ownership, fellow employees now have an incentive to confront cheaters – as it is likely to affect the incomes of all workers. For the cheater, the whole workforce has essentially become the principal. This significantly condenses the information gap and makes it much harder for the individual to cheat the company. To reiterate earlier comments, there will always be some remunerative incentive for an agent to cheat the principal, but when the workforce becomes the principal, replacing an individual or group of capitalists who can often appear distant from the goings on of the shop-floor, the ability to cheat vastly diminishes. As a result, although worker ownership does not completely resolve the principal-agent dilemma, it is the most likely route towards diminishing as much as is realistically possible.

As has been stated throughout, the inequality element of the dual-contradiction can only be resolved if the worker receives the total surplus value they have helped to create. This does not necessarily mean they receive it all as dividends. Surplus value is often used to pay for future investments, or perhaps pay off the debts of past investments.

> [I]n no conceivable condition of society can the worker receive the full value of his product for consumption. ... [T]he need for a social reserve and accumulation fund would remain and consequently even in that case, the workers, i.e., all, would remain in possession and enjoyment of their total product, but each separate worker would not enjoy the "full returns of his labour."
>
> Marx (1847:8)

Within a worker-owned firm, the workers have control of the surplus value they collectively create and have the final say in how that surplus should be used. With the example of the carpenter used back in Chapter 1, it is easy to see how much surplus value each worker creates. One employee takes the materials and tools provided, and produces a commodity, a table for example, and sells it at a higher price. Once the materials, tools and wages are paid for, the remaining surplus is easily calculable. Once all the tables have been sold, the carpenters may decide to share the total surpluses between them as dividends. Instead, they may decide to invest the surplus in better tools or better materials to earn an even higher surplus in future. However, in companies where some employees 'enable' commodities to be produced or sold rather than to actually produce the surplus value themselves, it becomes more difficult to derive how much of the firm's collective surplus value each individual should receive. This is perpetuated further within complex productive methods, where the producers themselves cannot calculate how much surplus value each of them has individually contributed.

Take for example a factory where the vast majority of the production process is undertaken by automated and robotic practises, where a small group of workers inspect the production process, maintain the machines and deal with any mechanical malfunctions. Although the workers are all producing a surplus value by operating and maintaining the machines, it becomes much more difficult to derive how much surplus value any particular worker has individually produced. In many respects, workers are only able to use the total surplus value produced by the whole firm (or a particular segment of a firm) to get any understanding of how much each employee has produced. Under these circumstances, it becomes difficult to calculate the total amount of surplus value produced or enabled by each worker and how to allocate it via dividends. As stated in Chapter 1, we must recognise that both 'producers' and 'enablers' are essential if the firm is to realise its surplus value through selling their products onto the open market. As a consequence, workers within an entire firm, or in the case of bigger firms, in an entire department, must accept that the total collective surplus value must be shared and dividends must be distributed proportionately. This can be done either in equal amounts across the whole workforce, according to how much work has been performed by each individual worker, as a percentage of pay for each individual worker, or perhaps some other democratically derived method. Either way, the most effective means to distribute dividends which best represents the surplus value produced by an individual worker is via worker ownership of the means of production. Capitalist firms and consumer cooperatives offer no profits for the firm's workers. State run enterprises offer some returns by the means of redistribution, but it is not reflective of effort applied. Although worker ownership will not enable workers to receive the precise amount of surplus value they have produced, it is by far the best means of doing so.

We should also mention at this stage that worker ownership can help to rein in the excessive amounts paid to corporate executives. As workers are now in control of their company, they can determine the heights of executive pay. There is nothing necessarily prohibiting worker-owned firms from offering positions with exorbitant pay packets. This is no problem under the subjective theory, as pay is determined largely via the labour market, but this can be a problem under the labour theory. Inequalities may exist within the firm, where workers who are producing an identical amount value receive a higher or lower income compared to colleagues. It is ultimately down to the workers, who have the final say, to determine which levels of inequality between staff members can be tolerated, most likely in accordance with the wider labour market.

> The only important exception to this used to be the claim of the workers to the "full produce of their labour", to which so much of socialist doctrine traces back. But there are few socialists to-day who believe that in a socialist society the output of each industry would be entirely shared by the workers of that industry; for this would mean that workers in industries using a great deal of capital would have a much larger income than those in industries using little capital, which most socialists would regard as very unjust.
>
> Hayek (1944:115)

Under a worker-owned firm, such differences in pay can be justified if the labour market and the consent of the workers allows. The difference Hayek makes above demonstrates another stark difference between the cooperative and (traditional) socialist models. Even with wage differences within worker-owned firms, it is fairly safe to say that levels in income inequality within the firm are likely to be much lower under worker ownership than under the conventional capitalist model. However, what a 'socialist' income distribution looks like is still up for debate[20]. This would also be an appropriate moment to clarify that although Marx was initially supportive of worker ownership, he would eventually lose favour with this model, even as a transitional arrangement from capitalism to communism[21]. This and other factors would perhaps explain why the state socialist model became the preferred means of replacing capitalism in 20th century leftist thinking. As we have shown, this state-centric approach would entail much of the same issues – surrounding incentives and social justice – as conventional capitalism had and continues to face.

We must also briefly discuss another type of weakness conventional capitalism tends to fuel and how worker ownership helps to resolve it. There are many occasions where it is the capitalist owner who is dealt an injustice, rather than their employees. For small businesses, owning and managing a firm is no easy task, it exposes the owner to a great deal of risk and responsibility. This can lead to a situation where small business owners are in fact exploiting themselves, rather than their employees, to ensure the firm remains sustainable. For many employees, the stresses and strains of work can be put aside at the end of the shift. For many business owners, there can often be no clear distinction between what is work and what is leisure, as the business must always come first. In addition, where the employees are often trained for a particular task, a business owner must learn a plethora of different skills they may have little background in, such as accounting, marketing, human resources, etc. They must carry out what often seems to be a never ending list of seemingly non-business related tasks.

In many instances, being a capitalist is never always as simple and easy as it often seems. However, on the back of this, it has often been argued that the capitalist owners of a firm still deserve the whole surplus value the workers produce. This is due to the list of reasons mentioned previously, as well as the fact that the capitalists themselves have taken the risk to start-up the enterprise whilst the workers have forgone the risk and are offered a stable rate of pay and security regardless of how the firm performs. This argument is still folly, for four reasons. Firstly, if the firm fails, where the capitalists only lose their savings used to invest, the workers lose their livelihood. The workers thus have more at stake. Only if the capitalist relies upon the enterprise for bare subsistence (along the same lines as the workers) can this be omitted. Secondly, as stated earlier, most workers do not have the time and money to invest in new enterprises. They are dependent on maintaining subsistence and never have the opportunity to start a business capable of employing people themselves. Capital (money to invest) is thus usually monopolised by the higher income/wealth brackets. Thirdly, risk and responsibility is best spread over a larger collection of people (the workers) than by one investor or a small group of them. More hands don't just make lighter work, they also make better (democratic) decisions. Lastly, being offered a stable rate of pay regardless of how the firm performs will not yield higher returns, especially compared to incomes which fluctuate for all workers according to effort applied, as is the case under worker ownership. As such, worker ownership would help to prevent the injustices many small business owners face, by spreading the risk, responsibilities and tasks between a larger group of people, increasing efficiency through the collective incentive to maximise income, as well as spreading the greater rewards that worker ownership brings.

Concluding Remarks

So far we have only touched on some of the potential theoretical benefits faced by worker-owned firms. Indeed, a lot more is yet to be explored. Nonetheless the worker ownership model has thus far been presented as the most likely cure to the dual-contradiction compared to the other proposals presented. Through worker ownership, workers are now more likely to receive an income which is more or less representative of the effort applied, whilst employees now have a substantial incentive to apply as much effort as possible to maximise their income. It goes without saying that the worker ownership model has historically been presented with a plethoric combination of critiques which will inevitably be addressed in much more detail in the coming chapters. Regardless, the theoretical resolution to the dual-contradiction should not be underestimated. As a result, any dilemmas, limitations or contradictions of the worker ownership model must outweigh the gains made from solving the dual-contradiction if we are to disregard it as a means of replacing the capitalist mode of production.

---

[17] It is important to re-emphasise Marx's (1848) hypothesis that wages are intentionally driven below the market rate to the point of basic subsistence. This is achieved by sustaining some form of unemployment, a 'reserve army of labour'. However, we will assume that despite pressures, for most the time market rates are derived through the natural processes of the market. This can lead to wages above and sometimes even below the rate required for basic subsistence.

[18] We must note that in theory, a minimum wage increase should, for the employer, pay for itself. As although the employer now has to pay a higher minimum wage to their workers, all of the employers' customers are now also earning at least the minimum wage. This gives customers a potentially higher disposable income, increasing sales and increasing profits for the employer.

[19] Whether pay is linked to performance in the largest of businesses is up for debate. Bebchuk and Fried (2004) argue that the ability many managers have to influence their own pay – regardless of performance – has largely distorted incentive mechanisms for these types of firms.

[20] Some may claim that cooperative ownership of the means of production is a form of socialism. This is no problem for those who believe socialism's meaning to be adaptable over time. For those who believe the concept of socialism to be static, it will likely represent state ownership, probably as we saw in the 20th century.

[21] Marx believed that capitalism would be superseded by a transitional 'socialist' (what he called, 'lower communist') stage, that would itself then be superseded into a (higher) 'communist' stage. Marx never widely discussed in much detail what the socialist stage would entail. That task he left to his followers, much to their misfortune. However, he conceded that this stage would be "still stamped with the birthmarks of the old society from whose womb it emerges" (Marx, 1875:10). This would theoretically leave open the idea of a market based system with a cooperative means of production. Marx himself even theorised this idea (Marx, 1894:317). Jossa (2005:12), who gives a very thorough account of Marx's view on the cooperative movement, theorises why this model lost favour with Marx and his followers: "One reason behind the scant attention given by Marxists to the cooperative movement to this day is the fact that Marx himself ceased to concern himself with cooperative firms following the collapse of the Paris Commune. And this may in turn be explained by the difficulties experienced by the cooperative movement from the 1870s onward".

Chapter 4: Worker Ownership

The basic concept of worker ownership may seem simple enough – workers owning the means of production – but in reality there is much more going on. The purpose of this chapter is to look into the concept of worker ownership more thoroughly, to understand what it really represents. To begin, we must first ask what form worker ownership must take within various contexts. Regardless of ownership, enterprises vary in size, structure and sector. Worker ownership will apply differently to companies which differ in these respects. Some previous academics have argued that workers should not in fact own the means of production but should still be able to manage the company and receive the profits they create. Others argue how workers should own the company but have less say in determining its future, giving more power to investors or the government for example. This work shall argue that both worker ownership and management are pivotal to the firm's survival, and that such approach is the best route to optimal efficiency, productivity and employee participation.

Ownership Structure

The main difference between capitalist, socialist or any other mode of production, comes down essentially to ownership. As the production of commodities is essential for supplying the wants and needs of a population, having the ability to own the means of producing those commodities is a powerful and potentially rewarding responsibility. Unlike capitalism and the previous socialist experiments of the 20th century, only worker ownership allows those who produce a commodity to fully gain the rewards of that production. Sole proprietorship can also be recognised as a form of worker ownership, as a self-employed firm is owned and managed by its sole worker. As the theory of the dual-contradiction has explained, when workers are locked out of gaining the full fruits or their labour, they become financially poorer than they otherwise would be, and hold little if any incentive to work any more efficiently than what is required of them to remain employed. Once workers own the means of production, they earn the profits they create on top of the wages they expect. Ownership gives the workers the power to receive the profits they themselves earn – it is not automatically syphoned away to wealthy shareholder-investors or the state. Indeed, it may be the case that once profits have been earned, the workers must pay taxes to the state, or pay back the debts from previous investments – but it is the responsibility of the workers to distribute these payments themselves. It is not in the hands of the investors to pay the taxes the company owes to the state. It is not in the hands of the state to pay the debts the company owes to the investors. Responsibility to distribute the company's surpluses lies solely with the workforce.

Partial Ownership

First of all there needs to be a distinction regarding how much ownership employees should take. As a result, before dealing with 'full employee ownership' we must first address the limitations of 'partial employee ownership'. In this context the firm is owned partly by the workforce with the remainder owned by 'external' shareholders. These external shareholders can be any of the actors we discussed in the previous chapter: investors, the state, customers, etc. There are multiple common justifications for this mixed ownership approach. Some may argue that rather than the workers or investors taking full ownership, they should instead share it, balancing out the rewards of success between them. Instead it could be argued that workers should share ownership with customers, or the state, or perhaps all of these actors. These scenarios however, can become untenable.

First of all, the distribution of the surplus value created by the workers will now be partly decided by external actors – a partial return to the dual-contradiction. Worker-owners would lose the sovereign ability to determine what happens to the surpluses they create. There are already remunerative incentives for investors to invest. There are already remunerative incentives for customers to buy commodities to fulfil their wants and needs. Worker ownership provides workers with a remunerative incentive to maximise the production of value, alongside the incentives of the investors and customers. A withering away of worker ownership is wholly unnecessary.

Secondly, flexible ownership arrangements would mean that ownership could be further stripped away from the workforce in future. Although partial employee ownership could sustain itself indefinitely, there will always be incentives by other actors to gain a greater share of the firm's surplus value. Potential investors may ask for shares of the company in exchange for investment capital. Customers may be offered shares, similar to a consumer cooperative, in order to ensure their loyalty to the company and to boost sales. A whole range of scenarios could take hold, all of which threaten the ability of the workers to determine the future of the surplus value they create. This leads ultimately to a state of affairs where ownership of the firm remains constantly unstable and flexible, and where the dual-contradiction could fully re-emerge. Ownership should not and must not be bargained away.

There may be exceptional circumstances where indefinitely diminishing employee ownership from full ownership to partial ownership may be necessary, but one struggles to imagine a scenario where that could feasibly be the case. Regarding the transition from capitalist to worker ownership, there may be a justification for partial worker ownership in the short run. In this scenario, a capitalist firm transfers shares of the company to its workforce at a permanently increasing rate until full worker ownership is reached. Although this is defined as partial worker ownership, it can be justified as a means of transition from a firm of full capitalist ownership, to joint capitalist/worker ownership, to eventually reaching full worker ownership. In the United States, this process is undertaken at a much smaller scale through 'employee stock ownership plans' or ESOPs. ESOPs are ownership transfer plans where the company rewards workers (usually as a remunerative reward at no cost) with shares of the firm. These shares are not distributed equally and can in some circumstances still be sold on the stock market. It should also be noted that ESOPs are not used as a method to fully transfer ownership from capitalists to workers, but function more like a bonus scheme. Methods of transition to a cooperative economy (where all firms are owned by their workers) will be examined in further depth later, but it should be understood that ESOPs must be used as a means of transitioning capitalist firms to fully worker-owned firms. If ESOPs lead to a permanent situation where the firm is only partially owned by the workforce, the same issues explained above – revival of the dual-contradiction, and ownership instability – will remain intact.

If full worker ownership is to sustain itself, it is essential that each worker owns an equal share of the business. If co-workers within the same company own differing percentages of the firm, the incentive dynamics are likely to differ. Some workers may gain a disproportionate say over the determination of the surplus value compared to others. It is also essential that all workers are worker-owners. If some of the workforce are members whilst others are not, the company could risk degenerating into a capitalist enterprise where only a minority of the workers are shareholders, thereby regenerating the dual-contradiction. As a consequence, each and every worker should be an equal shareholder of the firm, regardless of status within the firm, length of employment, or any other factor. Full employee/worker ownership[22] means equal shared ownership by all those who produce or enable surplus value production within the firm. Again, this must not be bargained away.

Full Ownership

According to a guideline by the UK Department for Business, Innovation and Skills, an employee-owned company is a firm where employees own at least fifty per cent of the company. For the remainder of this study, an employee-owned company will be defined as a firm with full employee ownership, where ownership cannot be flexible or withered away.

The BIS guideline refers to firms with a hundred per cent worker ownership as 'worker cooperatives'. However, worker cooperatives must follow a strict code of conduct (the seven cooperative principles), thus it is possible for a firm to be fully employee-owned without being a worker cooperative. There are also different approaches to how worker ownership can be applied. The BIS guideline also continues to highlight two distinct forms of employee ownership which appear most commonly.

These two methods are as follows:

1. Direct employee ownership – where employees become individual shareholders of shares in their company.
2. Indirect employee ownership – where shares are held collectively on behalf of employees, often through an employee trust.

BIS (2011:3)

Both approaches to worker ownership hold various advantages and limitations, which we shall explore with both respectively.

Direct employee ownership: Direct employee ownership, or stakeholder ownership, is when worker-owners have to purchase a share of the company when they commence their employment. If for example four partners establish a worker cooperative, each worker will own a quarter of the enterprise. If further in time the company employs another worker, they (along with the previous four) will own a fifth of the company. When starting up a small worker-owned enterprise, it is likely that all the members involved will be required to contribute funds to purchase physical capital – machines, tools, raw materials, computers, etc. In return for this 'capital contribution' each member becomes both an employee and stakeholder/shareholder of the company they have collectively established, this contribution ensures that each worker-owner has a direct stake in the business. All members are expected to contribute an equal share. The capital contributions of all worker-members are aggregated into a 'shared capital fund' used for purchasing the necessary physical capital for production. This is also the case for worker-members who join the company after the initial start-up process – when the company is already up and running. When the company decides to employ new members, they will also be required to pay a capital contribution. This is because new employees will most likely require additional capital to produce additional commodities for the company. If, for example, a joinery hires a new carpenter, that new employee will require their own tools and materials. Once an individual worker-member leaves, they are repaid their capital contribution from the capital fund[23], and they are no longer an employed worker nor shareholder of the enterprise. Surplus value can be paid into the shared capital fund to reimburse leaving worker-members or to invest in additional physical capital. It is important to re-emphasise that only the individual worker-members can own their respective share, they cannot sell it on or transfer it to another body in any circumstance – it can only be transferred back to the company when the worker-members terminates their employment.

There are, however, a great number of issues that arise from this method. To begin, as we explored in Chapter 1, most people are unable to obtain the means of production. Paying a capital contribution may be an unrealistic expense for many of the poorest. This could be a significant barrier to entry for many prospective worker-members. As has been noted by other academics in the past (Jay, 1977, Meade, 1980), even if worker-members can pay the initial capital contribution, this may represent a large share of their savings which are all tied up in one firm. If the firm goes bust, the worker-members lose their job and a significant chunk of their savings.

> For one thing, employees individually do not have personal access to savings
> in the necessary quantities. For another, even if they did, it would be unwise to
> for them to invest their individual savings heavily in the enterprise on which
> their employment and earned income also depend.

> Jay (1977:13)

As worker-members cannot hedge their savings in multiple firms, the contributory system has often been referred to as a 'having all your eggs in one basket' approach (Oakeshott, 1980). Although this is rarely an issue for the majority of directly-owned worker-owned firms which function successfully, there is always the prospect of this constitutional flaw emerging when the firm comes under financial pressure.

Another issue expressed by other academics in this field (Dickstein, 1991, Tortia, 2007) relates to reimbursements. Assuming our hypothetical worker-owned firm encounters a period of low profitability, not only will the incentive for worker-members to look elsewhere for more profitable firms increase, but the reserves kept in the shared capital fund for reimbursements will also shrink. Under these circumstances if a large number of worker-members choose to leave the firm, the firm may be unable to reimburse them, leaving the company with little or no reserves, placing the company in greater financial jeopardy. If the company can find as many new worker-members to replace the leaving worker-members, the capital contributions of the new members could potentially cancel out the reimbursements of the leaving members. However, attracting new members to a failing firm will be considerably difficult if more profitable employment is available.

Despite these theoretical limitations seeming legitimate and credible, in reality these concerns have been more difficult to observe empirically. One historically successful company which applies the direct employee ownership model is the Mondragon Corporation. The Mondragon Corporation is a group/federation of multiple worker-owned cooperatives in the Basque region of Spain. There is an abundance of both critical and complimentary academic literatures studying Mondragon since its foundation in 1956 (Morris, 1992, Kasmir, 1996, Erdal, 2012, Flecha and Ngai, 2014, Heras-Saizarbitoria, 2014). Regarding direct employee ownership, the Mondragon case study sheds some intriguing light on how this model is applied within the networked collection of worker cooperatives. Erdal (2012) notes that as of 2012, the capital contribution required to join the cooperative stood at €14,000 each. Rather than new members having to pay this outright or take out a private loan, this contribution is taken out of their salaries or the interest (dividends) accrued in their individual capital accounts. This process is known as 'accumulating deferred shareholding'. Put simply, their share in the company is paid for by the profits they help to create. As Oakeshott (1980) observes:

> With perhaps a tiny minority of exceptions, the level of these entry contributions at Mondragon has never exceeded six months of the lowest rate of shopfloor earnings. Thus in relation to average expectations of life-time earnings, the downside risk to which Mondragon workers are exposed is modest enough.
>
> Oakeshott (1980:53)

The capital contributions also appear not to have deterred new members from joining, with waiting lists for new membership positions being implemented (Morris, 1992). Regarding the issue of reimbursement, Morris (1992:32) states "[o]n retirement, the accumulated profits, by Spanish law, must be paid out within two years"[24], accounting for potential volatility in employment levels. As such, despite the many limitations noted earlier, the direct employee ownership model appears to work very well throughout Mondragon's history. Although this model can work well for large corporations like Mondragon, it could become seriously problematic when an individual firm, without the safety nets of cooperative federations like Mondragon, faces difficulty, as noted earlier. Firms using this method must take note of these flaws and apply procedures for the firm if it ever does face difficulty. As a result, the direct ownership model may be best suited to small worker-owned firms, preferably with few workers and little capital, where there is little need for large and expensive capital contributions. Worker cooperatives that form federations, like Mondragon, may also be able to sustainably apply this system, as large shared capital accounts can reduce the need for expensive capital contributions, and where numerous reimbursements of a particular firm can be covered off. As a result, if a worker-owned firm such as Mondragon believes they are capable of sustaining an effective direct employee ownership model, even through difficult times, there are few other reasons to express further concern.

Indirect employee ownership: The other approach to worker ownership is the indirect employee ownership model. If we were to refer to the direct ownership model as a 'stakeholder model', the indirect ownership model is more akin to a 'trustee model'. Under this arrangement, rather than having every worker-member listed as an individual shareholder of the firm, the firm is owned entirely by a trust where all its employees are its beneficiaries. A trust is a relationship where one party (the settlor) transfers the ownership rights of their property to another party (the trustee), for the benefit of the settlor. As a result, the settlor no longer controls the property rights *per se*, but does earn the benefits of that property (should there be any). Regarding a worker-owned company, the settlor would be the workers who collectively own the firm, who transfer the ownership rights of the company to a trust, where the workers are able to control the surplus value they produce.

The trust itself is usually a part of the company or closely related to it, as a result we can still refer to the company as being 'worker-owned'. As the trustee/trustees can only manage the trust to the benefit of the settlor (the workers), they should have no remunerative incentive, or indeed capacity, to cheat the workers or alter the core constitution of the firm. Worker-owners of a directly owned firm (like Mondragon for example) may prefer to transfer ownership to a trust in order to prevent 'degeneration' – that being the ownership of the enterprise being transferred to external actors, such as capitalist investors for example. As a result, this form of ownership better protects the ownership stability of the firm. Worker-owners cannot vote to sell shares of the company as it cannot alter the core constitution of the enterprise. As all the workers are beneficiaries of the trust, the firm cannot discriminate between which workers can become worker-members and which cannot – all must be members. Where a worker-owned firm using the direct model could hypothetically employ new workers without making them worker-members, with the indirect model, it becomes a lot more difficult to do so. As such, the indirect form of employee ownership substantially reduces the chances of degenerating the firm into a partially worker-owned firm, or degenerating completely to capitalist ownership. This is the comparative advantage of the indirect model of ownership over the direct model of ownership.

As individual workers are not individual shareholders they do not require the payment of a capital contribution upon starting employment. Doing away with capital contributions avoids many of the issues discussed earlier with the direct model: worker-members losing savings if the firm goes bust, the firm not being able to reimburse contributions for leaving worker-members, etc. This is another advantage of the indirect model. An example of an indirectly employee-owned enterprise is the John Lewis Partnership, a British retail firm that transitioned from capitalist to worker ownership in 1929. Erdal (2012:946) notes the distinctive advantages John Lewis enjoys:

> One of the reasons why the John Lewis Partnership has managed to last for over 80 years in democratic employee ownership is that its ownership is collective, effectively neutralising the dangers of individual ownership. The securities – stock or shares – that embody conventional individual 'ownership' carry the rights to information, power and profit. These powers cover not just this generation, but all generations in the future. The value of shares is therefore both high and volatile – the right to extract wealth from the people employed is projected into the infinite future. If such securities are held directly by the employees the result is that there is a high financial incentive for each generation to sell the company rather than hand it on to the next generation.

There are, however, a number of limitations. In practice, the indirect model can be difficult to implement for prospective companies and start-ups – primarily due to initial investment. When starting up an indirectly worker-owned firm, the workers may still require the use of their own funds to purchase the necessary physical capital. They will still need to provide some form of capital contribution, yet this investment cannot be linked to ownership. They would essentially have to lend investment capital to their own firm. Once surplus value has been produced, a share of that surplus would have to be given to the original worker-owners who provided the initial capital as a form of repayment, as would any other type of investor would expect. Once the firm is up and running, more employees may be required. These new worker-members may not have to pay any capital contribution, but they must accept that dividends per head may be smaller, as a sum of the surplus value must be repaid to the founding worker-members (or any other investors) who supplied the initial investment.

Even if a founding worker-member left the firm during the process of repayment, they would still be repaid, again, like any other type of investor. Any additional investment capital must come from retained earnings or outside investors, a further discussion on investment will be presented later in Chapter 7. Another, perhaps more trivial point to make, is that although future worker-members are not required to pay a capital contribution under this method, they may lose a sense of ownership that would come from directly investing in the firm. This is more than just an emotional attachment; capital contributions create a coercive incentive to ensure the enterprise does not fail and thus the initial contribution is not lost. However, the coercive incentive to remain employed and maintain subsistence along with the remunerative incentive to produce a surplus far outweighs the coercive incentive to ensure a component of a worker's savings remains intact. The individual sense of 'ownership' and 'stake' may be lost somewhat, but the ability of the firms success to allow the worker to maintain subsistence and possibly a surplus on top, will ensure the worker-member's spiritual and physical loyalty to the enterprise remains solid and unwavering.

The indirect approach to worker ownership may indeed be preferable over the direct approach in many respects, especially for medium to large sized businesses or capital intensive firms. As stated earlier, however, there is no single one method of worker ownership which is best suited to every firm. Indeed, these methods could be combined[25] or heavily adjusted, or new approaches altogether could be applied. For as long as total worker ownership cannot be threatened and the firm itself can be effectively sustained and maintained, any method can be seriously considered.

Solidifying Ownership

Regarding the overall discussion on ownership, it would seem only logical that the workforce must take full and all-inclusive ownership of the firm they work for. For new firms, or firms which are likely to remain small, the direct method of shareholder ownership may be more desirable. This ensures the firm receives initial investment from its start-up and that workers have a financial stake in the firm, but not one which commands a large portion of their savings and makes reimbursements problematic. For larger worker-owned firms, it may be advisable to transition to an indirect/trustee approach to ownership. This method avoids capital contributions which may be unnecessary for larger and well established firms, and also protects the sovereignty of the workforce from degeneration. This issue of ownership will come up again in Chapter 7, as ownership and investment have an unavoidable and pivotal link.

Regardless of which methods of ownership are used, the core principles of full worker ownership and sovereign worker management must be upheld. Upholding these principles will require implementing strong company constitutions. The complexity of the constitution will depend on the size of the firm and how many worker-owners it employs. Larger firms like John Lewis have constitutions which encompass the responsibilities of various institutions and democratic processes within the firm. The constitution of John Lewis outlines the codes of conduct, the employment conditions and to safeguard the core principles for the current and future workforce.

> The Partnership exists today because of the extraordinary vision and ideals of its Founder, John Spedan Lewis. He believed an 'industrial democracy' where employees shared knowledge, power and profit was a better form of business. That vision was set out in a written Constitution – a framework to define the Partnership's principles and the way it should operate. The Constitution has been revised on a number of occasions since then, in order to keep it fresh and up to date. Nonetheless, this latest edition is a direct connection to his original inspiration – it defines what we are.
>
> John Lewis Partnership[26]

The constitution sets out the origins of the company as well as to demonstrate how they are different to other firms in today's context. Transparency is essential for any form of democratic organisation such as John Lewis. Setting out the rules, rights and responsibilities of the firm helps to solidify its business model, whilst ensuring that necessary revisions can be made for when times change.

For smaller worker-owned firms there is less need for a large and complex constitution, instead, the firm could apply a basic constitution along the lines of the seven cooperative principles. The definition of a cooperative and its seven principles, according to the International Co-operative Alliance, can be found below:

> A co-operative is an autonomous association of persons united voluntarily to meet their common economic, social, and cultural needs and aspirations through a jointly-owned and democratically-controlled enterprise.

Co-operatives are based on the values of self-help, self-responsibility, democracy, equality, equity and solidarity. In the tradition of their founders, co-operative members believe in the ethical values of honesty, openness, social responsibility and caring for others.

The co-operative principles are guidelines by which co-operatives put their values into practice.

1. Voluntary and Open Membership

Co-operatives are voluntary organisations, open to all persons able to use their services and willing to accept the responsibilities of membership, without gender, social, racial, political or religious discrimination.

2. Democratic Member Control

Co-operatives are democratic organisations controlled by their members, who actively participate in setting their policies and making decisions. Men and women serving as elected representatives are accountable to the membership. In primary co-operatives members have equal voting rights (one member, one vote) and co-operatives at other levels are also organised in a democratic manner.

3. Member Economic Participation

Members contribute equitably to, and democratically control, the capital of their co-operative. At least part of that capital is usually the common property of the co-operative. Members usually receive limited compensation, if any, on capital subscribed as a condition of membership. Members allocate surpluses for any or all of the following purposes: developing their co-operative, possibly by setting up reserves, part of which at least would be indivisible; benefiting members in proportion to their transactions with the co-operative; and supporting other activities approved by the membership.

4. Autonomy and Independence

Co-operatives are autonomous, self-help organisations controlled by their members. If they enter into agreements with other organisations, including governments, or raise capital from external sources, they do so on terms that ensure democratic control by their members and maintain their co-operative autonomy.

5. Education, Training and Information
Co-operatives provide education and training for their members, elected representatives, managers, and employees so they can contribute effectively to the development of their co-operatives. They inform the general public - particularly young people and opinion leaders - about the nature and benefits of co-operation.

6. Co-operation among Co-operatives
Co-operatives serve their members most effectively and strengthen the co-operative movement by working together through local, national, regional and international structures.

7. Concern for Community
Co-operatives work for the sustainable development of their communities through policies approved by their members.

International Co-operative Alliance[27]

Although these principles apply to all forms of cooperatives, even those such as consumer cooperatives which incorporate the dual-contradiction, for worker-owned firms, these principles can be appropriately applied. As stated earlier, a 100 per cent worker-owned firm is not necessarily the same as a worker cooperative, but nonetheless, all worker-owned firms should, as far as they practically can, adhere to the principles that define a cooperative. We will therefore accept that the worker cooperative model can work as a template model for worker-owned firms, even if they are not technically constituted as a cooperative. It is quite possible for a non-cooperative worker-owned firm to be just as progressive, if not more so, than a conventional worker cooperative. This will depend on the worker-owners and how they wish their firm to be organised. This is one of the fundamental benefits of economic democracy, it allows those who know the business better than anyone to write the rules on how the firm is structured, whilst being able to change those rules when circumstances dictate.

Although constitutions and principles may be sufficient for a hypothetical worker-owned firm, for a cooperative economy there will need to be safeguards that prevent the degeneration of worker-owned firms, along with assurances that new as well as existing enterprises will be worker-owned, where the employees are guaranteed sovereignty. The details of these suggestions will be outlined in Chapter 12, where we begin to delve into how a cooperative economy – where the majority of firms are owned and managed by their workers – will be established and sustained.

---

[22] Some have implied how the terms 'employee ownership' and 'worker ownership' are not one and the same, as in some cases not all workers are employees (agency workers for example). For simplicity both terms will be used interchangeably, referring to all those who consistently produce/enable value for a particular organisation.

[23] In some cases such as Mondragon, during employment the personal capital account of an individual worker-member (which contains the sum of their capital contribution) will earn a rate of interest. This interest basically acts as the dividends which are paid to workers as profits. It remains essential that if all of the dividends the worker-members earn is credited into their capital accounts, they must be able to draw from it prior to them leaving the firm. If workers cannot access the profits they create, this will dent the incentive to produce/enable more value. This could also give workers an artificial incentive to exit the firm early to get a hold of their accumulated dividends.

[24] Dickstein (1991:24) claims that Mondragon pays out members who leave over a 5 year period.

[25] An employee-owned firm wishing to use a hybrid model may decide to hold a certain portion of the company's shares in a trust with the remaining shares held by the individual worker-owners. This ensures that workers have a sense of direct ownership but not to the extent where shares are ridiculously expensive for new workers or where reimbursements for leaving workers could put a financial strain on the firm.

[26] See the John Lewis Partnership's constitution at:
https://www.johnlewispartnership.co.uk/content/dam/cws/pdfs/Juniper/jlp-constitution.pdf

[27] See https://www.ica.coop/en/whats-co-op/co-operative-identity-values-principles

Chapter 5: Worker Management

> Thus the goal of a democratic organization should not be to suppress conflict, but to welcome it and use it productively. Freedom of expression is a value that should be widely embraced, for it enables an airing of alternatives that would otherwise not be considered.
>
> Gamson and Levin (1984:236)

Regardless of the structure of a worker-owned firm, the firm itself remains comprised of individual people. Human beings are complex creatures, who think and act in ways which can often be at odds with their own self-interest or the best interest of others. Neoclassical economic theory, which continues to largely dominate the economics profession of today, assumes that individuals act in a rational manner to maximise utility. Although this theory can often be at odds with reality, we have thus far tried to apply this theory as best as possible for the sake of simplicity. Nonetheless we cannot forget that individuals are likely to make irrational decisions. In the context of a worker-owned firm, such irrational decisions could threaten the livelihood of the individual, and potentially the livelihoods of their colleagues, many of whom they will have developed a close relationship with. The stakes could not be higher. How worker-owners interact with one another is therefore of high significance.

This chapter asks whether worker-owned firms can be managed at least as effectively as conventional capitalist firms. This also means asking what happens when co-workers of a worker-owned firm come to a disagreement regarding various decisions that must be taken. These decisions can vary in relevance, they could be new proposals up for consideration, or perhaps a review of current methods. When the stakes are high, emotions are likely to run high. The enterprise must be prepared for dealing with debate and deliberation in a productive and timely manner. Failing to do so, and the firm itself is at risk.

The Incentive Dynamic

To recall our early analysis of incentives, a worker-owned firm emits three likely incentives individuals will face:

- Coercive incentive: the individual worker requires employment at the firm to maintain subsistence. If they do not comply with the **MAEL** set by the firm, they are likely to be fired from the firm. Also, if they support the firm taking a decision that will lead the enterprise to collapse, their subsistence will also be threatened.

- Remunerative incentive: the individual worker has an incentive to apply as much effort as possible in order to maximise their income. For this to apply, there must be a link between work applied and reward gained. This is unique to the worker ownership model.

- Moral incentive: the individual worker may have developed an emotional attachment to the firm and developed personal relationships with other worker-owners of the firm. Along with personal incentives, they may have an incentive to better the lives of their colleagues, perhaps to feel a sense of moral worth or self-esteem, or perhaps simply due to an altruistic disposition.

In particular circumstances, there could be additional incentives of the three types that individuals may face. Regarding the three above, each are likely to vary according to the individual. If a worker is earning an income from another source which is sufficient to maintain subsistence, the coercive incentive is likely to be weaker. If an individual worker cares more for self-interest than to collective spirit, the moral incentive is likely to be weaker and the remunerative incentive stronger. The remunerative incentives are likely to be weaker in markets with low prospects for high profitability. A range of scenarios are likely. What is universal is that there is an 'incentive dynamic' at work – a desire to maximise utility for the individual and/or the group, and a means of achieving it. When all worker-members have an incentive to maximise the income of the firm, they must come to agreement on which method is best to achieve that aim. If a particular worker-member has no incentive – perhaps because they have adequate wealth to cover their subsistence, and hold no altruistic nature – they may not be inclined to do as other worker-owners would expect of them. If so, there is no need for that worker to remain employed, the firm is thus likely to fire them.

Worker-owned firms are therefore only successful when the incentive dynamic is functioning for all workers employed. This incentive dynamic is, unsurprisingly, a pivotal concept that will feature prominently throughout this study. The incentive dynamic will guide worker-members to take particular decisions, and will refrain them from taking others. It relies, to a large degree, on the assumption that individuals will predominantly make rational decisions, but benefits from the democratic principles of inclusive deliberation, transparency and collective decision making. One individual's choice is likely to affect the whole group, thus the whole group is responsible for making the crucial decisions, with the input of each individual and their particular take on things. If individuals are, for the majority of the time, likely to make the most rational decision, the collective decision making body of the worker-owned firm is most likely to make the most rational choice, as the lone voice of the irrational minority is outvoted by the confident voice of the rational majority.

Management Structure

Once workers are given sovereignty of the enterprise they work for, they are now accountable for its survival. They must decide which commodities to produce and in what quantity. They must oversee the production process, determining how many inputs should be bought, how many final products should be sold, and at what price. In capitalist firms, although workers are only employed if they produce or enable profit to be made, the workers are reassured in knowing that the capitalist investor-owners, or the executives they appoint, have the responsibility for managing the firm and making the big and difficult decisions. It has often been argued that this gives workers peace of mind, knowing that they needn't worry about how the firm is being managed. In exchange for this peace of mind, the workers must accept that the company owners should benefit from the risks being made and denounce any claim to the surplus value they help to produce or enable. For as long as the workforce are assured that their employment is safe and stable, there is little else for the employees to worry about regarding the management of the firm, so it is argued. This, however, is certainly no excuse for justifying the dual-contradiction. Indeed it could be safely said that the majority of workers would most likely favour financial dividends and the extra responsibility that comes with ownership over this hypothesised 'peace of mind'. Or to put it another way, the loss workers endure from the added responsibility does not outweigh the emancipatory effect of self-determination and the prospect of higher incomes. Also, there is no guarantee that the continued employment of the workers will be safe and stable in the hands of the capitalist investor-owners. Indeed, employee-owned firms tend to stabilise employment better than conventional firms in tough times (Pencavel et al, 2006, and Burdín and Dean 2009). Employees have as much to risk from the failure of a capitalist firm as the capitalists, if not more so. Where the majority of workers rely on their employment for subsistence, the majority of capitalist shareholders do not necessarily rely on the profits made by the firm for maintaining their own subsistence[28]. Allowing worker-owners to determine the future of the company they work for ensures that they gain a greater say in the decisions that affect employment risks. Worker management emancipates the workforce, allowing them to determine the destiny of their firm and the financial risks and rewards that come with it. If the employees of a company wish to receive the profits they help create they must accept responsibility for the firm's survival through the work they undertake. This responsibility is pivotal, and requires strong and sound processes and institutions to allow for the workforce to best utilise this responsibility.

Worker management can include a variety of forms that allow for the workforce to take decisions that vary in magnitude and significance. Like different forms of worker ownership, these forms of worker management will often depend on the size of the firm.

> The optimal organization for a small bakery cooperative is different from a large industrial cooperative. No one organizational form could function equally well under such different conditions of technology, skill and training requirements, scale of production and other factors.
>
> Wright (2010:168)

For smaller worker-owned firms, the workforce is also likely to be very small, comprising perhaps of only a few individuals. The management of this type of enterprise will likely be some form of direct democracy, where workers make decisions amongst themselves on minor shop-floor issues as well as issues of major impact, issues that are likely to determine the destiny of the firm. Minor decisions can be taken informally during the process of production – as workers tend to in capitalist firms – the only difference being that workers are now accountable to themselves rather than a hierarchy of foremen and managers. Worker-owners who must make small impact decisions during the production process are likely to decide amongst themselves on the shop-floor which decision to take, this will not require a lengthy process of debate and deliberation. On the other hand, more significant decisions can be taken in a more formal setting outside the production process. In this situation, employees meet to discuss the state of the firm and debate various matters which require resolution. This would usually occur in a designated time and place with predetermined codes of conduct and procedures.

Although direct forms of democratic management may be applicable for small worker-owned firms, how does this apply to larger firms? For companies with hundreds or perhaps even thousands of worker-owners, a more practical means of worker management must be applied. Under this context a representative form of worker management should be implemented. Worker-members will still deliberate amongst themselves on smaller issues, perhaps applying a form of direct democracy for each department or sub-division of the firm. For larger issues regarding the management of the whole company, the firm will need to appoint qualified managers. These managers could be similar to the managers we see in conventional capitalist firms, but who are democratically accountable to the workforce rather than appointed by shareholders external to the firm. In addition, as the dual-contradiction has been resolved and workers are incentivised to maximise efficiency and productivity, managers are not required to spend as much time monitoring indolent workers. This is opposed to the capitalist practice of managers spending a great deal of their time ensuring workers are performing the tasks set to a reasonable standard.

> [I]n the presence of information asymmetries about the actual effort offered by each worker, the cooperative firm requires less monitoring to achieve the optimal level of worker effort. Being also owners of the firm and choosing the person responsible for management functions inside their circle, cooperative workers develop relations based on solidarity and forms of peer monitoring which reduce monitoring costs. Consequently, the manager of the cooperative firm can devote more of his/her effort to organizational activity which increases the efficiency of the production process. Hence, with respect to working effort and to the related organization of the production process, governance in the cooperative firm is more efficient than in the capitalist firm.
>
> Alessandrini and Messori (2013:22-23)

Having a managerial team is essential for the firm to remain focused on collective targets and to ensure all the pieces that make up the firm are working in tandem towards the same common goals. All else being well, the incentives worker-owned firms enjoy make this managerial role much easier and effective.

Some have advocated that all aspects of management should be made responsible by the workforce, avoiding professional managers and hierarchies altogether. This form of absolute self-governance is perhaps the best model for smaller worker-owned firms where there is neither need nor resources to employ qualified managers. This however, is not practical for larger firms.

We have seen instances where pure participatory democracy has worked well, but this is limited to small enterprises with a stable work force. ... Pure participatory democracy has not worked well in larger, less stable enterprises.

Gamson and Levin (1984:231-2)

This is due to multiple reasons, the first of which comes down to the profession of management itself. Elster states that "workers lack the technical competence and market expertise which are required for successful management in a complex and constantly changing environment" (1989:94). Even with some form of job rotation – where workers within a single cooperative alternate differing tasks and roles – the ability to conduct significant managerial tasks requires a substantial amount of training and experience. Workers should only be responsible for the tasks they are competent in undertaking. Although future training for different roles should be encouraged, this is no justification for appointing ill-equipped employees to perform tasks they cannot effectively execute. This is the case for all tasks, not just those of a managerial nature.

The next issue comes down essentially to practicality and time management. Westenholz (1986) witnessed how the amount of time available to delegate various managerial responsibilities of varying significance can often be costly and time consuming. That and without an effective means of sharing responsibility, confusion can often follow regarding the allocation of tasks and the specific responsibilities of each individual worker. This can be particularly troubling in situations of high staff turnover, where new employees may be perpetually unsure of the tasks and roles they are expected to perform. If every managerial decision requires a process of debating and voting, this is likely to take a considerable amount of time which could be used more efficiently. There is also an additional issue regarding responsibility. If workers are constantly changing managerial roles, a situation may arise where no-one is willing to take responsibility for a long term failing. Consequently, managers of a worker-owned firm must be competent, must be responsible for a defined set of tasks and roles, and must have adequate time and resources to uncover failings and initiate reforms where needed.

In addition to conventional managers, workers could implement forms of representative democracy. Although managers are expected to take the day-to-day decisions of running the firm, the employees must be able to hold these managers to account, as well as vote on the major issues that impact the company. Workers would first of all establish a governing body, made up of all existing employees, which oversees the general state of the firm. This would be similar to the direct democracy model used by smaller cooperatives, but focusing on the larger issues. In addition, employees from various departments of the firm could be elected by the entire workforce to hold the managers to account on a more regular basis – to keep up to date with the developments of the firm and then to inform their departmental colleagues of these developments. There are many different forms of representative democracy that could take shape.

The example of Mondragon shows how a multi-layered form of democratic worker management can be used effectively. For each individual worker cooperative sitting underneath the wider Mondragon umbrella, the whole workforce comes together to form the 'general assembly'. This assembly is the sovereign body of the firm, who has the final say on issues on significant impact. The assembly also elect the 'board of members' on a one-member one-vote basis. The responsibility of this board is to appoint and supervise the chief executive, who manages the day-to-day operations.

> Again the key is that the person with the most day-to-day power is accountable
> to the elected representatives of the people he or she is managing. This creates
> the strongest possible incentive to keep them informed and to listen to their
> views.

Erdal (2012:947)

In addition to the board of members, workers at Mondragon also elect representatives to a 'social council'. The members of the social councils are elected by particular departments or segments of the firm at a shop-floor level, and deal with minor and individual-specific matters. All the worker-members of each department meet monthly, and advise their social council representative on which issues to discuss. This ensures that even within large representative democratic structures, there is still an important degree of autonomy within particular segments of the firm. For Mondragon, this method has been largely successful. Generally speaking, which ever approach a worker-owned firm decides to take, it is essential that accountability is concrete and that the whole workforce gets the final say on any issue of pivotal importance.

Ensuring that individual workers can remain directly engaged in the company's future must not be underestimated. Research by Lampel et al (2010) concluded that when a worker-owned firm grows, worker-owners can often lose a degree of autonomy and their ability for inclusive decision making. If employee-owned businesses are to innovate and grow, they will require greater worker autonomy:

Our results are consistent with past studies that looked at growth rates of EOBs [employee-owned businesses], but these studies also suggest that employee ownership per se will not deliver superior growth performance unless ownership is combined with greater participation in firm governance. When we turn to our survey data we find substantial support for this assertion.

Lampel et al (2010:13)

The profitability of EOBs correlates with giving employees greater autonomy in decision-making. EOBs that adapt their organisational structure and empower their front-end employees are more likely to sustain their performance as their size increases.

Lampel et al (2010:4)

Although the firm's constitutional arrangements regarding ownership and management must be concrete, there must still be a degree of flexibility within the structure of the firm that allows for innovative managerial methods to enhance participation.

The dividends that individual worker-owners receive should also, as best possible, reflect the effort applied and value produced/enabled. The larger a worker-owned firm becomes, the less likely any individual worker's dividends will reflect their own applied effort. If a worker-owner perceives that the effort they apply has no bearing on the income they receive, there will be no remunerative incentive to apply as much effort as possible, creating a partial return of the dual-contradiction[29]. "Pooling surplus dilutes incentives because it weakens the link between enterprise performance and the accumulation of individual capital." (Morris, 1992:34). Ireland and Law (1982) apply game theory to how profits are distributed. They claim that if total surpluses were equally distributed to all workers regardless of how many hours each employee has worked or how much value they have produced, there is a remunerative incentive for each worker to shirk and a remunerative incentive to convince fellow workers to apply more effort[30]. This way, the worker can earn the same amount of profit but by working less. If, on the other hand, profits are distributed according to hours worked or value produced, there is a remunerative incentive to apply as much effort as possible. In this case, there is no additional incentive to pressure colleagues to apply any more or any less effort, as a worker's income is dependent on the hours they work and/or the value they produced. Whether the worker's colleagues decide to apply more or less effort irrelevant to them, as this will affect their income and not anyone else's. This of course assumes that the decision by colleagues to apply more or less effort does not affect the viability of the firm as a whole, in which case there is a clear incentive to pressure colleagues to apply a different degree of effort. However, where viability is not of concern, such 'worker-on-worker' pressure is not necessary, as the incentive dynamic is sufficient to maximise each individual's level of effort applied. With all that being said, we should recall what was briefly mentioned in Chapter 3, that it is almost impossible to calculate the value produced/enabled by each individual worker in the majority of circumstances, especially in complex production methods. For smaller worker-owned firms, each worker's income will likely reflect effort applied. For larger worker-owned firms, they should ensure that dividends payments reflect the effort applied by each particular unit or sub-division of the firm as best as possible, perhaps through the recorded performance of each department, of each store, of each factory, etc. Firms can experiment with this. Perhaps a large enterprise could divide each worker dividends fifty per cent by the success of the firm as a whole, and fifty per cent by the success of the sub-division. Alongside this, the firm could decide to set aside a special fund to distribute bonuses to workers who display extraordinary degrees of effort or innovation[31]. Whichever approach may be taken, and regardless of the size of the firm, autonomy of work and realisation of reward should always remain paramount.

It goes without saying that the best ideas for reforming democratic processes and participation often come from the workers themselves. "A genuine commitment to democratic process means openness to the possibility that a new wave or generation of employees will decide to alter the system in significant ways" (Webb and Cheney, 2014:78). Experimenting with different forms of worker management structures is advisable for as long as the core principle of worker management itself is not withered away. Perhaps Mondragon's focus on multi-layered governance and autonomy provides a good blueprint for large and expanding firms. When designing an ideal model, perhaps firms could take account of the democratic methods used by political entities. Democracy is not always a simple or quick process, but it should be regarded more as an investment in the future of the firm rather than a wasteful use of time and resources. Particular democratic methods can never be applied universally or easily replicable, but they must be nourished, nurtured and tailor-made to the enterprise in question. Workplace democracy may not always be effective a hundred per cent of the time, but the results worker-members collectively produce, for the majority of the time, will far outweigh the negative consequences that come with the conventional autocratic and often militaristic methods that we see in the corporate world of today.

Informal Inter-worker Conflict

Establishing sound democratic institutions and processes within the firm is not enough. Unlike the dictatorial capitalist model, worker management will ultimately lead to more scrutiny and criticism between workers, the question is how will worker-owned firms manage this? Gamson and Levin's (1984) article *Obstacles to the Survival of Democratic Workplaces* offers a great deal of insight into this arena, initially stating that:

> If a democratically managed firm tends to be characterized by an inability to make decisions, by widespread and unproductive conflict among co-workers, and/or by a work force with inappropriate skills for the task of carrying out the operations of the firm, the firm will have a short life.

Gamson and Levin (1984:222)

Conflict between workers is likely to derive from a number of sources which differ in their severity. The first source of conflict comes down essentially to the work ethic of specific individuals. The incentive dynamic of the worker-owned firm ensures that workers monitor and support each other to ensure that working standards and ethics are kept to a high standard and wasteful practices are averted. As stated earlier, workers that attempt to cheat the firm are more likely to be caught compared to a capitalist firm, whilst the cheaters have less of an incentive to cheat in the first place. Nonetheless, the process of identifying a cheater and expelling them is likely to bring about a great deal of argument and confrontation.

Matters become complicated still if a particular worker has no intention of cheating or doing the company wrong, but still works at a less productive pace or has developed inefficient working habits. Confrontations like these are likely to take place on the shop-floor level between workers themselves at an informal level. Solutions are likely to be company specific. Nonetheless, in order to avoid spiteful and emotive arguments taking fold, it would appear obvious that formal procedures for dealing with informal disagreements may be a better solution. Managers are likely to be the first port of call, as they are responsible for their team and held to account by their team (and the workforce as a whole). Human relations officers are likely to play an important role in this process for larger firms. For smaller firms this HR role may be an additional responsibility for an employee with other primary duties, like we see with trade union representatives for example, or undertaken by an external consultant. Workers with grievances with other workers could discuss their issues with an HR specialist in a private setting in order to bring about a productive solution. Anonymity is likely to ensure that long lasting grudges between co-workers do not develop, whilst passing over the issue to a trained and qualified colleague in HR – who is likely to deal with the problem more delicately – can ensure that particular workers do not become disillusioned with the sorts of scrutiny that may be more likely within a worker-owned firm. Disciplinary committees made up of workers from various sections of the firm can ensure unbiased and impartial decisions are made regarding more serious matters. Better training and education could help to avoid unprofessional and unproductive methods of scrutiny before they develop, averting a potential source of confrontation.

An even better approach to avoid confrontation from bad working habits is to prevent those habits emerging to begin with and to address them early when they do emerge, for example, giving new workers adequate training. Apprenticeships are a good means of achieving this, especially for graduates who may not be used to the conventional workplace. Although most workers may favourably seek to improve the effectiveness of their work, existing workers who may be more resistant to change may also require formal methods of training to recognise the benefits of the more productive methods. Training it would appear, is the first initial solution to preventing and resolving co-worker conflict. Mellor et al concur, stating that "on our evidence a tremendous amount of training and support to nurture the process [of confronting and handling conflict] is needed to ensure that it is not counterproductive" (1988:117, bracket and comment added). Some situations may arise where scrutiny is too scarce. Gamson and Levin (1984) note how small isolated groups within the firm may be more tolerant of shirking and less likely to dismiss workers where personal relationships have developed. As mentioned earlier, dividend payments which are reflective or company and departmental performance could be trialled to prevent this. Quality management and a transparent form of cross-departmental scrutiny should also be encouraged to weed out wasteful elements of the firm. Indeed, there are also lessons to be learned here for our 'cooperative state', which will most likely have to reform the educational system to adjust future workers to a new environment of democratic management along with professional and diplomatic styles of communication between co-workers. More on this will be discussed in Chapter 12.

Formal procedures and better training is unlikely to prevent every cause of confrontation, but they are a safe bet. All humans inhibit an innate ability to conduct emotional argument and confrontation. Some are more likely to be provoked than others. Workers who display an overt taste for argument and conflict are unlikely to last long at the firm, this is no more unusual than what we would find in a conventional capitalist firm.

However, the increased tendency for workers of a worker-owned firm to scrutinise their co-workers to a greater degree requires a professional and rational set of procedures and common standards which all workers place their trust in. Achieving this is no overly complicated task. Gamson and Levin (1984) argue that each democratically controlled firm should establish a 'Formal Code of Social Statutes'. Similar to the constitutions required to maintain a cooperative's ownership status (as discussed in the previous chapter), the firm could also apply an extension to this constitution that includes formal codes of conduct.

> Probably the most important foundation for creating a common culture is the initiation of a written code of social statutes that describe both the rights and obligations of workers in the democratic work setting, as well as the methods by which the decisions will be made. The importance of this foundation is less in its permanence than in the process of transforming vague principles of democracy and equality into a concrete code of behavior.
>
> Gamson and Levin (1984:227)

Similar to the firm's ownership status, which solidifies the core principles of worker ownership and management, a code of social statutes would apply differently to each firm, specifying the responsibilities of each worker, and how to go about dealing with confrontation or a potential source of confrontation. These statutes can be revised to reflect how the firm changes over time, learning the lessons from previous experiences, positive and negative. Workers need to feel confident and committed to the firm's core values and principles. This increases the likelihood of greater participation and therefore increases their sense of workplace well-being. The constitutions of existing worker-owned firms such as Mondragon or John Lewis may be a good place to start. If conducted correctly, there is no excuse for company failure on the grounds of petty argument and shop-floor fall-outs. All in all, scrutiny and advice given between workers should be productive and welcomed where appropriate. The workplace of an employee-owned firm should not be a breeding ground for paranoia, with workers fearing each other, being watched behind their backs. The state of paranoia should be left to the world of corporate capitalism. Workers which own the company they work for should feel a sense of safety and stability, not fear and anxiety. Trusted formal procedures, quality training and a set of common standards and cultures should assist in building a workplace where hard work, pride and solidarity become guiding principles of work and labour. Employees need to see how their participation has a positive effect on the team, where they see their responsibilities as a pivotal part of the firm's overall strategy and purpose.

The perceptions of existing worker-owned firms raises some interesting points. Burns' (2006:4) survey of 96 UK worker-owned firms reveals that 84.1 per cent of companies "think better employee relations are a benefit of co-ownership", with the majority of these respondents 'strongly agreeing' with that proposition. This would imply that despite the theoretical potential for a greater number of inter-worker fallouts to occur under worker ownership, the reality of the matter implies quite the opposite, that worker relations actually improve.

Looking at the perceived disadvantages employee-owned firms mention, 65 per cent note how decisions in the firm happen more slowly, 53 per cent noting a tendency to avoid unpopular decisions and 46 per cent agreeing that the implementation of decisions happens more slowly (Burns, 2006). Burns (2006:3) does state that "Employee owned enterprises believe that the advantages of employee ownership easily outweigh any disadvantages". However, these perceived disadvantages should be addressed. The same survey suggests that a lack of government support and a lack of similar companies available to benchmark and compare against were mentioned as the biggest problems these firms faced. Perhaps resolving this would help to alleviate many of the issues raised. For a particular worker-owned firm, seeing how other worker-owned firms tackle similar issues is a win-win for both parties. Best practice is best shared. This remains much more difficult when worker-owned firms remain in an economic minority, as they currently are. Specialist and customised learning and development was also suggested as a potential remedy for the problems these firms face, a 'cooperative state' should take this on board.

Formal Inter-worker Conflict

Formalising informal arguments and conflicts may be a productive solution on the individual shop-floor level, but how are worker-owned firms to deal with formal sources of conflict – decisions taken democratically on the destiny of the firm. In conventional capitalist firms, workers are discouraged from interfering in the major affairs of the company, even when workers have a greater tacit knowledge of the inner workings of the firm compared to those managing and/or owning it. Worker ownership unleashes freedom of expression within the workplace. However, this comes with its own caveats. As the process of history has illustrated so many times, the destiny of any social entity, whether it be a country, a company, or a family, is likely to be determined by a few pivotal decisions taken in a short space of time.

Any turning point is likely to be marred with emotional argument and passionate debate regarding the preferred step forward. Worker-owned firms are no exception to this rule.

If the principle of the rational individual is to hold true for the majority of the time, the cooperative is always most likely to choose the most rational decision, where alternative, perhaps, irrational or less-rational choices are outvoted. These issues are more likely to be discussed in quarterly or yearly company-wide meetings, as opposed to anonymous meetings with HR or any other individual component of the firm. As stated earlier, worker-owned firms should still strive to employ good quality managers to take decisions accountable to the workforce, this is to avoid time-wasting on matters of a trivial nature. Issues of magnitude however, must be taken by the workforce as a whole. Issues of this kind could arise from a number of sources; a decision to be taken over a major investment, a decision on laying off a significant portion of the workforce, responding to difficult market conditions, etc. Perhaps a particular issue of major importance has been suppressed or put off, and workers suddenly find themselves having to take a decision unprepared and with everything at stake. Ideally, these sorts of situations should be avoided with good management, but this cannot always be guaranteed. A decision amongst the workers must be made.

Although a simple majority vote could put the issue to rest, the firm could risk disillusioning or perhaps even losing an essential quantity of its worker-members. Before the vote of a major decision is made, it is likely that the issue in question has been discussed at some length prior to the vote taking place during monthly or yearly meetings. These meetings are a formal setting for dealing with the company's major issues, and should at all costs refrain from becoming a space for workers to discuss informal grievances between workers, exacerbating conflicts which could be dealt with through HR, and wasting time and resources which should be spent on company-specific rather than individual-specific issues. In smaller worker-owned firms, or perhaps larger firms with departmental meetings, issues of an individual-specific nature could be brought up in monthly meetings in tandem with the other formal processes discussed earlier. Meetings should, as far as possible, be reserved for company-specific issues. For such meetings to be effective, participants should submit points of discussion which they feel are of major importance. Ideally, the meetings will be conducted by a meeting facilitator (MF), a neutral figure who is capable of commanding the respect of attendees. Ideally, this would be someone qualified in human resources who is trained to deal with confrontation should it arise. The MF is likely to structure the meetings, decide which points are to be discussed and arrange for action to be taken with management if various motions are voted upon.

Such meetings should be held regularly rather than improvised, however additional meetings could be called upon in special circumstances or emergencies. Such meetings should be given a fixed time, avoiding lengthy meetings that eat up working time, and to avoid meetings which are too brief and fail to tackle the issues at hand. The MF must also ensure that all worker-members attend the meeting (preferably within working hours) and that all workers actively participate in the meeting to ensure all opinions are aired. Without proper supervision, a situation could emerge where a few participants dominate the discussions of the meeting where others do not feel socially confident in voicing their opinion. Mellor et al (1988) also make this observation in their own research:

> Participants' inability or unwillingness to confront and handle conflict in a constructive manner was largely attributed to the following factors:
>
> (i)   lack of familiarity and experience in 'constructive criticism',
> (ii) inexperience in the conduct of, and unwillingness to participate in, meetings, and
> (iii) the development of perceived 'cliques'.
>
> Mellor et al (1988:116)

Good coordination by HR and the MF, along with adequate training should ensure that most worker-members are equipped to participating in meetings in a healthy and constructive manner. Such training could include 'model debates' where participants argue upon hypothetical issues to learn how to argue constructively and how to deal with a confident opposition. A code of conduct for meetings could be developed by the MF so all participants are aware of the methods of debate. Early prevention by HR can prevent informal individual-specific issues from being raised along with the prevention of perceived cliques or factions that emerge within the workforce. Indeed, there will always be some individuals who will not have the necessary social skills to adequately engage in such meetings and debates. As Mellor et al (1988:117) state, "[t]here is perhaps excessive optimism about the ability of people to develop the social skills necessary for effective participation in decision-making". Individuals who are unusually shy or nervous may not be able to demonstrate an ability to participate even with extensive training to boost confidence. In these circumstances, the MF could meet with these individuals one-on-one prior to the meeting, where the individual may be more likely to raise their concerns in a safe and trusting environment. The MF could then bring up these topics during the meeting on the behalf of the individual, but without direct reference to them. Once that topic is being discussed the shy individual may be more likely to voice their opinion. Meeting facilitators can experiment with methods such as these to ensure all meeting participants concerns are raised in a considerate manner. The more participants who engage, the better the democratic process will work.

Smaller firms are more likely to struggle with formal meetings and procedures. Worker-owned enterprises comprised only of a few individuals are unlikely to have the resources to properly train their employees to deal with formal meetings. They are also unlikely to have a dedicated HR representative who is trained to organise and structure meetings, or deal with conflict should it arise. As discussed earlier, the primary issues facing a smaller firm are likely to be dealt with informally, perhaps on the shop-floor level. When major divisions in the workforce emerge, and where there is not adequate resources, training or procedures to deal with it then external assistance will be required.

Mellor et al (1988) notes how cooperative development agencies (CDAs) were established to support new and small cooperatives, with one of their roles being to help defuse tension and to offer advice. CDA officers worked in a similar capacity to human resources and meeting facilitators, but with an added benefit of being perceived as a more neutral, trusted and professional figure. Although the use of such assistance may come at a cost for smaller enterprises, this may be a cheaper option compared to employing a HR rep and MF of their own. CDAs can also be of use for larger worker-owned firms where existing conflict and tension over a particular issue cannot be resolved with internal processes. Conflict resolution providers can be employed to assist the company with addressing an issue of this magnitude and to find a comprise the majority of workers can ultimately agree upon. In a capitalist economy, there are likely to be few providers who are trained in dealing with issues relating to worker-owned firms. The CDAs discussed in Mellor et al (1988) were publicly funded institutions which have since largely ceased due to political disinterest. In our 'cooperative economy', where worker-owned firms represent the majority of enterprises, private companies specialising in worker management and dispute resolution are likely to emerge, should the demand for such services be high enough. Trade unions may also have a role to play here. As a cooperative economy would no longer require trade unions in their current capacity (in the private sector at least), their *raison d'etre* may alter from conflict between employees and employers, to conflict between the employees themselves within worker-owned firms.

Regardless of which approach is taken, it is essential the enterprise can deal with any disagreements that emerge and reach a consensus on major issues that require the approval of the workforce. If this does not occur, the future of the company itself is it risk, along with the employment of all its worker-members. The theory of the incentive dynamic would imply that conflict is always likely to emerge at some point, but the worker-members will all eventually resolve their differences and agree on a plan of action for the sake of the firm.

Concluding Remarks

To conclude, is it clear that effective methods of worker management are an essential component of effective worker ownership as a whole. The two are interdependent. It can also be said without reasonable doubt there is an unsurprising link between employee participation in workplace affairs and the levels of work satisfaction and productivity that follow. Worker participation must be encouraged as much as possible within a practical and effective setting. Ownership alone will not induce workplace incentives. Employees need to have the ability to engage with their workplace practises, to innovate and pioneer new methods or products and will result in higher remunerative rewards. Workers' incomes need to fluctuate according to the effort applied if remunerative incentives are to be effective, this means giving workers the autonomy to determine how and how much effort to apply.

Workers also need the ability to express their concerns on various issues with the confidence that they will not be alienated by their co-workers or that decisions are not followed up with actions. Worker-owned firms need managers that can direct the firm yet remain accountable and transparent in the work they do. This must be met with a professional and delicate approach to human resources that deals with underlying issues in a productive and timely fashion. Worker management is not an excuse for endless meetings and debates on trivial matters, or a shouting-match of emotional argument. Meetings and decision-making should be seen as a form of investment in the company's future that deals with issues that genuinely affect the future of the firm. Good company training and education can assist workers on how to deal with individual-specific issues on the shop-floor, and company-specific issues in the conference rooms. Assistance will be required from external sources in some cases, a point of future discussion in Chapter 12 when we look closely at what our 'cooperative state' will be responsible for providing and facilitating. But for the majority of cases, the incentive dynamic will ensure that worker-members always have the best interests of the company at heart, and that means resolving differences, making decisions and boosting participation where possible. The fact that history shows us how workers can become their own bosses, can manage their own businesses and can make the difficult decisions, shows us that worker management is no idealistic or utopian endeavour, but a serious alternative to a frequently militaristic corporate hierarchy found in conventional capitalism – one that amounts to workers feeling more like impersonal cogs in a machine rather than foundational pillars of the enterprise.

---

[28]   They could simply cease trading, sell the assets, invest in something else and live off another form of income, either from that investment or through gaining employment themselves.

[29]   Under these circumstances, it must be stated that the remunerative incentive to shirk – as worker income has no reflection on effort – may be prevented by the moral incentive to increase income for every other worker. Meade (1980) compares this to the moral incentive to vote in general elections. Although an individual participating (voting) may have no effect on the outcome, a large number of voters still feel a civic duty (a form of moral incentive perhaps) to vote nonetheless. Whether the moral incentive to apply as much effort as possible outweighs the remunerative incentive to shirk, will depend purely on the individual. There will always be a free rider motive in any enterprise comprised of more than one individual. Therefore ensuring worker income reflects worker effort is the most effective solution.

[30]   See Ireland and Law (1982:69-72)

[31]   It is important that individual rewards and bonuses do not encourage too much competition between workers of the same firm. Not only is this potentially damaging to working relations if particular workers feel cheated, but individuals may inefficiently apply a significant amount of company resources to slightly better their own position at the greater expense of the company.

Chapter 6: Labour

The following section of research focuses upon more technical and economic aspects of worker ownership and management. That being said, we will stay true to our commitment not to bombard the reader with abstract mathematical equations; we must proceed to tell the economic story of worker ownership and management using words rather than numbers. For a more mathematical approach to comparing worker control with conventional capitalism, Vanek's (1970) *General Theory of Labour-Managed Market Economies* is a good place to start. Indeed, a lot of Vanek's work will be discussed in the coming chapters, with a sustained ambition to keep it simple and user-friendly.

Recalling the initial remarks of earlier chapters, we must remind ourselves, in basic terms, that humans are currently reliant of the consumption and production of commodities to ensure their survival. We need to consume commodities, like food and water, to stay alive. We need to produce commodities so that we can consume them, or exchange them for something else we need or want to consume. If a commodity is to be produced in an industrialised economy, it requires the ability to procure human effort and to procure the necessary means of production (materials, tools, machines, etc.). This chapter will deal with the former whilst the next chapter deals with the latter. In Chapter 1, we discussed the distinction between labour (the act of working) and labour-power (the capacity to do work). In reality, what an employee actually sells is their labour power, they sell their ability to perform the tasks set by their employer. However, for simplicity, we shall now use both terms (labour and labour-power) interchangeably.

Whether we like it or not, labour-power is often considered to act like any other commodity – something produced to be sold on a market whose price (the wage) is set by supply and demand. Like any other commodity, labour is usually exchanged for money. If the type of work being performed is scarce and can only be performed by a few talented individuals, the price of purchasing that labour-power will be more expensive. On the other hand, labour which requires skills that are abundant in the labour market will see a price which is relatively cheaper. Labourers compete for the same jobs in the same way that companies compete selling their commodities – the same pushes and pulls of supply and demand are in action. Thus, despite not actually being a commodity[32] (Polanyi, 1944), labour has all the hallmarks of a commodity. When moving from conventional capitalism towards a cooperative economy, not only are labourers competing for jobs, but they are also competing to become shareholders of an enterprise, along with all the responsibility that entails.

To recall the agent-principal nexus discussed in Chapters 2 and 3, not only will the company have certain standards they expect of the new employee (as would a conventional capitalist firm), the new employee will also have a certain degree of power over the company. The workers of a large corporate capitalist firm are sometimes comically referred to as robots, where the company can pull the levers of said robots in any which way they please. Under worker ownership this is still true to some extent, but the worker-owner-robot has now gained the capacity to pull the company's levers to a much greater extent. The company controls the worker and the worker controls the company. We cannot forget, however, that the worker-members of a worker-owned firm must still compete with other prospective worker-members if they are to gain employment in the first place. In the labour market, the pulls, pushes and pressures of supply and demand still function in allocating which workers are employed by which firm. Once these workers have been employed, they can begin to identify themselves as a partner of the firm, rather than a mere commodity, a mere robot. Put simply, the face of the labour market has changed, but it functions in roughly the same way. The way we perceive labour in a worker-owned firm is not the only difference we find comparing it to a conventional capitalist firm, as we shall see there are plenty more differences at play.

Demand for Labour and The Profit Principle

Let us know turn to the demand for labour. Similarly to any other type of business, a worker-owned firm will wish to employ additional labourers if they can produce/enable additional surplus value. Where capitalist firms are reliant upon their workers to produce/enable profits, the labour managed firm requires only the ability to pay the going wage rate to its workers at the very minimum. If a capitalist firm only earned enough to pay the wages of its workers and earned no profits for the business owners for a sustained period of time, the company would likely close down and the business owners would invest their money elsewhere. This would not happen in a worker-owned firm, as the purpose of the worker-owned firm is not to produce profits necessary, but to produce the best possible income for its worker-owners. This makes them more flexible to changes in market conditions, as we shall later reveal. However, in market conditions where competitors use profits to expand or invest, all worker-owned firms should strive to earn and increase profits if the firm is to survive in the long run. A worker-owned firm could function without earning a profit, but in the long run this may not be sustainable. Tastes and technology change, firms need to keep up with the trends and fashions in order to safeguard their long term sustainability.

The way in which we measure profit has massive implications for our study. This leads us to perhaps one of the most important distinctions between worker-owned firms and conventional capitalist firms – what we shall call 'the profit principle'. In usual circumstances it is the primary ambition of the conventional capitalist firm to boost 'total profits' in order to give a return to their investors/owners[33]. Total profit is easy to calculate, it is simply: total revenue minus total cost, the difference (if the figure is positive) is total profit. For the worker-owned firm on the other hand, rather than the main ambition being to boost total profit, instead the firm works towards increasing 'profit per head/worker'. Put simply, each individual worker is far more interested in increasing the dividend they are likely to receive, regardless of whether total profits increase or not[34]. Indeed there could be a situation where a worker-owned firms' total profit increases, but due to more worker-members joining the firm, the dividends are now shared out between a larger number of recipients, meaning profit per head has decreased. The same effect could happen in reverse, where total profits decrease but due to reducing the workforce the profit per head increases.

This distinction between maximising total profit and maximising income per head will be referred to as 'the profit principle'. Although the principles of increasing total profit and increasing profit per head may seem at odds, the two ambitions can often lead to the same microeconomic decisions and outcomes (Drèze, 1976). Regardless of the outcomes, we need to understand the process. The effects of the profit principle will become clearer as the chapter progresses. There is another important principle which must also be noted. Rather than using the term 'profit per head' we should instead use the term 'income per head', where income = profits + wages. In a worker-owned firm, profits and wages can be interdependent. Assuming *ceteris paribus* (nothing else changes), a firm which decides to increase wages for all its workers must simultaneously expect dividends to be smaller at the end of the year, as increased labour costs eat into profits. Alternatively, the firm could decide to cut wages, but dividends are likely to be higher at the end of the year as labour costs have shrunk. Regardless of which decision the company takes, the income per head should remain constant. As a result, it is in the interest of each worker to maximise their long term income per head.

So how does the profit principle affect the demand for labour in a worker-owned firm? The question to this is simple. If the incentive dynamic is at play, the employment of any new worker must at the very minimum keep income per head for the existing workers the same, but preferably, increase income per head for the existing workers. In strict economic terms, new staff members will only be employed if it is in the interests of the existing workers to employ them. If increasing the size of the workforce means the income per head of existing workers decreases, there will be no remunerative incentive to employ. Recall however, that the incentive dynamic is comprised of coercive incentives, remunerative incentives and moral incentives. There could be a moral incentive to employ new worker-members, for example if the firm's locality suddenly suffers an increase in unemployment. Worker-members may be happy to sacrifice a portion of their income to help their neighbours get back into employment. Alternatively, there could be a coercive incentive to employ new members, a company may have to adapt to a change in the law and employ a health and safety officer, for example. Although there is no remunerative incentive to employ that officer, there is a coercive incentive to employ him, as the firm will otherwise have to close, threatening the incomes of all workers. Keeping the company alive is the most important aspect for the existing workers. If there is a coercive incentive to employ, they will likely employ. If there is a coercive incentive not to employ, they will not employ. The same is true of remunerative incentives, but the pressure is not as strong. Keeping the company alive is more important than a short term increase or decrease in income per head.

The main reason for employing or not employing new workers in a profitable worker-owned firm comes down to whether income per head will increase or decrease. Meade explains in more economistic terms how this relationship functions.

> If one more partner is accepted into a Co-operative, he will add to the revenue
> of the Co-operative an amount equal to the value of his marginal product ... in
> a Co-operative he will receive the same share of the total surplus as do all the
> other partners ... if, therefore [his marginal product is greater than the share of
> the total surplus] ... he will add to the surplus of the Co-operative something
> more than the existing surplus per head, so that the surplus per head can be
> raised for all the partners. Thus the existing partners will wish to build up the
> partnership until the value of the marginal product of labour is equal to the
> average earnings per worker.

> Meade (1972:405, bracket and comment added)

Let us go through this statement step by step. The 'marginal product' is the extra value created or enabled by employing one more worker. If a company sells a commodity at £10 each, and an additional worker is able to produce an extra 20 commodities per day for that company, the workers marginal product has a value of £200. After (non-labour) costs have been taken into account, the surplus/profit made by the worker is added to the total surpluses made up of all workers. The new worker is now guaranteed a share of this surplus, as are all other workers. This share is the same as the income per head concept discussed earlier – it is the total income the worker receives from the firm. Due to the profit principle, raising the total surplus of the firm is not the key objective. The main aim of the firm is to maximise income per head. As such, the marginal product of labour (MP) must equal income per head (IPH). So why must they be equal (MP = IPH)? Put simply, this means the firm will hire/fire the right amount of labour to maximise income per head. The firm will add one more unit of labour (hiring an extra worker) if this will increase income per head. The firm will retract one more unit of labour (firing an extra worker) if this will increase income per head. Eventually, the firm will reach a point where either adding or retracting one more unit of labour will reduce income per head, this is the point of equilibrium – the optimal and most efficient number of staff to employ. This is not just the case with labour, there is an optimal level of all inputs and outputs of production. The firm needs to procure the right amount of materials, tools and machines to allow the labourers to produce the right amount of commodities at the most efficient rate.

> [T]he firm should only increase its labour employment whenever the net contribution to total income by the last man employed is more than the income per labourer currently earned, and reduce its employment whenever the opposite relation prevails between current income per labourer and the incremental income
>
> Vanek (1970:3)

To understand this further we must look at what were to happen if marginal product did not equal income per head (MP ≠ IPH). Firstly there is the scenario where marginal product is lower than income per head (MP < IPH). In this case, the value produced/enabled by the additional worker will not cover the cost the remaining workers have of paying that new worker a wage and sharing a portion of their dividends. Hiring this worker will reduce the income per head of the remaining workers, there is therefore no remunerative incentive to employ that new worker. Leaving aside additional workers for a moment, and focussing exclusively on the existing workforce, income per head may still be greater than marginal product. In this case, there may be a remunerative incentive to reduce the workforce until a point where the firm has the right number of employees to maximise income per head, where MP = IPH. Let us now look at the opposite scenario, where marginal product is higher than income per head (MP > IPH). In this case, the additional worker would produce/enable more value than income per head of the remaining workers. Therefore employing this worker would raise the income per head of the existing workforce, thus giving them an incentive to employ them. If MP > IPH remains even after employing that new worker, the firm will continue hiring more staff, and thus continuing to raise income per head, until a point where MP = IPH. As we have discussed, employing any more workers above MP = IPH would lead to a situation where MP < IPH. Achieving equilibrium between marginal product and income per head will lead to a point where the workers can maximise their incomes. Vanek (1970:22) points this out on several occasions in his *General Theory*, stating that in the short run "it immediately becomes apparent that in equilibrium the income per labourer of the labour-managed firm must equal the marginal value product of labour".

Although this may be the case in the short run, this may not be the case in the long run. Workers may tolerate a short term reduction in income per head for as long as it yields a higher return in the long run (especially for the original workers). If long run income per head is expected to be lower, Vanek's above point should hold true. This may be particularly true for apprentices, who are unlikely to increase income per head (at least by a great deal) in the short term, but as their skills develop over time, they are likely to make a larger contribution in the long run. However, as with the theory of marginalism more generally, it may be difficult for the company to estimate whether hiring or firing an additional worker will produce a higher income per head or not. This ability will depend largely on how value is created and measured within a particular firm, and the resources available to that firm to accurately measure the financial contribution of each worker. For other companies it will simply be a case of rough estimations, a process of trial and error. If the new worker does not increase (or maintain) income per head, they or maybe another member of staff could be made redundant, that or the workforce decreases naturally over time through attrition[35] back to the original level.

The question of whether the workforce should be reduced is frequently a complicated and at times emotive matter. Once again this comes down to the profit principle (whether it will increase or decrease income per head) and the incentive dynamic (the coercive, moral and remunerative incentives to do so). For one reason or another it may be in the best interests of a worker-owned firm to decrease the size of its workforce. There could be a remunerative incentive for the majority of the workers to make redundant a minority of the workers if it becomes apparent that income per head could be increased for the remaining workers as a result. Potential reasons for this will be outlined in Chapter 8. In this scenario the workers have to make a decision between reducing the workforce and receiving a higher income (assuming they are not one of the unlucky few) or whether to sacrifice this additional income in order to spare the unlucky few from unemployment. This is a battle between remunerative and moral incentives. What is more likely to occur is a coercive incentive to decrease labour – that decreasing labour is the only way to keep the firm alive for the remaining majority of the workforce. This situation can become difficult, as the remaining workers still have a moral incentive to keep those workers employed.

Developing close working relationships with colleagues, and then having to choose between their job or your own can be a potentially traumatic experience for the unlucky firms which face financial difficulty. If we are, however, to stick to the principle of the rational individual, as uncomfortable and unrealistic as that may sometimes be, the only rational choice is for the redundancies to go ahead. If the workers temptation to abide by the moral incentive (to keep an unsustainable amount of staff) outweighs the coercive incentive (to go ahead with redundancies to keep the firm alive for the remaining workers), the firm could fail and all workers will potentially become unemployed. As will be discussed later, support systems can be put in place to reallocate workers between departments and employers. But at this early stage we must simply justify the need for worker-owned firms to employ at the optimal level, the level where either a decrease or increase in labour will decrease income per head. The theory of the rational individual would imply that despite moral and social implications, the worker-owned firm will always employ an amount of labour which is sustainable, and if remunerative incentives outweigh moral incentives, the worker-owned firm will employ the optimal level of workers where income per head is maximised.

Supply of Labour

As with the demand for labour, the supply of labour only changes in a few ways, again, primarily due to the profit principle. In a capitalist labour market, workers seek to find positions usually for the highest wage. Other aspects are considered as well, for example the level and type of effort expected to perform, distance from the place of work and consequential travel cost, the hours of work, annual leave, etc. In most cases however, especially for the lowest paid, the wage rate will be the most pivotal factor. When workers in a cooperativist labour market look for alternative employment, they will likely pay most attention to three figures; the total income per head they are expecting to earn; and the two constituent parts of this figure; wages and dividends. As with conventional capitalism, the wage is the money earned to maintain subsistence at the very least. This is usually paid weekly or monthly. Worker-members of a worker-owned firm are unlikely to pay themselves below the necessary minimum where they can absolutely avoid it. Going below this minimum would not only harm the well-being of the existing members, but would also deter new members from joining and entice existing members to look elsewhere. As a result, any 'cooperative state' would not (in theory) need to legislate a minimum wage. Worker members are also unlikely to give themselves a wage which is too high and is therefore not financially sustainable for the firm. The end result is therefore a wage rate which is sustainable for the firm and gives its workers the means of subsistence at the very least. The second figure prospective workers will look at is the expected dividend. This is the bonus each of the existing workers have earned in the past, and is most likely to be paid annually. This figure will give some indication of what the new worker-member is likely to receive should they apply a similar degree of effort as the existing workers had the previous year. New workers may also wish to discover the average percentage of profits which are released as dividends to the worker-owners each year. If this percentage is low, this could mean that a greater proportion of the profits have been reinvested into the firm, meaning a higher percentage and thus a higher dividend is likely to be earned in future. Alternatively, the percentage could be low because the company has a problem with debt and may not be unable to service debts in the future, questioning the survival of the firm in the long run. Either way, this figure will a likely point of discussion between the prospective worker-member and the company in question.

By adding the wage and dividend figures together the new worker-member can calculate the expected total income per head for the year ahead. If this figure is higher than the worker's current total income, they are likely to switch. It must also be noted that some workers will have a preference for a higher wage and lower dividend, or a lower wage and higher dividend. Most will probably prefer the former to the latter. Issuing a higher wage can be the more riskier option, as this is akin to cashing out early on the dividend expected at the end of the year. Of course, the company may experience a downturn later in the year, where profits are drastically reduced. If the company has issued a higher wage in anticipation of earning a similar rate of profit from the year before, the company could soon find itself in financial difficulty. Although the 'higher wage lower dividend' option could be safeguarded by paying for this year's higher wages from last year's profits, any financial downturn could lead to wage reductions in the subsequent year, which for workers may be difficult to adjust to. A lower wage and higher dividend approach may be more tempting in markets where turnover is more volatile – where there is little likelihood of knowing whether profits will be higher or lower one year to the next. This option provides for longer term wage stability. The decision the workers must take regarding wages and dividends is one of the most important, as it is one of the few factors of production the company can adjust regarding its cost.

So what are the consequences of this change from workers seeking to maximise wages, as observed in capitalist economies, to now seeking to maximise income per head? The most obvious change is for sectors where companies are competing for workers with a scarce skill set; these firms are more likely to present themselves as more profitable compared to their competitors[36]. In conventional capitalist companies, workers with a scarce skillset can expect to earn a higher wage and continue on that wage, sometimes regardless of the amount of effort they apply compared to the effort expected from their employer. This is particularly true of the highest paid executives. In Bebchuk and Fried's (2004) work *Pay without Performance*, it is argued that the greater power managers wield over shareholders has led to a situation where managerial pay can increase regardless of whether performance increases or decreases.

The opposite is the case for the working majority, as we have seen, where pay is rarely linked to effort applied, and due to low bargaining power, workers pay can remain at the very minimum. As Atkinson (2015) claims, wages for the working majority rarely correlate to marginal product. The use of zero hour contracts in the UK is an obvious example, where pay is more linked to the bargaining power of the employees rather than value produced/enabled[37]. Since the fall in UK trade union membership stemming back to the industrial disputes of the 1970s and 1980s, the ability of workers to bargain for a better wage has largely diminished, particularly in the private sector. The rise of more flexible and precarious working practices has been the result of this long process. As a result, it would appear that bargaining power seems to have much more of an impact on wages under conventional capitalism than marginal product alone, for both rich and poor. As Bebchuk and Fried confidently proclaim, "managers have used their influence to obtain higher compensation through arrangements that have substantially decoupled pay from performance." (2004:6). These individuals are not kept in check by those who own the company, and so are given the capability to set the rules. In a worker-owned firm, the level of income a higher earning individual receives will now be more dependent on the effort they apply, especially if a lower wage and higher dividend approach is taken. In addition, the remaining worker-owners are more likely to be critical of instances where other workers earn a higher income per head but are perceived not to be raising the income per head for the remaining workers. As stated in the previous sub-section, the existing workforce needs to be under the impression that both new and existing worker-members will at least maintain current income per head, or preferably increase it, for the existing workers. The examples highlighted in Bebchuk and Fried's (2004) research are therefore less likely to occur in a cooperative economy. For workers with skills which are more abundant in the labour market, we would expect to see little other change.

Bringing together the forces of supply and demand, we can begin to observe how particular factors may lead to particular outcomes regarding labour and worker ownership. Meade (1980:93-96) explores a model considering the gains and loses from expanding or contracting employment. This can be roughly narrowed down to demand-side and supply-side factors between worker-owned firms and prospective employees that we have discussed so far. Meade's (1980) model will be revised and extended to take account of additional scenarios and outcomes. The first two relationships to display have been discussed earlier in this chapter. The first term is the expected income per head of the existing workers of an existing worker-owned firm (IPH), the second is the expected marginal product (the surplus value produced or enabled) of a specific prospective worker who is looking to join the firm (MP). Two scenarios illustrate whether the firm will hire this prospective worker.

1.   MP > IPH
2.   IPH > MP

These first two scenarios demonstrate the profit principle. In scenario 1, the marginal product created by the prospective worker is higher than the income per head currently enjoyed by the existing workers. The existing workers are therefore likely to employ that worker, as total income per head is expected to raise for all workers as the new worker is much more productive. In scenario 2 the opposite is true. The income per head of the existing workers is higher than what the prospective worker is likely to create. Income per head will decrease for the existing workers if they employ that person. It is also important to state that moral incentives have been disregarded here, as we are simply discussing the remunerative (and potentially coercive) incentives at work.

Now we will add another feature to this analysis – the income per head expected to be earned in another worker-owned firm (AIPH)[38]. This distinction will show us which company the prospective worker is likely to seek employment with, the original firm or an alternative firm.

3.   MP > IPH > AIPH

In scenario 3, the surplus value created by the new recruit will be higher than the income per head currently earned by the existing workers. This means the existing workers have a remunerative incentive to employ that worker, as found in scenario 1. In addition to this, the original firm is earning a higher income per head than its competitor, meaning the prospective worker is most likely to choose the original firm for employment rather than the alternative firm. The alternative firm has an even greater incentive to employ the prospective member if their skills are scarce, not only due to the fact that they are likely to raise income per head for the remaining workers, but also because they will be diverting a profitable worker away from the original firm. The alternative firm may produce an artificial incentive to convince the prospective worker to choose them over their competitor, to turn MP > IPH > AIPH into MP > AIPH > IPH. This could be done by offering the prospective worker an increased wage or a bonus in addition to their yearly dividends.

There is now also an additional factor to consider. As the income per head in the original firm is higher than the income per head in the alternative firm, those working in the alternative firm have an incentive to leave it and join the original firm. This is similar to the incentive investors of capitalist firms have, to transfer their capital out of a less profitable to a more profitable firms. If the difference between the two firms is negligible, the workers in the alternative firm are more likely to focus on ways to marginally increase income per head. If the difference between the two is more substantial, the incentive to leave is much greater. Of course, having an incentive to leave your current firm and to join another one is not the same as actually doing so. Would there be an incentive for the original firm to take on employees of a firm that was less profitable? Even if there was an incentive, could the original firm afford to do so? These are all hypothetical questions that must be answered before coming to concrete conclusions. If however, workers do start to leave a particular firm and seek employment elsewhere, the position of the company they are leaving will slowly deteriorate, creating a negative spiral effect. The more workers who leave, the greater income per head will diminish for the remaining workers, until a situation emerges where wages cannot be paid, inputs cannot be purchased and debts cannot be serviced. The only way to avoid this situation would be to ensure that a supply of labour to replace the leaving workers can be found. These workers are likely to come from firms with an even lower income per head. What we finish with is a situation where the companies with the lowest income per head are likely to fail, and in all likelihood this will be due to factors much more serious than consequential labour shortages.

4.   AIPH > IPH > MP

In scenario 4, again, there are multiple forces at play. First of all, the income per head of the existing workers is greater than the marginal product the prospective worker is likely to produce/enable. There is no incentive for the workers to employ that recruit. Secondly, the income per head expected in another worker-owned firm is higher than what the existing workers are currently earning and what the prospective worker is likely to gain from the original firm. For the prospective worker there is no chance of gaining employment in this particular industry. Solutions to this depend of why the MP figure is so low. If this figure is simply down to the fact that the worker cannot produce/enable enough value compared to others, this could be solved with greater training to convince and demonstrate to employers that they can be more profitable to the firm. Alternatively, if there is a lack of demand for the firm to employ more workers (having reached the optimal level of labour) the prospective worker could look for positions in different sectors, perhaps where there is more demand[39].

Now let us look at these scenarios again, but let us now change the prospective worker (MP) with an existing worker at the original worker-owned firm (MPE). This means that rather than companies making a decision as whether to employ a new worker, they are now making a decision as whether to make an existing worker redundant. Once again, all of the following postulations are assuming that there are only remunerative and coercive incentives at play. As a result, we will be assuming that moral incentives to keep existing employees employed will not feature. As cruel and unrealistic as this might seem, it will present the most economically efficient outcome regarding the context. As stated earlier, there may be a coercive incentive to downsize the workforce, if for example, the company comes under financial pressure and the employment of the entire workforce is at risk. Let us move forward with that in mind.

5. MPE > IPH > AIPH
6. AIPH > IPH > MPE
7. IPH > AIPH > MPE
8. IPH > MPE > AIPH
9. MPE > AIPH > IPH
10. AIPH > MPE > IPH

In scenario 5 the existing worker is producing/enabling a rate of marginal product which is higher than the income per head of the remaining workers. This figure is also higher than the income per head found at alternative companies. In this case, there is neither an incentive for the firm to dismiss the existing worker, nor is there an incentive for the existing worker to seek employment elsewhere. Again, there is an incentive for the alternative firm to employ that worker but this would require artificial incentives that the alternative firm would not normally offer to recruits. The existing worker is likely to be dismissed in scenario 6, and is unlikely to find employment elsewhere. Similar to the case of the prospective worker in scenario 4, the existing worker will need to convince their fellow worker-members that it is in their best interest to keep them employed. Further in-house training, along with more productive methods and techniques could be a starting point. If however, there is no likelihood of that worker being able to produce/enable an adequate amount of surplus value, they are likely to be laid off.

The only difference between scenarios 6 and 7, is that although no employer is likely to keep/take the existing worker, in scenario 6 the worker has an incentive to find an alternative employer, whereas in scenario 7 they have an incentive to stay at their current company. In scenario 8, again, the original company has an incentive to dismiss the existing worker. Although the existing worker has an incentive to remain employed at the original company, they will be able to find employment at alternative companies if they are dismissed. In scenario 9, the existing worker has an incentive to find employment at an alternative firm, as does the alternative firm having an incentive to hire them, but the original firm has an incentive to keep the worker on. The two firms are likely to compete for their employment. Lastly, in scenario 10 we see that whilst the existing worker has an incentive to join an alternative firm, there is no incentive for that alternative firm to employ them. The original company has no incentive to dismiss them.

All these scenarios demonstrate how demand and supply factors, along with differing incentives, can determine who works where and why. If the forces of supply and demand are to reach a state of equilibrium, a situation should emerge where MP and/or MPE = IPH = AIPH. At this stage all parties are at an optimal level where there are no conflicts of interest. It is important to re-emphasise that moral dimensions have not played on any part of the results shown thus far. Other non-financial factors have also not featured in this model, but will undoubtedly have an effect on supply and demand. Nonetheless Meade's (1980) model is a good thought experiment which illustrates the new effects a cooperativist labour market would face.

Entrepreneurs and Labour

So far we have only discussed the supply of labour for an existing firm. A new worker-owned firm with a desire to expand will need to hire workers to facilitate business growth. This scenario will depend on who is setting up the company, a group of workers, or an individual entrepreneur/founder. For new firms with an individual entrepreneur, the entrepreneur would have to bargain with their first employees in a similar way to how they may bargain with their first investors. The first employee must accept that the entrepreneur is to receive a larger portion of the surplus value during the initial start-up period. We would expect this as the entrepreneur has already expended time and effort to come up with a new commercial concept, starting the initial phases of planning the company's birth, as well as being rewarded for building the capacity to employ new workers. As we have discussed earlier, however, these feats are by no means a justification for the dual-contradiction – the workers who set about bringing forward the entrepreneur's vision to life equally deserve the fruits of their labour. Although surpluses must eventually be distributed equally, during the firm's initial start-up phase, the entrepreneur will be entitled to repayments from the company to cover any initial financial investments put forward by the entrepreneur. Honorariums (financial bonuses) could be utilised to recompense the non-financial contributions made by the entrepreneur, including the entrepreneur's initial time and effort to establish the business. These bonuses will be essential to incentivise the initial risks taken and innovations achieved by the entrepreneur. As time progresses, the entrepreneur and the subsequent workers employed would start to share the surpluses equally, although the entrepreneur may remain on a higher rate of pay, again, as an added reward for their initial efforts. It nonetheless remains essential that the incentive dynamic remains healthy and stable for the non-founding employees, as without their labour, the aspirations of the entrepreneur would not have been realised. On the other hand, the rewards of the entrepreneur for their innovation must be adequate enough for them to want to begin this endeavour to begin with – for without this endeavour, the subsequent employees would not have had the capacity to produce a subsistence and surplus by these means.

> But to build a business out of an idea takes more than just the application of
> an inventor: it takes joint commitment and problem-solving by whole groups
> of people. Shared 'psychological' ownership is often the result. And
> psychological ownership becomes enormously stronger when it is matched by
> real ownership.

Erdal (2011:70)

There is an indisputable interdependence between the entrepreneur and the worker. The same can be said with the investor who lends the start-up capital. All parties have an interest in the success of the firm. The best method of realising this collective interest is through worker ownership and management, as the workers (along with the initial entrepreneur) have the greatest interest in its survival.

It could be argued that the conventional capitalist business model better suits individual entrepreneurs in starting their own business from scratch, with the potential to employ workers in future if the company achieves greater success. This however, is not strictly true.

> [T]he model firm is established on the initiative of a single individual and where the firm concerned is intended to become a cooperative, the relevant ownership rights and management functions are apportioned among a plurality of individuals only after the establishment of the firm. Examples of this procedure include a number of forest cooperatives in the Pacific Northwest, which were originally set up by single promoters.
>
> Jossa (2015:273)

There is no obvious downside to an entrepreneur deciding to start their own business and then, if the company is ready to expand, invite a prospective employee to become a partner in the firm. Although this may impact the entrepreneur's profits in the short run, as profits must now be shared, in the long run the entrepreneur may in fact increase their profits. Worker ownership ensures that the workers the entrepreneur employs also become entrepreneurs themselves to an extent. Similar to investors pondering whether to supply the entrepreneur with investment capital, the new workers will ponder as to whether this endeavour has the potential to produce a higher income per head in future compared to what they currently earn or could earn. Although the entrepreneur of a worker-owned firm may potentially earn less to begin with compared to the conventional capitalist approach, due to the maximised incentives of the workers, the entrepreneur could in fact earn a higher income through sharing the profits. The reason for this is simple, the collective absence of the dual-contradiction. Worker ownership breeds new and innovative ways of working, more efficient and productive approaches, ideas that the entrepreneur could not had thought up or implemented alone or with non-shareholding employees. If the incentivised workers can grow the company in ways the entrepreneur could not have otherwise achieved, all parties share in this greater reward. To use a culinary analogy, the entrepreneur gains from a smaller slice of a much larger cake. Sharing the responsibilities of running the firm can also be beneficial. A small firm where a single individual is performing all the managerial responsibilities can be arduous and stressful, sharing these roles out to those who are both willing and able can help to resolve this. As such, worker ownership can complement the plans and successes of individual entrepreneurs. There is no reason to tolerate the dual-contradiction for small firms and start-ups, its abolition should be embraced as a means of achieving collective entrepreneurialism.

It has been argued (Jay, 1980) that entrepreneurs should own 100 per cent of the start-up company until a certain threshold of employees is reached, after which ownership should then be shared equally amongst those employees. For example, a capitalist start-up firm would only be required to transform into a worker-owned firm once it reaches a workforce of say 100 people. The problem arises as to why the company owner who employs 99 workers would wish to employ a 100th? Not only would this re-establish the dual-contradiction and everything it entails, but it would also act as a coercive incentive and artificial barrier to growth and expansion. Clearly this approach in untenable. To reaffirm earlier statements, worker ownership cannot be bargained away, regardless of whether the company in question is pre-existing, or a new start-up firm with an individual entrepreneur. Worker ownership must be a guiding and unbreakable principle of this new political economy. By the same token, worker ownership and individual entrepreneurship are not incompatible. Quite the contrary, they should be complements. If incentives and responsibilities are shared, the rewards are likely to be greater for all parties, as we have explored.

The case of a start-up worker-owned firm comprised of multiple entrepreneurs (as opposed to just the one) carries additional implications. Regarding the distribution of surpluses the issue becomes much simpler, as all parties share equally in the surpluses created as would be expected in an existing worker-owned firm. Finding a group of individuals to start this business venture could potentially be more challenging. For groups of friends or family members this could be relatively easy, the same could be said for a group of colleagues looking to start their own enterprise. Pooling together individuals who have never previously met can be more difficult.

> [T]he creation of new enterprises to fill market gaps and to exploit new technologies is by its nature more easily undertaken (and therefore more likely to be undertaken) by an individual than by a spontaneous workers' co-operative sprung ready-made from the dole queues.
>
> Jay (1980:26)

There is a great deal of truth in this, however, this does not mean that support structures cannot be put in place to support and nurture collective entrepreneurialism. Public employment offices, shared workshops and private sector start-up facilitators could all play a part within a cooperative economy. This will certainly be a point of discussion in Chapter 12. For as long as the principles of full worker ownership and management are adhered to, the means in which new enterprises can be set up is something that can be experimented with.

A Cooperative Labour Market

As mentioned earlier in the chapter, labour is treated as a commodity within capitalist labour markets. Labour is just one of the essential inputs that are required to bring goods and services to market. The Meade model we have just explored also treats labour as a commodity, especially where the drive to increase income per worker is based solely on coercive and remunerative incentives. There is of course the question of moral incentives. Ideally, a worker-owned firm would not wish to reduce its workforce unless absolutely necessary, and even in that case additional steps can be taken. The best model of this is the Mondragon Corporation. This federation of worker cooperatives has diversified across multiple markets and sectors where demand fluctuates between the goods and services it collectively sells. If in a particular instance, a particular cooperative within the federation suffers from a lack of demand for their goods and services, in normal circumstances it would have to reduce output and reduce its workforce. Under conventional capitalism, this can be potentially devastating for the workers who would lose their jobs, as their means of subsistence has been stripped away. For Mondragon however, the firm is keen to reallocate workers between sectors with differing demand.

As Mondragon is unique in having its own university, it can easily retrain workers to become equipped with the skills for different industries and markets, this ensures that the actual number of redundancies are kept to a minimum. This model has been used successfully at Mondragon on multiple occasions[40]. This largely successful approach applied at a microeconomic level could be replicated on a macroeconomic level. Wolff (2012) critiques the barbarity of conventional capitalism when it comes to labour reductions, and acknowledges the role labour saving technologies has to this effect. He proposes how workers self-directed enterprises (WSDEs)[41] could buck the trend.

One way to accomplish this would be to create a fund (by surplus distributions from WSDE boards) and a government agency to administer it. Any WSDE that faced a need to lay off workers would qualify for assistance. The agency would survey and interview workers to determine those most interested in new and different jobs. It could provide training, relocation, and other services to effect employment changes from enterprises and industries needing fewer workers to those seeking expansion. In this way, unemployment would be eliminated without compromising various incentives for labour-saving technological progress and without ignoring patterns of citizens' demands for certain goods and services.

Wolff (2012:126)

Although lay-offs and redundancies will always be a necessity in a market economy, the concept of worker reallocation between different firms and industries presents an interesting proposal to mitigate the worst effects. Attempts to humanise and de-commodify the labour process must always be welcomed when presented. Job centres and other forms of unemployment agencies may be the first place to look when searching for potential agencies to take this task on. Of course, attempts to reallocate workers will be futile in a macroeconomic context where unemployment is generally high and employment prospects bleak. The extent to which a cooperative state should seek to deal with these underlying macroeconomic failures is a debate for another time, however, the worker reallocation scheme proposed by Wolff (2012) may be one innovative and progressive place to start.

There is also another point to consider when analysing worker redundancies due to automation or other labour saving technologies. When worker-owned firms install labour saving technologies, there may not necessarily be a need to shrink the workforce. One potential solution would be to reduce the number of hours worked whilst keeping salaries constant. That way all workers can increase their overall income, as the new technology increases productivity, whilst the workers can reduce their working hours to improve their work-life balance.

In capitalism, where workers are excluded from choices about technology, they choose between labor and leisure based on the wage given by their competition in the labor market. In contrast, workers in WSDEs make labor/leisure choice together with and as part of their decisions about technological change.

Wolff (2012:133)

When moving from capitalist ownership to worker ownership we may expect to see less turnover of staff as a result of workers wishing to readjust their work-life balance. Despite rapid technological gains over the last century, many people in advanced economies still find themselves with less leisure time and more precarious working hours. In Keynes' (1930) *Economic Prospects for our Grandchildren* he predicted that within a century the working day would be stripped down to 3 hours per day, or 15 hours per working week. In today's context of growing insecurity at work, that ambition seems more like a pipe dream, at least with the current economic model. Worker ownership enhanced with labour saving technologies has the potential to relieve this pressure and bring Keynes' hypothesis a step closer to reality.

Concluding Remarks

By and large the main practical functions of the labour market under conventional capitalism and worker ownership have altered very little. The profit principle – the difference between maximising income per head rather than total profits – is perhaps the most striking difference. Regarding demand, worker-owned firms will seek to employ individuals who will produce a surplus value for the firm that will ideally increase the income per head for the remaining workforce. Regarding supply, the individual worker will wish to maximise their income per head and will seek employment where that can best be expected. The discussion on labour and employment will not end here. As will be demonstrated in the next two chapters, the profit principle will reveal multiple other features which will present worker-owned firms with multiple other challenges.

---

[32] Labour cannot be a commodity as humans are not 'produced' solely to be sold on an open market for the purposes of performing work. The question as to why humans procreate is much too complex for a simple footnote! Nonetheless, we can agree that we are not born simply to work for an employer.

[33] "In the case of capitalist enterprises profit-maximisation has been a dominant assumption but various 'managerial' models such as those of sales maximisation, growth maximisation and managerial utility maximisation have been advanced to reflect the idea that ... ownership may be divorced from control, giving managers a significant degree of discretion to peruse objectives which may differ from those of shareholders." (Ireland and Law, 1982:10).

[34] See Vanek (1970:2-3).

[35] Workplace attrition is the process of workers leaving the firm by their own accord and the firm not replacing them. Workers may be reaching retirement, or may find more preferable employment elsewhere. The rate of attrition is commonly referred to as the rate of staff turnover.

[36] This would also occur for workers with an abundant skill set if there are labour shortages throughout the economy. In a heavily globalised economy where there is greater labour mobility

between nations, such shortages are unlikely to occur. Therefore we should assume that labour scarcity is most likely to occur for those with a scarce skill set.

[37] See Atkinson (2012:147)

[38] The **AIPH** could represent the average income per head for a group of firms in a particular market. Alternatively it could represent the income per head of a particular firm, under oligopoly or duopoly for example.

[39] If there is little demand for labour throughout the economy in general, we would expect greater government intervention to correct this. The market system we are postulating in this model is capable of reaching full employment, even if such a likelihood is unrealistic empirically.

[40] See Morris (1992:23-25).

[41] In the interest of clarity, Wolff's **WSDE** concept is almost identical to the worker-owned firm/worker cooperative model we have been discussing.

Chapter 7: Capital

It is widely held that the most serious problem co-operatives face is a lack of finance.

Thornley (1981:62)

There is no certainty that producing a commodity will yield a profit, the producer has to take risks. To take a risk, an investment must occur, either of money or time or some other scarcity. As a universal means of exchange, it is likely that money will be used to make an investment in a particular company, to purchase tools, materials, labour power, etc. Money which is used solely to produce profit (more money) is known as capital, or financial capital. Under capitalism, a capitalist would use money to produce a commodity, sell that commodity for an amount greater than the cost of producing that commodity, and then use that greater sum of money to produce more commodities, and so on. This process continues until the producer believes that the risk of further investment is too high and/or their investment will yield no further profit. The question then arises as to why would anyone invest and take this risk? There are multiple reasons for this, but front and foremost it must be emphasised how risk is an everyday element of human life, where risks and rewards constantly vary from multiple sources, financial or otherwise. We take risks when we believe there is a chance that we will become better off as a result, whilst acknowledging that we could also become worse off.

Economists would argue that the purpose of risk taking is to maximise our utility, to increase the things that give us satisfaction as much as we can. When presented with an identical risk, some people are more likely to take it than others, depending on their state of mind, their financial well-being, their health, etc. If capitalism has taught us anything it is that humans, on aggregate, are willing to take enough risk to maintain the subsistence of humanity and at a minimum, although there is frequent disagreement on how well this wealth is distributed. These are important concepts to keep in mind when discussing why worker-owned firms would want to invest and how they would go about it. The issue of procuring investment is perhaps one of the greatest sources of critique for worker ownership. This chapter will shed greater light on the matter, with the aim to address the many obstacles worker-owned firms may face when presented with the task of procuring investment.

Capital Demand and The Market Dynamic

When discussing investment in business, there are two likely contexts an enterprise will find itself in; a start-up which requires initial investment; and an existing firm which requires additional investment. For the start-up firm, the question 'why invest?' is a simple one, without the initial investment the firm will not be able to acquire the means of production - the materials, tools, land, and labour power, etc. There are also two types of investment sources a business can call upon; internal (capital acquired and saved within the firm, for example company profits used for reinvestment) and external (investment from any source outside the company, from a bank for example). For start-ups, internal investment from retained earnings cannot occur as the company has yet to make any earnings, internal investment can only come from the individuals who intend to start up the company, from their own personal savings. For external finance, enterprises will most likely have to access capital markets. Capital markets are usually comprised of stock markets and bond markets. For the sake of simplicity, we will assume that capital markets also include loans from banks and other financial institutions. Both start-ups and existing companies must be able to access external investment if there is a fully functioning capital market within a cooperative economy. Returning to our question of why invest, although it would appear obvious why a start-up firm would require investment, there answer for existing enterprises can be more nuanced.

The profit principle - the difference between maximising total profits and maximising incomes per head - can alter the incentive for the worker-owned firm to invest. Similarly to our discussion on labour, the profit principle also plays a significant part in the realm of investment. Let us take a hypothetical example to demonstrate such alterations. Assume the worker-members of a medium sized worker-owned firm are preparing to vote upon whether to approve a major investment in the firm. This investment will fund an expansion of the firm, hiring new tools, machines and workers to produce more commodities. Whether the firm intends to reinvest internal funds or source investment from external actors is irrelevant at this stage, the only important feature to remember is that there will be a financial cost to the current worker members for investing, a cost in which there is no absolute guarantee of remunerating. Regardless of this, the worker members in this example are reasonably confident that the venture will be profitable for the firm - that total profits will increase and the investment will make an adequate return. However, each individual worker will have to calculate whether the loss in dividends endured in the short run will be higher or lower than the return they receive from that investment in the long run. If the future returns are lower than the sacrifice made today, the worker will likely reject the plan, wanting to take their dividend now rather than investing it for something smaller in return in future.

There is one particular reason why income per head may decrease. One aspect of the investment plan is to hire additional worker members, who will inevitably take a share of the profits they help to create once the new tools and machines are up and running and producing the additional commodities. In this sense, the size of the cake has increased, but as new members have joined, everyone's slice is smaller.

> The conclusion was that to some degree the workers' co-operative would be less inclined to make the kind of new investment which would increase employment without increasing distributable rewards per head of the pre-investment members of the co-operative.
>
> Jay (1977:25)

Of course, this effect may not necessary materialise. In theory both total profits and income per head could rise simultaneously. As technology constantly improves, the tools and machines the worker-owned firm purchases are likely to be more productive compared to the company's existing stock. More productive tools and machinery means that more commodities can be produced more quickly and/or require fewer workers to operate them. Under these circumstances, the new worker members operating the new stock are themselves likely to produce a higher income per head compared to the original workers, meaning that income per head for the whole company will increase. Dickstein (1991:24) states that the workers "can only benefit from increased investment if it results in greater productivity and therefore greater income for the workers". Also, this process is not necessarily unique to the worker-owned firm. For a conventional capitalist firm, where the major investors are likely to make the investment decisions, they are almost certainly likely to approve a profitable investment decision for as long as it does not lead to stock dilution. Stock dilution is when a company increases the number of shares traded, thereby decreasing the value of the original shares. As a result, shareholders are typically apprehensive toward investment decisions that include share dilution, as their share of future dividends will decrease[42]. Any final decision is dependent on how much knowledge the investors have of the investment decision and how much power they actually have to approve or disapprove the decision. Let us not forget that those who own the firm but who are external of it, are less likely to know the inner workings and goings on of that firm. The worker-owners of a worker-owned firm are best suited to make the most rational decision regarding whether to invest, as they know the company inside and out.

The question we must now ask is whether workers would in any circumstance accept a lower income per head as the result of major investment. The answer to this depends more upon what the firm is selling and its market conditions more than anything else. We cannot analyse a firm in isolation. We assumed earlier that our hypothetical worker-owned firm, which was considering whether or not to make a particular investment, was operating in an open market. If we now assume that this firm operates a monopoly, we see no difference to the hypothesis outlined earlier. If investment decreases income per head, the workers of that monopolistic firm are in no hurry to initiate that investment. There is no threat of a competitor firm, which does invest, coming forward to take a greater market share. Where competition is present (whether it be market perfection or oligopoly), there is a threat from competitors. This threat can come primarily in two forms. Firstly, our worker-owned firm may be considering investment because there is higher demand for the commodity they are producing – investment is required to produce more commodities. If they fail to invest due to the 'bigger cake, smaller slice dilemma', competitors are likely to step forward who do invest and thus take a greater market share. Although this competitor worker-owned firm would suffer a lower income per head in the short run, the aim here is to take the original firm's market share, in an attempt to maximise income per head in the medium to long run. Secondly, our worker-owned firm may be considering to invest in new technology to update their product range in line with new market tastes. Again, if they fail to do so, competitors will invest in the new technology and are likely to take a greater market share as a result. The commodity of the original worker-owned firm now appears obsolete to the consumer. If the worker-owned firm is not willing to sacrifice some portion of its income per head, it may be at risk of losing all of it if it cannot keep pace with market trends and developments. The cake/slice dilemma has also been discredited by other academics:

> Especially in the context of real situations where technology and product
> designs are changing over time, modernisation and corresponding investments
> may be imperative at virtually any cost.
>
> Vanek (1970:305)

> Now that [the cake/slice dilemma] could be true if the only or normal reason
> to borrow money was to expand in the sense of to increase your productive
> capacity. But in almost all enterprises you have to keep investing in order to

stay in business, coping with changes in tastes, technology, and new methods;
and all that requires significant capital expenditure on a quite sufficient scale to
give enterprises an incentive to be in reasonably good standing with investors
so that they can borrow in the future, and to be seen to be in that position.

Clayre (1980:78, bracket and comment added)

Competition between co-operatives will provide an incentive to new
investment, as will the natural desire of each co-operative to maximise its
income per head and to protect future employment.

Jay (1977:16)

Competition is not just likely to come from existing competitors, but also from new
companies that emerge in the marketplace. The more we move away from a monopolistic
market and more towards market perfection, the easier it is for new enterprises to enter the
marketplace. When there are limited barriers to entry, new firms can challenge the market
share of the older companies. Let us take another hypothetical example. A medium sized
worker-owned firm is about to take a decision on whether to invest in new labour saving
technology – machines that produce at least the same amount of products as before but
requires fewer workers to operate them. This new technology will replace the older means of
production and could produce more commodities to cater towards an increase in demand.

All this means fewer workers will be required in this particular part of production.
Although we discussed in the previous chapter how labour saving technology can be used to
reduce the existing workers' hours (at the same wage) rather than making those workers
redundant, in this case we will assume that a reduction of the workforce is necessary. As also
discussed in the previous chapter, federations of worker-owned firms such as Mondragon
often seek to reallocate workers from sectors with less demand to sectors with more demand,
in order to minimise redundancies. In this scenario however, the enterprise cannot reallocate
these workers to other parts of the company and will have to be laid-off. Reducing the
workforce due to implementing new productive methods is likely to increase income per
head for the remaining workers. Consequently, there is a remunerative incentive to invest. On
the other hand, there is a moral incentive not to invest as the leaving worker members may
not have secured new employment and are likely to see a significant drop in their standard of
living, at least in the short run until they find alternative employment. If the firm does not
invest, the whole future of the business could be a risk from competition in the market.

Investing is indeed the right option. Although the firm may assist the leaving workers to find new employment, there is an alternative. The leaving workers could start up a new enterprise to compete with the firm they have just left. These workers are already accustomed to the products they will produce, and will be seeking to take a share of the market the original firm is looking to expand further into. Vanek (1970:4) refers to this as a "bee-swarm effect" as new and existing competitors rush to compete for a greater market share.

A similar effect would occur if the original company fails to expand and instead concedes a portion of its market share to others in the marketplace. Starting a new firm from scratch is never easy, but these workers with their previous experience are more likely to succeed than most. Indeed some have argued that easy market access for start-up firms is essential to keep worker-owned firms, and the markets they operate in, as competitive as possible. Meade (1980:74-75) goes as far to say that "there is much heavier reliance on ease of entry of new businesses than under capitalism". Under a market system and cooperative economy, if there is demand for a particular commodity, a worker-owned enterprise will be incentivised to supply that demand. We shall refer to this affect as the 'market dynamic'. This market dynamic is essential if worker-owned firms are to remain competitive and efficient. In order to secure current levels of income per head, and to potentially increase it in future, the market dynamic of our cooperative economy must ensure that competition and survival spur on investment and expansion, whilst the incentive dynamic ensures that worker members are constantly contributing new product ideas and innovative production techniques. With that being said, our attention must now be turned to how prospective worker-owned firms are likely to procure investment capital and how existing worker-owned firms are likely to procure investment capital once they have decided to invest.

The Supply and Demand of Internal Investment

For a well-established and profitable worker-owned firm, internal investment is perhaps the most convenient and obvious source of investment capital. In Chapter 4 we explored how internal investment is likely to function for start-up worker-owned firms depending on whether the workers owned the firm directly or indirectly. This start-up investment came from the savings of the workers setting up the firm. If the workers decide to use a system of capital contributions, where investment is tied to ownership, then this type of capital is known as refundable capital. If, on the other hand, the workers decide to lend their private savings to the firm without any link to ownership, it is known as internal debt financing. An example of this was explored in the preceding chapter, where we discussed worker-owned firms that are started by one entrepreneur who then employs workers once the initial investment by the entrepreneur has been made. In this case the company pays back the investment made by the entrepreneur as if they were an external investor. In reality, most start-ups will require an amount of capital only available through external sources. To re-emphasise an earlier comment, most workers and would-be entrepreneurs do not have access to the means of production. Put simply, most people do not have sufficient savings to start up a new company which is capable of maintaining their subsistence. As a result, the ability to finance a start-up with only the internal savings of its prospective entrepreneurs is a highly unlikely prospect for the majority of people. The ability to procure external finance, for both start-ups and existing firms, will be discussed later. With that being said, the remainder of this section will be concerned primarily with another form of internal finance, that being reinvestment – the investing of profits an existing firm has already earned.

Reinvestment is a typical source of finance for other types of enterprise regardless of ownership and management practices. Worker-owned firms within the Mondragon Corporation are insistent upon taking a set share of the surpluses created and reinvesting those surpluses back in the company. Other firms, which have no mandatory threshold for reinvestment will be required to consult the worker members for permission on whether to reinvest and by how much. Management are likely to establish an investment plan with estimations on costs and returns, including total net income for the company and income per worker. The worker-members will then decide on whether to approve the investment. The money will come either as a share of the last year's surpluses or from a fund of reserves comprised of multiple years surpluses. Regardless of how the savings have been accumulated, the worker members will have to decide whether it is in their own interest to invest. Investing means sacrificing dividends now for a potentially greater return in future, whilst failing to invest means taking dividends now but potentially dealing with more strenuous market competition in future should their competitors decide to invest[43]. Let us once again assume the investment decision is likely to be approved, and the new machines, tools and materials are purchased and workers employed, with the income per worker expected to increase. Along with the bigger cake, smaller slice dilemma, there is also another dilemma which may deter investment stemming from another source. Even if investment is likely to increase income per worker, there is the question as to whether each of the worker-members who agree to the investment plan and consequently sacrifice a slice of their dividends will be employed for long enough for that investment to yield them a good enough return. This issue has been well documented before.

But consider a case in which elderly Mr Smith is about to reach retiring age, while young Mr Brown has just joined the co-operative. If part of this years surplus[44] is ploughed back into the concern [business], Mr Brown will gain from the future yield of the machine at the expense of Mr Smith who will lose part of his share of this year's surplus

Meade (1980:91, bracket and comment added)

In this scenario, the only way each worker can realise a return from investment is by continuing their employment with that firm and earning a larger dividend each year from that investment. No rate of return can be gained from retiring or switching employers. Indeed, from this perspective it is more likely that an investment decision will be based more on the age of the decision makers rather than on total profitability. As a result we can call this a 'rate of return dilemma', as the rate of return for individual workers from a particular investment will be based more on the length of employment than any other factor. This dilemma may not even come down to an issue of retirement. Some professions, which entail arduous, dangerous or just generally distasteful tasks, are likely to have a high rate of staff turnover. Worker-members which are seeking employment elsewhere are unlikely to want to sacrifice this year's dividends for an investment they will never see materialise. This artificial barrier to investment must be, and can be, overcome. Mondragon's mandatory profit retention scheme is a simple and effective solution to this. Each year a percentage of the profits earned must be set aside for reinvestment over the long term. This form of profit retention acts more like a form of internal tax, so worker-members are unlikely to feel like they are sacrificing something they could otherwise opt out of or democratically reject. As the figure saved is a percentage of earnings, the workers income per head will still vary according to effort applied, ensuring the incentive dynamic remains active. This form of profit retention also prevents a short-termist desire to eat up all the dividends today with disregard for the company's potential change of fortune in future. Although there is a coercive incentive to ensure the company remains profitable over the long run, profit retention acts on that incentive, setting it in stone.

There are additional measures the company could take to avoid the rate of return dilemma. If the firm wants employees to make a larger contribution, it could offer workplace investment bonds[45]. For those unfamiliar, a bond is a type of loan which is sold by a debtor to a creditor. The debtor uses the money gained from selling the bond to fund an investment. The creditor pays for the bond at a figure called the principle. Once the bond expires, the debtor repays the principle to the creditor plus any interest accrued. It is expected that the profit made from the investment should cover the cost of repaying the principle plus a rate of interest. The expiration of the bond depends on its length, some can be as short as a year, others can last for decades. Interest is also usually paid during the lifetime of the bond at set points, therefore the longer the maturity of the bond, the more interest the debtor is likely to pay. In the case of a worker-owned firm, the firm could offer its worker-members workplace investment bonds for purchase[46]. The workers can pay for this with their salaries or savings. The company pays out interest throughout the lifetime of the bond and once the bond expires, the company will pay the participating workers the principle plus any outstanding interest. The company pays for this by deducting debt repayments from its income. The dividends for all workers will be reduced in order to pay back the company's debts, but as participating workers own these debts, they will be repaid the bonds principle and earn interest on top of their dividends and wages[47].

As the bonds have no relation to ownership of the firm, a participating worker could leave the firm during the life of the bond and be paid the principle and interest after they have left the company. For members close to retirement, this can be an effective additional method for the company to procure internal investment without the anxiety that older workers may feel in that they might not share in the rewards of that investment. Rather than older workers sacrificing a share of their income for potentially nothing in return, they now have an incentive to invest so they can reap the rewards throughout their retirement. Such investment could even be integrated within the workers' pension schemes. Like any form of debt, the company must ensure that the rate of interest it offers to its bondholders is sustainable. In addition, participating workers should not be given a special status or privileges over non-participating workers. If this were to arise, the use of bonds internally should be prohibited where possible, only to be used when absolutely necessary. Ideally, the participating workers of such a scheme would be made anonymous, as not to spur the development of bond-owning and non-bond-owning cliques within the workplace.

So what are the remaining objections to self-financing? Vanek's research illustrates further complications, one of which alludes to the fear that workers who own the company's assets and its savings could simply sell off the firm for a one-time financial reward. We will refer to this issue as the 'degeneration dilemma'. One such argument proposes a situation where the worker-members of an employee-owned firm believe that they can earn a greater rate of return by depositing funds in a savings account at a bank rather than by continuing te operation of the firm[48]. Put simply, they could earn more money elsewhere and without expending any effort. As a result, the workers sell off the assets of the firm and plough their savings into a more profitable alternative, earning a higher passive income. This process may not be problematic if undertaken by a few firms, but if replicated across a wider economy we could witness a significant drop in productive activity. In contemporary capitalist economies, the workers may sell off the assets to private investors who degenerate the firm into a conventional capitalist firm. Although in this case productive activity continues, the re-emergence of the dual-contradiction cannot be tolerated within our hypothesised cooperative economy. This dilemma is difficult to resolve without the necessary judicial reform. Under a cooperative state, the aim of the laws and institutions in practice would be to prohibit investor ownership in favour of worker ownership. Consequently, degenerating a worker-owned firm into a conventional capitalist firm would not be allowed or indeed desirable.

The prohibition of investor ownership would also likely extend to new businesses as well as existing firms. Nonetheless, the workers could still sell off the company's assets to make a one-time reward without transferring company ownership. If workers across a whole economy continued to perpetually degenerate their firms, two scenarios are likely to occur. Firstly, a situation would emerge where the large decrease in supply (for the goods and services the workers are no longer producing) pushes up prices, leading to higher rates of profitability, and thus increasing the rate of return in productive activities to at or beyond the rate of return of the alternative non-productive activities. Not only this, but fewer productive industries means less investment, meaning banks will not be able to sustain higher rates of return for its savers. This would mean degenerated businesses being regenerated and equilibrium being reached between productive and financial investments.

This rather unlikely scenario may emerge within a closed economy, but in an open economy degeneration cannot be sustained. Empirical studies show that employees are not likely to bleed the company dry[49], instead they are likely to invest and expand the company to the reward of both existing and future workers. Consequently, mass-scale degenerations are highly unlikely to occur in a competitive cooperative economy to the extent Vanek (1971) feared. Regardless of this, a cooperative state should still implement laws to deter liquidation purely for one-time gains. One country has already demonstrated how this could work.

> Spanish cooperative law prevents workers from benefiting from the increased
> value of their enterprise's assets if they should sell the firm or liquidate it. If a
> cooperative enterprise is liquidated, the revenue goes to the state.
>
> Morris (1992:33)

Even without the necessary laws in place, existing British worker-owned firms have enacted clauses in their company constitutions that achieve the same ends.

The practicality of a law to gift the revenues of liquidation either to charity or to the state, will depend on whether worker-owned firms could sell their assets prior to liquidating the firm. Workers would have an incentive to sell off their valuable assets prior to liquidation and once the firm has been liquidated, there may be no further assets of saleable value to give to the state. Under a cooperative state, firms that wish to liquidate should be required to notify the relevant authorities of the assets they hold and the assets they have sold prior to liquidation. This should keep the process transparent and avoid any potential fraudulent activities. Ideally, the moneys made from liquidating a firm should be awarded to cooperative development funds (which will be examined later), that offer loans to new worker-owned firms. This 'phoenix tax' can ensure that the death of existing firms can support the birth of new firms.

Despite Vanek's objections, there is nothing inevitable about degeneration for a worker cooperative or any other type of worker-owned firm. Mondragon has been operating since 1956, John Lewis has been worker-owned since 1929 and in Italy, Imola Ceramica stands as one of the oldest worker cooperatives in Italy, having started back in 1874. Although degeneration is indeed possible under current legislative arrangements, there is nothing inherently flawed within the worker cooperative model that leads it to natural degeneration. With the correct legislation in place, the issues Vanek supposes of degeneration all but dissipate. As such, the fear of degeneration within a cooperative economy should not become overstated.

To conclude this subsection, it would appear that despite many potential drawbacks to internal financing of investment capital, the majority of issues can be easily resolved. Workplace investment bonds, if used correctly, can give workers nearing the end of their employment an added remunerative incentive to see the company succeed once they have left. Mandatory saving thresholds can ensure the company can access emergency reserves if necessary or use the funds for future long term investment. In addition, Vanek's arguments against self-financing can be resolved quite easily using legislative reform to prevent degeneration into capitalist form, whilst the interdependent relationship between productive activity and financial markets ensures that large scale liquidations should not occur for as long as the respective industries remain profitable. One final thought must be given to the allocation of risk. One legitimate point Vanek (1971) makes is that whilst external financing allows the workers and investors to share risk to a variable extent, with internal investment the workers take all the risk. This is something we have discussed before, regarding capital contributions and workplace investment bonds. Depending on the amount at stake and the riskiness of the investment, the firm could apply internal reinvestment only for small scale investment or perhaps investments with a lower degree of risk. The riskier and larger investments could be financial through external investors. Each firm must calculate for itself whether investing internal funds is a wise choice, whilst the additional level of transparency and accountability that we would expect to see under worker ownership would imply that investment decisions are likely to be taken on more rational grounds compared to conventional capitalist firms.

The Supply and Demand of External Investment

For a cooperative economy to function effectively, capital markets must function effectively to allow worker-owned firms to access external finance. We have already touched on some of the benefits of procuring external finance rather than investing internal funds, most of which are relatively straightforward. Firstly, external finance may be demanded for the reason outlined earlier regarding the sharing of risk. The sharing of risk between workers and investors allows for alternative perspectives on the practicality and profitability of the proposed investment. Although the added transparency and accountability found in worker-owned firms should allow for more rational investment decisions to take fold, acquiring an external opinion on the viability of the investment – from a party which also has a direct stake in its success – can be a valuable added benefit. It is important to re-emphasise that the external investors will have no say in the decision making process of the investment or the company in general – the firm is both owned and controlled exclusively by its workforce. For a cooperative economy, under no circumstances can the firm and its workers transfer ownership and/or management responsibilities to any third party, regardless of the success or failure of the investment. The process for dealing with debt defaults and issues of a similar nature will be dealt with shortly.

The next reason for seeking external finance is even simpler, most firms (both at the start-up phase and for existing firms) may not have the necessary funds to finance the investment itself. Vanek rightfully notes how many worker cooperatives have been unable to establish and sustain themselves due to the lack of available external funding and the often total reliance on internal funds[50]. Access to a fully functioning and efficient capital market is therefore essential. So what are the drawbacks of external finance? An obvious drawback is that with external finance, workers will have to pay interest from future gains made from the investment, rather than earning the total future gains from investment, paid for with current savings. Like all forms of debt, there is a price to pay for getting what you want before having the ability to pay for its total cost. Worker-owned firms are no exception to this rule. In highly competitive markets, firms need this ability to invest in order to sustain their position in the market.

The demand for external finance is clearly present, so how effective are capital markets in supplying worker-owned firms the necessary finance capital in contemporary capitalist economies? The answer to this is relatively well documented. Capital markets are at best sceptical and at worst hostile towards supplying worker-owned firms with finance capital. Vanek's thoughts on this are perhaps the clearest.

> Probably the single most important obstacle to the spontaneous development of a labour-managed system within a capitalist environment is what we may call "the dilemma of the collateral." In a nutshell, this dilemma is the reluctance of banks and other potential lenders to lend without collateral – that is, without a share of "own" funds of the labour-managed enterprise – coupled with the tendency toward degeneration of labour-managed firms into partnerships, or other forms of second-class employment situations, where self-financing and collateral are present.
>
> Indeed, especially for a small or newly entering firm, it is almost unthinkable in a western economy to receive full external funding – that is, funding which carries only income and repayment obligations, without participation in control by the lender and without participation by the borrower in financing.

Vanek (1970:317-18)

Vanek's preference towards methods of external finance over internal financing is well documented. The inability of labour managed firms to access external finance is thus especially worrisome from a Vanekian perspective. Additional research since the time of Vanek's (1970) *General Theory* have also discussed this issue. In Cornforth's (1983) research on the reasons for the success and failure of worker cooperatives, he alludes to research taken in 1980 outlining the biggest perceived problems faced by British worker cooperatives. The result was unsurprising. The biggest perceived problem for both existing cooperatives and start-ups was the inability to obtain finance. It is fair to say that this view has changed very little over time.

> Co-operatives often attempt to attract capital using the same rewards and incentives and under the same public policy umbrella as investor-owned firms. Needless to say, this is a difficult strategy as investor-driven financial institutions seldom understand co-operatives nor are they excited by the idea of capital as a tool with a limited return.
>
> Webb and Cheney (2014:74)

A survey by Burns (2006) found that 42 per cent of employee-owned firms experience at least some difficulty generating investment, with 37 per cent citing "a lack of understanding from banks, accessing finance for investment, and a shortage of expert advisers with experience of employee ownership as typical problems" (Burns, 2006:9). The inability of capital markets in contemporary capitalist economies to finance worker-owned firms is due mainly to the firms' position on ownership.

> One disadvantage that is often raised about this model is that businesses can't access external capital – they can't sell shares, so they can't go to the stock market, which means potentially they can't grow at the same speed as PLCs. This means such companies have to finance themselves either through retained earnings or through debt
>
> Mayfield, Purnell and Davies (2012:218)

When conventional capitalist firms wish to invest, they can use retained earnings or borrow capital as can worker-owned firms. Unlike worker-owned firms, however, capitalist companies can transfer a share of the company's ownership to investors. The investors pay the company for these shares in return for a slice of the profits the company makes. The company uses the money from this sale to invest. How this sale takes place depends of the type of firm in question. Private limited companies can choose who purchases shares in the business, that's assuming they wish to sell shares at all. Public limited companies offer shares to sell on a stock market, where any investor can buy or sell those shares. These companies do not need to risk their own funds nor do they have to pay any interest like they would with a conventional form of debt. The only potential cost the company has depends on whether the company wishes to buy back the shares it has sold once the investment has borne fruit. If the investment makes the company more profitable, the market price for its shares are likely to be higher than what they were to begin with due to the increased value of the firm. Buying back these shares will thus come at an added cost. This difference can be perceived in a similar way to interest on a debt repayment. On the other hand, if the investment is unsuccessful and the company becomes less profitable, the price of its shares will decrease as the value of the firm decreases and there is less demand for those shares. In this instance, although the share price has decreased, due to lower profits, it may be more difficult to buy back the shares it had originally sold. Lastly, the company may not wish to buy back its shares at all, however this means there will be a higher expectation by the firm's shareholders to pay out dividends. These dividend payments, again, can be perceived as a form of interest payment. This type of financing, involving the sale of shares, is generally known as 'equity financing' and can only be undertaken by firms who are prepared to dilute ownership.

So how are worker-owned firms able to obtain finance capital without offering a share of ownership? The only option is to borrow. This type of financing is known as 'debt financing', which along with equity financing, form the two primary means of obtaining external investment capital. As mentioned earlier, financial institutions and investors in general are often perceived as being more hostile towards lending capital to worker-owned firms. This comes down to the 'collateral dilemma' Vanek (1970) alluded to earlier. Investors wish to insure their investment with some kind of collateral. This ensures that if the investment fails and/or the firm becomes bankrupt, the lenders will be able to recuperate their initial investment. Transferring ownership is one way of doing this, as the investors – who now control the company – can choose to liquidate it and recuperate their investment. Worker-owned firms must provide some form of collateral that does not include transfers of ownership and/or control. A worker-owned firm could pledge a specific asset against a loan as collateral. Ideally this would be a non-essential asset, meaning that if the firm could not repay its loan, the asset would be appropriated by the creditor to cover their loses, but the firm could still continue to function. An example of a non-essential asset would be unused land owned by the firm, intellectual property, or anything else of value that does not impede future production. If on the other hand, an essential asset was used as collateral, the firm would be unable to continue production and the firm would be liquidated. If the firm pledges no specific collateral, and if the firm goes bust, the company would be liquidated and the firm's assets would be sold off in order to repay outstanding debts[51]. For a cooperative economy, any remaining value (should there be any) could be subject to the phoenix tax. The higher the risk, the higher the interest rate. The more collateral the worker-owned firm pledges, the lower the interest rate of repayment is likely to be. Worker-owned firms are likely to convince banks and other creditors, as best they can, that their investment is protected. The more protected a creditor feels, the lower the interest rate. There is also a case here for worker-owned firms to use a portion of their own reserves along with other sources of investment, thereby combining both internal and external financing.

> As a rule, lenders are particularly well-disposed towards firms which self-finance their investments because they know that the use of self-owned resources is a sign that the firm is confident of success. And this is an additional explanation for the fact that the interest rates charged by external providers of funds tend to increase in an inverse proportion to the self-funded share of a firm's investments.
>
> Jossa (2015:275)

Banks and other financial institutions are also likely to play an important role in any cooperative economy:

> Instead investment would be financed, as now, from a free capital market and from retained earnings, with banks continuing to play the role in short and medium term finance which they play now.
>
> Jay (1977:14)

Along with conventional institutions such as banks offering debt financing to worker-owned firms, there may also be additional forms of debt financing that offer more benefits to both creditors and worker-owned firms. The most obvious option which comes to mind are corporate bonds. The discussion on bonds earlier referred to workplace investment bonds that would be offered as a form of internal financing for worker-members who are likely to cease employment in the short-term. Corporate bonds however, are a form of external financing that function along the same lines. Corporate bonds can be issued to external investors who wish to invest in the firm, but who also wish to diversify their portfolio. Put simply, rather than investing a whole chunk of money in one firm, which may go bust, investors prefer to invest across multiple companies. This is known as 'hedging', where investors spread risk across multiple investments rather than putting all their eggs in one basket. To remind the reader once again, the safer the investor feels regarding their investments, the lower the interest rate is likely to be. Corporate bonds are a goods means of achieving both lower risk for the investor, and potentially lower interest rates for the worker-owned firm.

There are also different types of bonds which worker-owned firms could issue, the first of which concerns transferability. Transferable and non-transferable bonds work similarly to the distinction between private limited companies and public limited companies when discussing stocks and shares earlier. With a non-transferable bond, the company can choose which investors can purchase its bonds with the certainty of knowing that those bonds cannot be sold to other investors during the bonds' lifetime. For example, some companies may wish only to issue bonds to its customers, such as loyalty members for example. One successful example of a labour-owned and managed firm using investment bonds is the John Lewis Partnership, a British company which trialled its 'retail bonds' to staff and customers in 2011, raising over £50m in the process (BBC News, 2011, Mayfield et al, 2012). On the other hand, transferable bonds can be purchased by anyone and can be traded on the bond markets similarly to how shares are bought and sold on the stock market. Fluctuations on the bond market – changes in the price the bonds are sold for along with fluctuations in the interest rate – are determined primarily by the degree of confidence investors have in that firm. Like any form of debt, bonds also have their downsides.

> Total reliance on fixed interest borrowing to finance investment, which is sometimes 100 per cent gearing, leaves an enterprise extremely vulnerable to bankruptcy in a trading recession because capital's reward has to be paid whether or not any trading surplus has been earned.
>
> Jay (1977:18)

> Although the bond carries a promise to pay interest at a certain rate, there is always some probability of default, and the probability of loss to the lender increases as the proportion of equity capital in the financial structure decreases. Accordingly, the lender will demand a higher rate of return; the cost of loan capital rises at the margin.
>
> McCain (1977:357-58)

Like all forms of debt financing, regardless of the performance of the company, they are still expected to repay the original sum borrowed in addition to paying the rate of interest that was guaranteed from the issuance of the debt. For highly successful companies this can be a blessing, as high rates of profit makes the debt repayments relatively inexpensive. Successful firms which issue stocks and shares are not afforded this luxury[52]. For investors, this is highly undesirable, as potentially higher returns from stocks are likely to be more enticing than bonds with a fixed rate. On the flip side, if the firm faces financial difficulty, the firm may not be able to keep up with debt repayments, potentially pushing it towards insolvency. For investors, in this case bonds may be preferable to shares as they are guaranteed a rate of return on their investment, where with shares they are not guaranteed any dividends from the company (as this is the company's choice, not the shareholders) and the shares themselves could lose all value if the markets lose confidence in the sustainability of the firm. With corporate bonds, investors know that they will be repaid their initial investment (the principle) and are guaranteed a predetermined rate of interest. Nonetheless, worker-owned firms could issue another type of bond which allows for variable rates of interest. These types of bonds can be referred to as 'performance indexed bonds', where the rate of interest is determined by the success of the investment, perhaps pegged to income per worker or a similar indicator[53]. As an example, rather than issuing a bond with a fixed interest rate of 6 per cent, the firm could instead issue bonds where the rate or interest is variable to the company's success, say for example between a boundary of 3 to 9 per cent. This still gives certainty to investors regarding the rate of return they are likely to receive, but also gives the firm a reasonable degree of flexibility regarding interest payments. It means that for unsuccessful investments, the company will not be overburdened with unrealistically high rates of interest, whilst on the other hand it gives investors an added reward should the investment be more successful than expected. The rate of interest actually paid will be decided along the lines predetermined by the firm and the investors.

These terms of issuance should prevent the firm from taking active steps to artificially reduce the rate of interest should the investment be highly profitable. This very point has been argued by Fanning and McCarthy (1986), who argue that worker-members could simply pay themselves higher wages, consuming the investors contributions, and then declare bankruptcy prior to bond maturity. This is unlikely to occur in the majority of cases where workers require a sustainable income, whilst special legislative reforms enacted by a cooperative state could be introduced to prevent such fraudulent practices. In addition, these performance indexed bonds are most likely to be used for medium to long term investments, as performance-based interest cannot be calculated prior to the outcome of the investment. If the firm cannot pay even the lowest band of interest, or perhaps even the principle, the usual process of liquidation discussed earlier will take fold.

The last type of bond to discuss are unsecured bonds – known in the US as debentures. Unlike secured bonds, unsecured bonds offer no collateral. This means that if the worker-owned firm is unable to repay the debt to its bondholders, the firm will not go into liquidation and the bondholders lose all of their investment. Some unsecured bonds may even come with interest rates with unlimited variability. That means the firm can choose what rate of interest it pays, whether it be nothing at all, or a rate which is well above the market average. These offer the most flexibility for the firm, whilst simultaneously offering the most risk and potential reward for investors. Worker-owned firms which issue debentures have an incentive to offer a reasonable rate of interest if they wish to issue bonds once gain in future. Investors are not likely to back a firm with a history of defaulting on its debt or offering low rates of interest. In a best case scenario we would hope to see worker-owned firms and bondholders develop a constructive and mutually respectful long term relationship, where both parties share in the risks and rewards.

In reality there needs to be an equality in the risks and rewards taken by creditor and debtor. Investors need to be reassured that their investments are safe and that there is some degree of insurance against debt defaults. By the same token, worker-owned firms need some degree of flexibility if their investment does not yield the financial result expected. It is neither in the interest of the firm, its investors or indeed the wider economy if firms are going bust due to excessive debt burdens or by investors losing all of their capital to unfavourable terms of agreement. If these concerns can be effectively addressed, using the multiple examples given so far, the lack of interest given to worker-owned firms by conventional investors can be reversed. Diluting ownership through shareholding is not a prerequisite to safe and profitable investment. In a highly globalised economy investors must not be treated less favourably compared to other, particularly capitalist, economies. If investors prefer the security provided by bonds compared to the added risks and volatility of shares, we would expect to see an influx of investors moving funds into a cooperative economy, and the inevitable reduction of interest rates that goes with added supply relative to demand. The successful case of John Lewis shows that there is a great deal of optimism and enthusiasm for this form of financing. Indeed, Meade, (1980:195) confidently states how it should be no more difficult for a worker-owned firm to access fixed interest finance than the capitalist firm currently does.

Regarding debt from the perspective of a worker-owned firm, we must not see a situation where excessive borrowing leads to the majority of a company's surpluses being spent servicing debts. If this is the case, the workers are unlikely to receive dividends and the link between effort applied and reward gained will be lost. This would establish a hybrid version of the dual-contradiction, where profits are being syphoned off to investors by the means of debt repayment, whilst the workers hold no remunerative incentive to maximise effort applied. Learning the lessons from the last chapter, an over indebted worker-owned firm is unlikely to attract new worker-members, whilst existing worker-members may become more incentivised to leave the firm and join a more profitable competitor. The investment must produce a higher income per worker if the investment is to be approved and for workers to remain at that firm.

By and large it would appear that performance indexed bonds, if used correctly, offer the best balance for both workers and investors. McCain (1977:382), who broadly discusses and consequently approves of the performance indexed bond model, states that "[g]iven an appropriate financial environment, the worker co-operative clearly can be no less efficient than the capitalist corporation", that being from the perspective of the capital market as a whole.

Other Sources of Investment

Given the continuous financialisation of contemporary capitalist economies, loans from private banks and the issuing bonds are not the only means by which worker-owned firms could procure investment. Several examples show how alternative sources of investment have developed throughout this process of greater financialisation. We shall also use this opportunity to offer further scrutiny of Vanek's LMF model.

The Mondragon Model

To recall earlier comments, the Mondragon Corporation is a federation of worker cooperatives based in the Basque region of northern Spain. The company was started in 1956 by a catholic priest, José María Arizmendiarrieta ('Arizmendi' for short), and a group of his former students who started their first worker-owned firm in the town of Mondragon. Start-up capital came from individual pledges by members of the local community who were willing to back the plans of Arizmendi and his cooperators. The more extensive amounts of capital required to expand the federation became more difficult to come by.

> When in 1959 the banks, not having wealthy backers to hold responsible,
> refused to lend them any more money Father Arizmendi started a bank,
> making the original cooperative founders the directors. The bank then

became the centre of a vigorous entrepreneurial process, mentoring and
funding the formation and development of all 120 businesses.

Erdal (2012:946)

This bank was called the Caja Laboral, and would become an essential pillar of the
Mondragon experiment. Mondragon would go onto establish a university, consumer
cooperatives and other amenities for the local population. Mondragon became not just a
federation of companies, but a bedrock of the local community. The creation of Mondragon's
own bank was a direct response to the lack of interest and willingness of conventional
financial institutions to invest in a firm with alternative ownership and managerial practices.
The bank would gain a lot of support from local residents, both employees of the firm and
non-employees, as locals set up saving accounts which would feed into the development of
new cooperatives. In addition, a large portion of the firms' funds came from the retained
earnings of the cooperatives the bank had helped set up. Consequently, the Caja Laboral
presents us with a sort of hybridised fusion of internal and external financing. Replicating
Mondragon's success across a cooperative economy would be rather difficult. For one, not all
companies will have the resources, capacity or skillset to establish their own banks. Some
larger conventional capitalist companies in the UK have established their own financial
institutions, such as Virgin Money, Tesco Bank and Sainsbury's Bank for example. Although
these examples show a capability of larger companies to establish profitable financial
institutions, their *raison d'être* differs greatly from that of Caja Laboral. The purpose of Caja
Laboral is not simply to earn a greater profit for Mondragon, but to expand and grow the
family of worker cooperatives and to spread its core values and beliefs across the local
economy. Caja Laboral is a cooperative development institution front and foremost. Whether
cooperative federations would develop in a cooperative economy is largely unknown. It
cannot be said whether the development of federations like Mondragon are designed as a
response to the difficulties of conventional capitalism and its indifferent financial institutions,
or whether in fact it is a natural tendency of worker cooperatives to develop new companies
in different markets and come together to create something bigger. Regardless, the
Mondragon case shows how financing need not be a case of either internal or external, but
can potentially be a fusion of the two.

The Italian Model

The Italian model is strikingly similar to the Mondragon model just discussed. In Italy all
cooperatives are required to allocate 3 per cent of their surpluses to a cooperative

development fund[54]. To compensate this, cooperatives are taxed at lower rates compared to conventional business types. Like the Caja Laboral, these cooperative funds are designed to finance cooperatives across the country. It's important to emphasise that all forms of cooperative are engaged in this system, including firms such as consumer cooperatives which still contain the dual-contradiction. Indeed these other forms of cooperative also often struggle to obtain finance due to their own form of fixed ownership. As a result, the Italian model does not distinguish between different types of cooperative as all struggle to obtain finance using conventional methods. This model is also more beneficial for companies which are not a part of a larger cooperative federation like Mondragon. All cooperatives allocate their surpluses into a fund of their choice, and these development agencies invest in cooperatives across the country. One could say this model is similar to the mandatory profit retention scheme used at Mondragon, but with the added benefit of ploughing money into an account with the reserves of multiple other companies. Although these cooperatives are essentially being taxed by these funds, such cooperatives may rely on the funds established to finance extensive investments when their own retained earnings are not sufficient. If cooperatives fail to commit to any specific fund, they are required to pay the 3 per cent surplus to the Ministry of Internal Development, again, as if it were a form of tax. Italy's large cooperative sector has ensured that a large pool of investment funds have been set up to provide alternative forms of investment, again, as conventional actors in finance may be unwilling to do so. Earlier it was suggested that a phoenix tax, designed to prevent incentives to degenerate worker-owned firms, could also be syphoned into these development funds.

In a cooperative state, it can widely be assumed that all financial institutions will be required to invest in worker-owned firms if they are to survive. Such financial institutions will in themselves be required to become worker-owned, so the bias in favour of conventional capitalist firms is likely to dissipate. As a result, the need for a cooperative state to demand all firms to contribute towards cooperative development funds may not be as strong or indeed necessary. Although governments could experiment with different types of mandatory contributory systems, the Italian model is, by and large, mainly a response to sustain and bolster the existing cooperative sector within Italy's wider conventional capitalist system.

The Digital Model

Due to the growth of the digital economy that emerged out of the internet boom of the 1990's, and consequent technological advancements in telecommunications, new ways of procuring investment away from the conventional types have sprung up. Peer to peer lending is one example of this. In this case online intermediaries are used to connect individuals borrows to individual lenders, at a mutually agreed rate of interest. Online crowdfunding is another example, especially for cooperatives. Social media can be used to connect with individuals who are sympathetic to worker ownership or the cooperative movement for example. Conventional institutions like banks are typically regarded as middlemen between those who wish to save and those who wish to borrow. The digital model starts to break this approach down, linking creditors directly to debtors. From this stage a means of investment can be established, where a particular project advertises itself to particular groups in hope of achieving the desired amount. As with corporate bonds and bank loans, this is a form of debt financing, where the firm borrows and ultimately pays back the loan plus interest. Due to the perceived undesirability of worker-owned firms to conventional investors, however, these digital means are an alternative form of procuring investment that avoids these conventional methods.

There is one particularly interesting case of an investor who was previously embedded within the conventional methods of finance, who had been persuaded by the worker-owned model. The Argentinian economic crisis that spanned from the late 1990s to early 2000s created an environment where investors were shutting down factories and relocating their capital overseas. This led to the *fábricas recuperadas*, or, recovered factory movement, where workers took control of the businesses they had once been employed by. Bredan Martin, a former Wall Street investor decided to find ways of supporting the cooperatives that emerged in Argentina. The Working World was formed to do just that.

> Instead of following traditional investment underwriting techniques, we decided that we would put finance in the hands of working people without making them put down collateral or take a debt burden that could threaten their wellbeing. We tied our loan returns to project success to make sure we would never take back a single dime that we didn't help generate. We began to pioneer non-extractive finance directly to cooperatives in Buenos Aires.

> It was a match made in heaven. Despite the prevailing conventional belief that these businesses were risky investments, we were starting to see returns on our investments in just a few months in spite of our non-extractive model. We learned that workers weren't just assets on a balance sheet to be cut as traditional business would have us believe, but rather incredibly valuable partners in investment.

The Working World[55]

Since the initial loans in Argentina, this company has since expanded into the US and Nicaragua, again, in communities that have been hard-hit by poverty and economic decline. Although this particular firm is based in specific areas across the Americas, it presents a model which could be replicated across national borders using digital means. The Working World used its online outreach to find potential projects that require investment, and also to locate donations from willing supporters. Co-operative & Community Finance Ltd is another example[56]. This company relies exclusively on sympathetic individuals and organisations to invest capital. This money is then invested into all forms of cooperatives, including employee buyouts and other forms of worker-owned firms and cooperatives. Similarly to the Mondragon and Italian models, this is a way of worker-owned firms coping with conventional capitalism. For a cooperative state, these means of investment would still be effectual, even if not as necessary. Nonetheless, they present an additional and interesting insight into how worker-owned firms can succeed even outside the economic mainstream. They also demonstrate how the mobility of finance has allowed investment to move into less conventional sectors of the economy. Having a physical presence like a bank is less pivotal in an age moving more and more extensively into online platforms, where locality draws less and less relevance.

The Vanekian Model

Lastly, we will evaluate Vanek's model for financing labour managed firms. To recall, with the Vanekian model, all firms are essentially unowned, but where the fixed capital is owned either by the state or private investors who charge the labour managed firm for renting them. These firms are not allowed to reinvest their own funds, there must be a total reliance on external funding. Under Vanek's model, as the rentier owns the productive assets and rents them to the workers, the rentier has the power to set the terms and conditionality of their use. One may rightfully ask what is wrong with Vanek's model, where workers have management and control but not ownership of the productive assets. The issue is that those who own assets usually hold more power than use who use them. It is possible that the capitalist or state rentier who lease out the assets could claim ownership of the company and its total profits, re-establishing conventional capitalism and the dual-contradiction. In a normal political setting this transfer would hardly be difficult – transferring ownership in the context of a cooperative economy however would be much more complicated both legally and politically.

In addition, would workers treat the assets with the same level of care and respect? It has been argued that workers will be required to compensate the assets owners if the asset depreciates, whereas the asset owners pay the workers if the asset increases in value. The practicality of constantly revaluing the company's assets – especially for large scale productive firms – is highly impractical. Another issue comes down to the limits of non-ownership – how does one decide what should be owned by the workers and what should not. Should the workers own the clock on the wall? Can they own the batteries to operate that clock? If not, would they have to ask their asset owners for new batteries every time they needed changing? As ridiculous as this hypothetical example may appear, it remains an important question – where does the boundary between ownership and non-ownership lie? Lastly there is the question as to what happens if the capital owners suddenly decide to pull out, either immediately or at the end of a contract? This scenario has the potential to sink the firm altogether, as without the necessary equipment and machinery, production will cease. As a result, Vanek's model is a good second best approach in a world where worker ownership (as we have discussed) cannot be applied, yet as we have stated previously, the reasons Vanek gives for objecting to worker ownership are either easily resolved or not present at all. Degeneration can be prevented, either by legislative reform or by the laws of supply and demand. Self-financing on the other hand can be properly applied when the considerations we have noted earlier have been taken into account. There may be no harm in experimenting with Vanek's model if there is the enthusiasm to do so. Nonetheless, model we have been outlining, where workers own and control the firm, offers a clearer and simpler alternative to the conventional capitalist and state socialist models both we, Vanek and other academics have sought to reveal.

Concluding Remarks

The purpose of this chapter has been to prove that under relatively simple conditions, both the demand and supply of financial capital should be available within a cooperative economy. The market dynamic and the incentive dynamic ensure that workers have an incentive to maximise their income per head, but this means at times accepting a lower income per head in the short run in order to sustain their incomes in the longer run. Regarding supply, the main disadvantage worker-owned firms currently face in conventional capitalist economies is the lack of willingness for investors to invest in those types of firms. In a cooperative economy, comprised of worker-owned banks, this would not be an issue. Financial instruments like the performance indexed bonds demonstrate how investors can choose between differing matches of risk and reward. Newer means of investing within the digital economy, along with the methods developed at Mondragon and in Italy show how the conventional capital market could be avoided altogether in some cases. By and large however, we should not expect to see too greater divergence in the demand and supply of financial capital in a cooperative state.

---

42 With stock dilution, both the value of the share and the likely dividend received are likely to decrease.

43 What if no company invests? This is also a problem found in conventional capitalist economies. The best solution is either for government to create added incentives for companies to invest – for as long as the results of investment are in the best interests of the company, taxpayers and consumers – or for the government to invest itself, creating a superior competitor that private firms would have to compete against and invest as a result.

44 For simplicity I have substituted the term 'total net labour earnings' (or TNLE) used by Meade (1080) with 'surplus'. For all intents and purposes the two terms are identical in meaning.

45 In a footnote to Vanek's (1971) essay *The Basic Theory of Financing Participatory Firms* (Chapter 8 in *Essays*), he refers to 'redeemable savings deposits'. These are similar to bonds in all but name, but are referred to as a type of external rather than internal funding. This concept is developed perhaps for Vanek to be able to continue his justification for discrediting internal sources of finance.

46 If such bonds are used extensively throughout the workforce we could see a return of the 'having all your eggs in one basket' approach we found with capital contributions. Ideally, such bonds should be set aside for those who are most likely to leave the firm in the short run. If workplace investment opportunities are to be universalised throughout the firm, they must not constitute a major part of employees' savings, as workers would lose both their jobs and their savings if the firm were to go under.

47 As interest from the bonds must be paid out of total profit, those with the bonds will see their dividends reduced so that their bonds receive interest. It is important that the reduced dividend and the bond interest adds up to a sum greater than what the dividends would have been had the bonds not been released – otherwise there would be no financial incentive to purchase the bond. This is another reason why workplace bonds should be reserved for those likely to leave, as this problem would not arise after they depart the firm.

48 See Vanek, J. (1971) 'Some Fundamental Considerations on Financing and the Form of Ownership under Labour Management', Chapter 8, in Vanek, J. (1977) *The Labor-Managed Economy: Essays*. London: Cornell University Press.

49 See Erdal (2011:53-57)

50 See Vanek, J. (1971) 'The Basic Theory of Financing of Participatory Firms', Chapter 9, in Vanek, J. (1977) *The Labor-Managed Economy: Essays*. London: Cornell University Press.

51 The extent to which the workers lose out from the bankruptcy will depend on the type of liability the firm has chosen. With unlimited liability companies, if the firm were to go bust, the worker-members would be required to pay-off any outstanding debts the company owes to its creditors. This makes individuals personally responsible. Alternatively, the firm could choose limited liability, where the worker-members are not personally liable for the debts of the company were it to go bust.

52 Highly profitable capitalist firms are expected to pay their shareholders larger dividends, whilst the price of the company's share are likely to sky-rocket, making it more expensive to buy back.

53 For a more mathematical understanding of performance indexed bonds, see McCain (1977).

54 See Webb and Cheney (2014:74).

55 See http://www.theworkingworld.org/us/about-us/

56 See https://coopfinance.coop/

Chapter 8: Output

Once two of the main prerequisites of production have been procured – labour and capital – a firm can begin to produce output. Output is the total amount of commodities (goods and services) produced within a given space of time. Output is sold either to consumers for direct consumption, or sold to other companies as an input for the goods and services they are wanting to produce and sell. For any company, regardless of ownership, the output produced needs to at least cover the total costs of production, including labour costs. For conventional capitalist firms, output needs to exceed total costs of production in order to create a profit. If the company does not produce a normal/minimum rate of profit, the investor-owners will divert their capital elsewhere to more profitable ventures. For worker-owned firms however, although earning a profit is highly preferable, it may not be necessary in some cases. The *raison d'etre* of production is not to earn a profit *per se*, but instead to earn at least the rate of subsistence for the workers, which is factored into the normal cost of production. These points have been raised before. The purpose of this chapter is to evaluate whether a worker-owned firm would produce at the same level compared to a conventional capitalist firm under similar circumstances, and if there are distinctions, what are the likely economic impacts. Unsurprisingly, the profit principle explains most of the likely deviations that could occur under the right conditions. Once the discussion on output has concluded, we will consider all the points raised in the previous chapters and begin to further explore the concept of the cooperative economy and the cooperative state needed to create and sustain it.

The Market System and the Principal Balance

Output is produced by a firm in order to sell it onto the open market. In the previous two chapters we have explored why labour and capital are best distributed via a market system. For prospective workers, a market system allows them to choose which worker-owned firm to join compared to the alternatives. The final decision on which firm to join is usually determined by the highest amount of total income a firm is willing to offer. It also serves firms as they may require additional or replacement worker-members; the market gives them access to labourers with a variety of skills. For capital, markets are also the best mechanism as investors can choose which firm holds the right degree of risk and reward. For firms, a capital market is essential as retained earnings are often not enough for major and necessary investments. The question now is whether markets best serve output. The answer is relatively straightforward – the vast majority of alternatives to the market system have proven to be either ineffective or less efficient than the market system. The debate between markets and central planning is an old one. We do not wish to take up too much time regarding this matter, as it has been explored many times over by many other writers. Back in Chapter 3 it was implied that the free market mode of distribution is preferable to other modes of distribution such as central planning. The reason for this is simple, the ability to plan for the production of every commodity along with the ability to distribute every commodity is an extremely complex, if not impossible, task with the current technology we have at our disposal. This is not to mention the huge loss of freedom consumers would if governing authorities have the ability to decide which commodities are allocated to whom. Hayek's (1944) *Road to Serfdom* gives a good account of how planning and commanded distribution cannot work in tandem with economic freedom. If the scarcity of all commodities were to be abolished, and all goods and services were free to access and could be produced in any amount with no cost, this would not be an issue. For many goods and services, particularly in the digital sphere, this could indeed be possible[57]. For the majority of commodities however, this is not applicable. Even with the most inclusive of democracies, a system of planning in a world of scarcity, even if practically possible, would still produce artificial winners and losers.

> The interconnectedness of peoples, countries, and economies around the
> globe is a development that can be used as effectively to promote prosperity as
> to spread greed and misery. The same is true for the market economy: the
> power of markets is enormous, but they have no inherent moral character.
> We have to decide how to manage them.

Stiglitz (2012:9)

> Market forces—the laws of supply and demand—of course inevitably play some
> role in determining the extent of economic inequality. But those forces are at
> play in other advanced industrial countries as well.

Stiglitz (2012:26)

There is nothing inherently just or unjust about a market system, it is how such a system is applied that we must be most concerned with. Under a conventional capitalist system we see markets used to distribute wealth in a certain way, one which has brought about significant injustices. A market system facilitating a cooperative economy would see very different results, one which would reap the benefits of resolving the dual-contradiction. There is an important question as to how worker-owned firms deal with negative externalities – the non-financial consequences of production, such as pollution for example. Businesses in a market system, whether they be capitalist or cooperative, will always ignore externalities to some extent. Raworth (2017) argues that economists should drop the concept of the 'externality' to begin with, as the effects of pollution, climate change, overfishing, overuse of antibiotics in agriculture, etc. are not external, they are (or will be) experienced by someone somewhere. There is room, however, for at least some optimism when it comes to worker ownership. For example, worker-owners are unlikely to want to pollute a river they and their local communities are dependent upon. Investor-owners, who may never have visited the workplace or said communities, are likely to be indifferent, ignorant or simply unbeknown to the pollution taking place. For as long as dividends payments are sufficient, and there is no apparent threat to future dividends, there is no real reason for investor-owners to take issue with the externalities the firm produces. Worker ownership, alternatively, helps to embed the process of production into local communities and ecosystems. That said, worker-owners will struggle to offset all of the known and unknown consequences of their company's actions, this is where government needs to set up. It is not just the role of government to resolve the externalities already identified by others, but to actively identify externalities themselves and resolve them accordingly. Left to their own devices, markets will not resolve the adverse non-financial effects they cause. This is perhaps the greatest contradiction of the market system.

There are many other arguments for and against planning and market based systems. We are concerned with the implications these two distributive systems have in a cooperative economy, where the means of production are owned and managed by the workers of each respective firm. The main attribute the market system gives to worker-owned firms is discipline. This can be illustrated with the concepts used throughout this research already. In our current world of scarcity, workers need to maximise their income per head in order to maintain their subsistence at the very least, with the hope of improving their standard of living over time. This is the incentive dynamic. Workers then join or form a worker-owned firm when the demand for a particular commodity can be supplied in exchange for subsistence or beyond. This is the market dynamic. In order for that worker-owned firm to continue supplying that demand, it must be competitive and well-disciplined in that particular marketplace. This can be referred to as the 'principal balance'. Without using its name, this principle has been alluded to before. The principal balance is simply the balance between maximising income per head and workplace satisfaction[58] on the one hand, and remaining competitive in the market on the other. A hypothetical example can be used to illustrate this. For example, worker-members of a particular worker-owned firm may decide to increase the price of their commodities in order to pay themselves a higher wage. Increasing wages may be decided to entice new workers to the firm, to appear to be more competitive in the labour market. If this is achieved however, the price of the commodities sold may now be uncompetitive, as other companies sell their commodities for less. The firm thus loses business and has to adjust prices and wages back to at least their original state. On the flip side, a firm may wish to decrease its prices in order to become more competitive and attract more business, but this must be paid for by lowering the wages of its workers. However, if the workers do not see a long term gain in this, they may be enticed to leave the firm, as the firm is no longer competitive in the labour market. To avoid this, the firm would have to increase prices and thus wages back to their original state. In both cases the principal balance has been disrupted and has had to return back to a state of balance. If worker-owned firms are able to find the principal balance, and if the markets for labour and output are in a state of normality[59], neither self-exploitation nor self-excessiveness should occur.

> Finally, the employees' participation in management has increased their involvement in and understanding of the firm's problems. This results in greater flexibility among the employees, and as a consequence, there are fewer difficulties in implementing unpleasant decisions. It should be emphasized here that this flexibility has not lead to self-exploitation.
>
> Westenholz (1986:146)

Once workers own the company they work for, some commentators may be under the false assumption that workers, who no longer have a dictatorial superior to hold them to account, may become indolent and begin to collectively shirk. Once again, this will affect competitiveness and the life of the enterprise. Firms which consistently produce goods of less quality or produce goods less productively, in order to expend less effort, are likely to fail, as the market has not effectively disciplined them into action. Only when there is no coercive or remunerative incentive for the company to remain sustainable will such an undesirable occurrence take place. The appeal of worker ownership alone will not yield results, they must be backed up with the willingness and resolve to make the firm a competitive and sustainable success. It is the role of an accountable and transparent management team to remind this to the firm's workers. The profit principle is also likely to affect expansion and investment decisions. As explored in the previous chapter, the market dynamic provides an incentive for worker-owned firms to supply new demand in new or existing markets, if this is certain to increase income per head. However, some expansion and investment decisions may be the result of the principal balance. If the firm does not keep up with market trends, their commodities may appear obsolete, the firm will lose its competitiveness and they could lose their market share. The workers will have to sacrifice a portion of their income per head just to remain competitive. Not all workers will be specialised in the arts of business and economics, they must be regularly informed by management and representatives on the state of the company as well as being given forecasts for the results of various decisions and options the company has presented to them. Like any democratic entity, well informed rational decisions rely on quality information for all available options, worker-owned firms are no exception.

A Planned Cooperative Economy?

So what would a cooperative economy look like without the free market system of distribution, and with perhaps some form of planning instead? The answer is simple, without a free market mode of distribution, there is no market dynamic at play, which in turn means there is no principal balance, at least in the normal sense. Under most forms of planning that have been trialled historically, the means of production are not owned by the workers or by investors, but are instead owned by the state or some other form of governing authority. The concept of a planned *cooperative* economy is therefore relatively unexplored territory. Nonetheless, we shall try to make sense of this hypothetical concept. Front and foremost, as there is no longer a market dynamic, it will have to be replaced with something else, perhaps something we can refer to as a 'contract dynamic'. Under this system, worker-owned firms are awarded contracts which allow them to function and sell commodities to the government, or distribute directly to consumers under the government's guidance. In this scenario, the workers are not truly sovereign, if they break the contract between the firm and the government they will be forced to cease production. The firm cannot negotiate another contract with another buyer, as the government is the only buyer (a monopsony). As a result, worker-owned firms cannot earn a profit by setting and altering prices, but by setting and altering the purchase of inputs. This restricts the incentive dynamic towards making production more efficient but creates no pressure to lower prices than what the government demands. The price for the products sold could have been cheaper under a market system, but the contract sets prices at a rate agreed by the government and the company. This creates a sort of consensual monopolistic price setting arrangement.

Competition between worker-owned firms is not present in an economy where only one firm can receive the government's contract. If a firm cannot win a contract, there is no purpose in its survival. The firm must be awarded the contract before it obtains the necessary capital, labour and inputs. The government cannot issue multiple contracts for multiple firms to sell the same type of product, as this would create different types of the same product and would create discrimination between consumers who are distributed commodities of differing quality or preference – a black market would emerge. The government could only realistically allow one contract for one company to produce all of one particular individual commodity. If the contract dynamic were to be in force, there would be no principal balance.

Under the contract dynamic, there would be a coercive and remunerative incentive to appease the demands of the government who issues the contracts and who holds the ultimate bargaining power. As there is no competition between worker-owned firms, there is no longer an incentive for firms to innovate their products. The 'principal balance' implies that workers must sacrifice some of their collective income in order to remain at least as competitive as they have previously been. Without the prospect of competitors taking a larger market share, there is no incentive to innovate. In addition, any new product must first be agreed upon by the government before it can be produced. Innovation thus carries a higher degree of risk, as the government may not issue contracts to allow for the production of a new good or service. Consequently, as there is no market dynamic in force, there is no immediate incentive to expand or develop new products. This cannot be a better situation than where we currently find ourselves, let alone one in which worker ownership takes fold.

There is also the potential threat of a partial return of the dual-contradiction. If the worker-owned firm cannot produce its products more efficiently and productively, the total income per head the workers are likely to receive will stagnate. The reason for this is no surprise. Firms cannot freely invest to expand into other markets, as they have no assurance they will win the contract. Firms also cannot alter their prices as a response to demand and supply fluctuations as prices are fixed by the government's contract. If workers' incomes do not alter according to the effort they apply, there will be no incentive for them to apply any more effort than the MAEL required for them to meet the government's demands and expectations. If the Soviet experiment has taught us anything, it is that citizens prefer an economic system which innovates and progresses in line with emerging trends. Even if a system based on economic planning could determine how much to produce, could decide which firms were to win which contracts, and could regulate the price for each product produced by each firm, an economic model which fails to innovate and evolve will not remain stable for long, especially in democratic countries[60].

The principal balance is an essential component of an effective worker-owned firm and cooperative economy. The ability to maintain subsistence along with the potential additional gains enterprises can award their worker-members will always entice them into production. The discipline that emerges in a competitive market system displays the realistic scope of these gains, and the means in which they can be achieved. One cannot realistically predict whether the market system will be more effective over planning for all eternity. Advancements in technology could change this, and new approaches to matching supply with demand could emerge. Until will get to this hypothetical point, we must accept the truths of economic reality, and they state with some vigour, that planning combined with worker ownership is not the optimal proposal for replacing conventional capitalism.

The Supply of Output

Marginalism

The principal balance allows us to understand some of the basic decisions worker-owned firms will take regarding output. Moving on we will use this concept to explore in more depth how worker-owned firms respond to various changes and fluctuations in the marketplace, and how they differ from conventional capitalist firms.

In conventional microeconomics, the quantity of commodities a firm is willing to supply is usually determined by the relationship between marginal cost and marginal revenue. Marginal cost is the cost of producing one additional product. Marginal revenue is the gain made by selling one additional product. Ultimately, the firm will seek to produce and sell its products at a rate where marginal cost is equal to marginal revenue (MC = MR). If these two are not equal, the firm is likely to alter its output. To illustrate this, let us imagine a situation where marginal cost is not equal to marginal revenue (MC ≠ MR). Let us first imagine that the marginal revenue for selling one additional product exceeds the marginal cost of producing one more additional product (MC < MR). In this case there is an incentive to produce/sell that additional commodity as the revenue for selling it exceeds the cost of making it. This could, for example, be the result of demand being higher than supply of the product in question. In this case the marginal revenue of the product has been increased relative to marginal cost as consumers are now willing to pay extra for the commodity as it had become scarcer. The firm will keep producing/selling that commodity until the point where selling one more product will only cover the cost of producing it.

Now let us look at the opposite scenario, where the marginal cost of producing one more commodity is higher than the marginal revenue of selling it (MC > MR). Is this case, the firm would not receive enough revenue from that product to cover the costs, and thus there is no point producing/selling it. This could happen, for example, if there is more supply than demand for the product in the marketplace. The over-supplying of that commodity may have reduced its price, reducing the marginal revenue to a position where marginal cost exceeds it. The firm may be able to reduce supply with the hope of increasing the product's price back to the original level, increasing marginal revenue to the point where is balances marginal cost. As a result, the point where MC = MR is the point where firms can maximise their total income. There are multiple reasons why marginal cost or marginal revenue can increase or decrease, however, the relations between supply and demand are perhaps the most useful for this chapter's purpose.

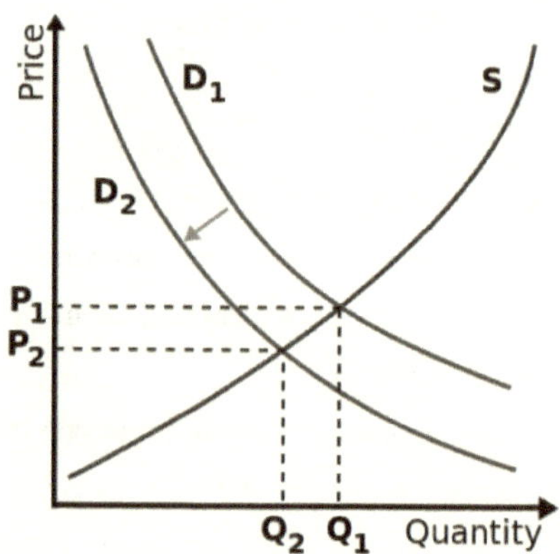

Figure 6

We can see from Figure 6 that when the market price of the product decreases, due to a decrease in consumer demand for example, the firm is incentivised to lower the quantity of that product supplied, as MC > MR. By the same token however, if the price of the product increases back to the original position, the firm will increase supply, as MC < MR. The firm will always seek to adjust the quantity supplied according to price in order to achieve MC = MR. This is only a basic introduction, in reality there are many more forces at play. Nonetheless, this theory demonstrates the basic pressures and forces that help us to understand why firms supply the amount of output they do.

Marginalism Adjusted to Worker Ownership

So how does this basic theory of supply and demand alter when taking worker ownership into account? This distinction is drawn from the profit principle: the distinction between maximising total income and maximising income per head. It has already been noted in the previous two chapters how worker ownership can affect the supply and demand of labour and capital. Decisions on hiring new worker members and dismissing them, along with the decision on whether to invest, have all been determined by the primary focus of the worker-owned firm to maximise income per worker (rather than maximising total income). But what happens when a factor relating to output occurs which is out of the firm's control? For example, how would a worker-owned firm react if the market price for the commodity they sell suddenly increases?

For a conventional capitalist firm the answer is simple, an increase in the market price of the product they sell means that MC < MR. There is more revenue to be made relative to cost from producing an additional unit. The firm will keep producing more commodities until MC = MR. The costs of increasing production must also be taken into account. The firm will hire additional workers, purchase a greater quantity of inputs and possibly invest in more fixed capital. For as long as MC = MR, total profits for the firm can be maximised, to the approval of the firm's shareholders. There is nothing to suggest that this principle should alter under worker ownership. Increasing output would indeed increase total profit. There is also nothing to suggest that worker-owned firms have higher marginal costs, even though they are expected to earn dividends on top of the normal labour costs which partly make up the MC figure[61]. However, the simple MC = MR dynamic does not factor in the consequences of the profit principle. Under the profit principle, a situation could theoretically occur where marginal revenue exceeds marginal cost (MC < MR), but the worker-owned firm may instead decide to maintain or decrease levels of output, rather than increasing it as the capitalist firm would. Under the profit principle, worker-owned firms will supply output at a rate that maximises income per head (IPH). We should remember that total costs are divided between workers and total revenue is divided between workers. As a result, increasing output as a response to the MC < MR dynamic must increase IPH, regardless of whether total profits increase or decrease. Whether MC < MR results in an increase in IPH will depend on the size of the firm's workforce. Employing an additional worker will increase costs per head but may not necessarily increase income per head by the same amount or more. This is ground we have already covered in Chapter 6, ground that we must now build upon to understand changes in output.

The Ward Effect in Theory

There has been much speculation and postulation as to whether worker-owned firms may in fact decrease production and employment rather than increasing it, as a direct response to an increase in the price of the goods they sell. This unusual process has been referred to as the 'Ward Effect', named after Benjamin Ward (1958) who wrote *The Firm in Illyria*, one of the first mathematical approaches to evaluating workers control of the means of production[62].

Ward notes that when the market price for the Illyrian firm's commodity starts to increase, the workers may have a remunerative incentive to decrease its workforce and thus decrease output.

Under normal circumstances, when the price of output (a commodity the firm produces) increases, the conventional capitalist firm will supply additional output, as seen in Figure 7. For the worker-owned firm, it has been suggested that the opposite will occur, as seen in the Figure 8. It is implied that if prices were to increase, the firm will reduce output, whilst if prices decrease, the firm will increase output.

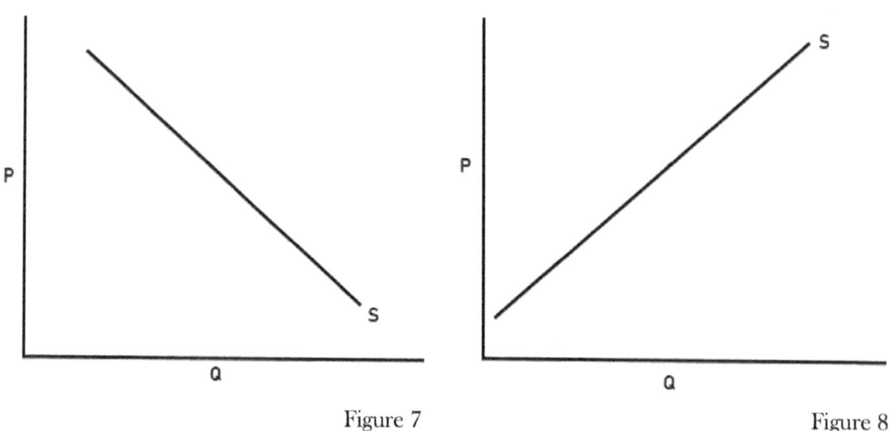

Figure 7   Figure 8

Although it may be difficult at first to see how this process would actually unfold in reality, we must deal with it in theory. Ward's (1958) research is largely mathematical, there are no hypothetical examples or case studies. The argument is made purely through the medium of economic theory. It goes without saying, that a negative relationship between output price and output production, as implied by Ward, would be highly detrimental if such a process did take hold in reality. Increased prices stemming from increased demand, which leads to lower output and lower employment is not economically sustainable. The Ward effect, if indeed true and consistent, would discredit the worker ownership model and the general desirability of establishing a cooperative economy. Consequentially, the Ward effect must be examined in great detail in order to reveal its likelihood and level of threat.

Let us look at how this negative relationship between prices and output could come about. As we know, a conventional firm would normally increase supply to take advantage of the higher market price for their output, bringing marginal cost up to the new higher marginal revenue. With the Ward effect however, the company may in fact be able to increase income per head much further by decreasing output as opposed to maintaining output or increasing it. So how could this happen? Ward (1958) assumes market perfection, so unopposed monopolies cannot be formed which reduce output and employment in order to artificially increase price. Monopolies are usually a source of negative supply schedules, but cannot be in this case. The reason must come from someplace else. Meade provides a non-mathemtical explanation, demonstrating this through a hypothetical 'product X'.

> But the short-run effect in the Co-operative system will be to reduce, not to increase, the levels of employment and output which will maximise earnings per head in the X-industry firms. A rise in the selling price of X will, of course, in itself raise both the value of the marginal product of labour and the average earnings per head in the X-industry firms; but it will raise the value of the marginal product of labour less than the average earnings and it will thus mean that the average earnings could be still further raised if one worker was dismissed. The value of the reduction in the firm's output would be less than the amount paid by the Co-operative to the dis-missed worker; and the remaining partners would gain by his dismissal.

Meade (1972:406)

Let us go through this quote step by step. The relationship between marginal product and income per head has been discussed in Chapter 6, where we assumed that for worker-owned firms, marginal product should equal income per head (MP = IPH). If the marginal product of a worker is lower than the existing income per head (MP < IPH), the worker will not be employed, as the total cost of hiring that worker (shared out between all the workers) is greater than the total profit that worker will make (shared out between all the workers). If, on the other hand, the worker's marginal product is higher than the existing income per head (MP > IPH), the worker will be employed. With moral and social aspects set aside here for the moment, all firms are expected to adjust employment to a point where MP = IPH. An increase in the price of the firm's output can destabilise this relationship. Meade (1972) demonstrates that if the price of output increases, income per head will increase further than the marginal product (MP < IPH). This also means that as a whole, income per head could be increased further still if labour was reduced, and thus the remaining workers will have a remunerative incentive to dismiss them. As a result, it is claimed that an increase in the price of the output the firm sells will lead to a reduction in both output and employment. A hypothetical example of how the Ward effect could function for a particular firm has been provided within the endnote to this chapter.

The Ward Effect in Reality

So does this assumption really hold true? Front and foremost, the model which Ward (1958) applies uses a set of fairly basic yet stringent assumptions. One such assumption is that the firm in question only produces one product. In reality, firms are unlikely to sell only one product. In complex market economies, firms, regardless of ownership structures, are likely to tap into multiple markets to diversify their product range and income stream. Producing just one type of product is risky, especially if the market price for that product is volatile. Producing multiple products, as we would expect most firms to do, can ensure that the firm can adjust and maintain itself should one of its products suffer a market shock. Like the example of Mondragon used earlier, a worker-owned firm could transfer workers from sectors where MP < IPH into sectors MP > IPH. Ireland and Law (1982) reveal that for a firm producing two products, should one of the those products experience an increase in its market price, the firm will readjust and consequently increase (rather than decrease) employment and output for that product[63]. "Multi-product firms might obviously shift members' labour from one production section to another according to profitability while paying the same dividend in all sectors" (Ireland and Law, 1982:25). This fairly simple and realistic alteration to Ward's (1958) model eliminates the prospect of the negatively-sloped supply curve (the Ward effect).

But what about the firm that does only produce one product? There are other factors that limit or forbid its effects. The Ward effect is a short-term phenomena. It is assumed in Ward's (1958) model that the Illyrian firm cannot alter its inputs (capital) in the short run, but can alter employment in the short run. The ability to alter only labour and nothing else is important. This means that the firm cannot adjust its operations to a potential scenario where an increase in production and employment (as a result of the output price increase) could lead to an increase in income per head. Instead the model bounds the firm to a position were income per head can only be increased by reducing output and employment. This assumption is oversimplified. In reality, employment in a worker-owned firm cannot be decreased at whim. Any reduction in staff numbers would have to be democratically voted upon, which leaves an important question: why would workers vote for lay-offs when they could potentially be the ones who are laid-off?

> Our view is that in organizing a coalition mode of production, workers are interested not only in the pecuniary rewards from current employment, but also in long-term aspects of their utility maximisation, in particular, with their income employment security.
>
> Miyazaki and Neary (1983:159)

The coercive incentive not to reduce labour, but instead retain it at current levels, would outweigh the remunerative incentive to gamble for a higher income per head. This is also without mentioning the moral incentives to retain employees, which in itself is often a very strong factor, as will be discussed in more depth later. Ward's (1958) model fails to grasp the moral dimensions of reducing the workforce out of want rather than need. The practicality of reducing the workforce for remunerative gain will be difficult for any company, let alone a worker-owned and managed firm.

> Of course, in any real situation, involving all the dimensions of labour, reductions in output with higher prices should be considered most unlikely, as, indeed, this would imply that the working collective would be engaging in self-mutilation in a period when everybody's income is increasing, in order to secure further increases (often only very small or hardly perceptible ones).
>
> Vanek (1970:385)

Even with democratic approval, the assumption that the firm can alter employment in the short run remains oversimplified. Along with the process of voting for redundancies, the process of beginning and concluding a redundancy process can take some time, prolonging the ability of the firm to lay off workers in the short run. Offering redundancy packages or having to repay any capital contributions will also costly, dampening any incentive to reduce labour in the first place[64]. In addition, many firms will have outstanding orders and contracts that will require existing levels of employment. Only in highly flexible labour markets, which are in themselves highly undesirable, will companies have the ability to reduce its staff size at relatively short notice. As Bonin, Jones and Putterman (1993:1399) state, "the negatively sloped supply curve is attributable to an unrealistic specification of freely variable labor in Ward's model". So what about a longer period of labour downsizing? Although employment could be reduced over the long run through attrition (waiting for workers to retire or leave off their own accord), the price of output could rebound during that time, removing the remunerative incentive to reduce the workforce, if there even is one. As Ireland and Law (1982) demonstrate in their models, even when labour is fully flexible and capital is fixed, risk adverse firms would increase production as a result of price uncertainty[65].

Although the Wardian model only allows labour to be adjusted in the short run, if we assume labour can be adjusted in tandem with variations to capital and all other factors, the model becomes even more untenable. If the firm can simultaneously adjust labour and capital, it can amend its production methods to allow for an increase in income per head as a result of further production and employment. This joint flexibility has been proven by Ireland and Law (1982:74) to do just that, claiming that "individual hours worked will be higher if capital as well as membership are variable". This is especially the case if marginal product can be increased using newer and more productive technologies. It would make sense to assume that investing in more productive technology, increasing employment to operate that technology, and producing more output as a result, can realistically increase income per head further than by simply decreasing employment and settling for a lower rate of output using the existing and no doubt older and less productive technology.

On the topic of marginal product, another point should be raised. The Ward (1958) model assumes that all employees are equal in the work they perform and the effort they apply. However, not all workers are as productive as each other. As a result, reducing employment and output will not necessarily lead to an increase in income per head. It could in fact decrease it, especially if workers essential to the process of production are cut. Workers are employed to fulfil set roles and responsibilities that are pivotal to the production process. Like withholding an essential ingredient for a recipe, taking out one worker from the mix could derail the whole production process, to the detriment of all remaining workers. This is yet another gamble for those considering employment cuts.

> For these reasons with firms with many outputs and with many variable inputs the extreme paradoxical results of an increased selling price leading to reduced employment and output may disappear.

> Meade (1972:409)

A simultaneously flexible labour and capital market can then, in theory, make the Ward effect possible but not inevitable. As Ireland and Law (1982:73) state, "the comparative statics [the end result] of a change in product price will be extremely complex when all of individual hours, number of members and level of capital are variable". Most of the decision makers in businesses will not be fully qualified spreadsheet-ready economists. Working out how to maximise income per head by mere pounds and pence will not be an obvious or indeed a worthy endeavour. Only for alterations and investments of significant scale will these questions be raised or indeed answerable.

The Ward effect appears to lose all credibility when all of the factors discussed so far are taken into account. For those with a good knowledge of economic theory and a good knowledge of the real world of business, the Ward effect's oversimplicity as a concept almost matches its oversimplicity to disprove. There is however, one more avenue to explore. In the extreme and unlikely event that the Ward effect should come to fruition in one particular firm or even industry, there is one remedy: the market dynamic. Ward's (1958) analysis assumes a perfectly competitive market system where no monopolies take hold, but still assumes a negative supply schedule could emerge. Even if we now give Ward the benefit of the doubt and assume that worker-owned firms casually react to increased market prices by reducing employment and output, this is still missing that one essential concept – the market dynamic. Although assuming perfect competition, Ward (1958:583) rightfully notes that his analysis has not included the entry of new firms into the market or the expansion of existing firms into new markets. Meade (1972:410) goes on to imply how this factor is vital for a cooperative economy, stating that the market dynamic may in fact be more essential for a cooperative economy than it is for a conventional capitalist economy. If existing worker-owned firms were to decrease output as a response to market price increases, new firms are likely to enter the market to take the market share the existing firms have surrendered. As discussed in Chapter 6, these new firms could well be made up of the former employees of the firms that decided to reduce output. The market dynamic therefore makes the Ward effect a self-readjusting mechanism. Let us explain how.

If the market dynamic were in full swing, enough new firms could spring up to eventually lower the heightened output price back to its original level as the new firms flood the market. This is especially the case in highly globalised economies where wide-scale foreign competition is abundant[66]. Existing firms in different markets may be enticed to enter additional markets where the output price is high, again, ensuring that competition is prevalent. As expressed earlier, it is in the interest of firms to enter multiple markets to ensure all of their eggs are not in one basket. The Ward effect therefore cannot persist and sustain itself in a competitive market economy where the market dynamic is present. It is because of this, and all the other reasons previously explored, that the Ward effect has never taken shape in reality.

Any cooperative state must ensure that the market dynamic is functioning effectively. This means maintaining strong competition laws and effective regulatory bodies to ensure that monopolisation, collusion, market failures and barriers to entry can be avoided wherever possible. A cooperative state should also remain alert to the Ward effect should it ever occur in reality. If it does, state led action to prevent it should be considered as necessary as preventing monopolisation, collusion and other forms of market failure. Tax policies to mitigate or prevent the Ward effect could be put in place should it somehow filter through into the economy at large. Tax benefits for firms that increase employment could be trialled to artificially increase income per head as a result of expansion. It could also act as a disincentive for firms considering lay-offs in general, as reducing employment would nullify these benefits. If the Ward effect is a more infrequent occurrence, a windfall tax could be introduced that directly targets firms that decrease employment and output solely as a means of increasing income per head for the remaining workers. Initiatives of this sort would need to be experimented with much prudence and care, as tax policies are often riddled with perverse incentives, leading to unintended and undesired consequences. However, as we have seen thus far, the need for such initiatives to begin with is highly unlikely.

> Strongly backward-bending supply functions of national product need not be feared in any realistic situation.
>
> Vanek (1970:391)

Demand Shocks

The discussion surrounding the Ward effect has allowed us to see what happens when the market price for output increases. If an increase in demand is one of the main reasons why market prices for output would increase to begin, what would happen if demand decreased instead? For a conventional capitalist firm, a decrease in the demand for the firm's output would usually constitute a reduction in the market price for that output. Consequently, the revenue the firm receives for selling its goods decreases relative to its costs – to use our earlier example, marginal cost is now higher than marginal revenue (MC > MR). The firm will thus reduce output, in attempt to reduce marginal cost, to the point where MC = MR. Reducing costs could mean a reduction in labour costs. Under these circumstances we would expect the firm to consider a variety of methods to reduce labour costs, such as a reduction in hours, wages or through redundancies.

As we have assumed the Ward effect should not be present a reality, the worker-owned firm will have a positive supply curve. For a worker-owned firm experiencing a demand shock, we would therefore expect to see a situation where MC > MR and MP < IPH.

As a result, at face value one would expect employment and output to be reduced, as we would expect for a conventional capitalist firm. The evidence of how worker-owned firms react reveals some interesting developments. Pencavel et al (2006) and Burdín and Dean (2009), who have analysed cases in Italy and Uruguay respectively, both conclude that variations in employment as a response to price fluctuations are much less prevalent in worker cooperatives compared to conventional capitalist firms. Rather than reducing employment in times of low demand, worker-owned firms are more likely to alter wage rates and working hours. In a market where firms are price-takers in their specific market "the wages of co-op workers are expected to be more variable than the wages of workers in capitalist firms" and that "the co-op worker's earnings are predicted to vary with the firm's product market conditions and with the firm's input prices and its fixed costs" (Pencavel *et al*, 2006:26). This is unsurprising. The moral incentives to keep workers employed is a lot stronger in worker-owned firms compared to conventional capitalist firms. In addition, we may not expect to see reduction in working hours or wages for those workers on a subsistence wage, as this would leave these workers unable to maintain their subsistence.

Creating and maintaining employment is clearly a primary aim of the worker-owned firm. In addition, workers are likely to be earning dividends on top of their wages in the good times, so when the bad times do arrive, workers can reduce their income without going below the rate of subsistence. Workers can either maintain their current wage rate and accept lower dividends or a loss at the end of the year, or accept lower wages throughout the year and be compensated with any surpluses gained at the end of the year. If the firm believes the demand shock is temporary, wages can be paid for with accumulated savings, which can be compensated with the surpluses gained in future years. The key point here is that the higher incomes earned by workers enables them to be more flexible during difficult times whilst avoiding redundancies wherever possible. If this added flexibility were to be commonplace within a cooperative economy, it may be safe to assume that overall wage rates would become more elastic, whilst overall employment levels would become more inelastic. The research undertaken by Pencavel et al (2006) and Burdín and Dean (2009) also demonstrates the concept of the principal balance in reality. Worker-owned firms are consciously adapting to market changes whilst simultaneously defending the interests of the workforce. This is important, as it shows how the various concepts used throughout this research are actively shaping the realities of existing worker-owned firms in various market economies.

Previous empirical work therefore provides several insights. First, the extreme implication of Ward's model – where worker cooperatives had a negative sloping supply curve and reduced their employment and output when output prices increased – has rarely been confirmed. Second, employment and output are less sensitive to product market shocks in cooperatives than in capitalist firms. Third, the evidence supporting the standard assumption that cooperatives exclusively maximize income per worker is not conclusive. In contrast, cooperatives' objective functions could include firm employment levels as a maximand.

Burdín and Dean (2009:519)

It is thus perhaps not surprising that firms owned by their workers—and who therefore share in the profits—have performed better in the crisis and laid off fewer employees.

Stiglitz (2012:104)

The one principle that has been challenged by the empirical analysis is the profit principle – the idea that the worker-owned firm seeks to maximise income per head rather than maximising total profits. We should perhaps rephrase this concept with the empirical evidence in mind. We can thus redefine the profit principle as: the idea that the worker-owned firm seeks to maximise both income per head and maximise total employment. This theory has been captured in the UK based evidence on employee-owned businesses (EOBs) put forward by Lampel *et al* (2010)[67].

EOBs create jobs faster. EOBs experienced greater employment growth than their non-employee owned counterparts in the period of economic growth from 2005 to 2008 (an average increase in employment of nearly 7.5% per annum in EOBs compared with less than 3.9% in non-EOBs).

Lampel et al (2010:4)

It has also been argued that worker-owned firms take a more consistent and long term approach to risk, rather than the short term and volatile swings we frequently observe under conventional capitalism. Lampel *et al* (2010) have something to say on this issue as well.

The report finds that employee ownership is a more resilient model: employee-owned firms have a lower risk of business failure, and during the recession they have outperformed the market, demonstrating higher rates of sales growth and job creation.

Lampel et al (2010:3)

Concluding Remarks

The discussion on output for worker-owned firms has merged together many of the key concepts used so far throughout this study. This discussion has also raised important questions regarding the mode of distribution more generally. On that front, the free market model is arguably the most effective mode of distribution for a cooperative economy. Systems of planning all present unnecessary challenges and impracticalities. The market dynamic and principal balance are pivotal features for the survival of any hypothetical cooperative economy. The former ensures supply will always meet demand, primarily due to the incentives to produce commodities and earn a profit from their sales. The latter ensures that such firms will always remain disciplined and competitive, driving forward the motions of human progress. Any cooperative state must ensure the market system is competitive and prevents monopolistic tendencies from taking hold. Markets can never be entirely perfect, nor can they always be efficient, as such a cooperative state must understand and react to market failures quickly and effectively.

The largest challenge for the worker ownership model in this chapter has been the Ward effect. As has been argued, the supply curve for worker-owned firms should always be positive in normal circumstances, and the Ward effect should rarely, if ever, transpire in reality. For the Ward effect to occur, all of the following must occur all at once:

- The firm only produces one product;
- The size of the workforce can be altered at any moment, to the democratic consent of the workforce;
- The firm cannot adjust capital as quickly as it can labour;
- There is total certainty on the market price of the firm's output over the long run;
- The firm can effectively measure the marginal product of each worker;
- There is no possibility of competition from new and existing worker-owned firms entering the market;
- There is no possibility of competition from foreign firms entering the market.

For all of this to occur at once is almost unimaginable in any real world situation. Although the worker-owned firms' supply curve would be positive, the fluctuations in employment and output may not be as volatile compared to conventional capitalist firms, as Burdín and Dean (2009:519) also conclude, "employment and output are less sensitive to product market shocks in cooperatives than in capitalist firms". Where capitalist firms are more likely to alter employment, worker cooperatives are more likely to alter wages and dividends. This chapter has demonstrated how maximising income per head may not in fact be the single most important priority, but where job creation and job stability also present a significant factor.

With all being said, a cooperative economy functioning in an effective market system would see very similar levels of output compared to a conventional capitalist economy. The only difference being, the benefits of production would now be shared between those who actually produce and sell that output. Incentives to maximise income per head and to sustain (and possibly create) jobs would lead to an expected increase in the quality and/or quality of the output produced. This puts the worker-owned firm at a competitive advantage to the conventional capitalist firm.

---

[57] See Mason (2015)

[58] Workplace satisfaction could include a number of attributes that are likely to vary according to each individual worker, these could include: expending the least amount of effort required, working in a good workplace environment, additional perks such as company cars, gym memberships, etc. Along with maximising income per head, all of these positive attributes must be balanced with competitiveness and market discipline.

[59] By normally, we mean the labour market is not in a state of high unemployment and the output market is not in a state where prices are so low the workers cannot cover the costs of production (including labour/subsistence).

[60] I have deliberately missed out the basic public services which are owned and distributed by the government as these are an exception. One would not expect such services to be privatised into worker ownership under a cooperative state unless there was a significant weakness in the moral incentives required for these sectors to function efficiently.

[61] Under worker ownership, a part of the marginal cost stems from labour costs - wages plus dividends. Dividends are not essential for the worker-members, as the wages should be adequate to cover subsistence, but dividends are essential if the firm wishes not to lose its workers to a firm which does offer dividends in addition to wages. Under conventional capitalist firms, a part of the marginal cost also stems from labour costs, which only covers wages, as workers do not receive dividends in these types of firms. However, the capitalist firm is also expected to earn a rate of 'normal profits' for its investor-owners, otherwise they are likely to withdraw their investments and direct it towards a more profitable venture. Normal profits are therefore also considered a part of a capitalist firm's marginal costs. With this in mind, and all else being equal, the marginal costs of a conventional capitalist firm should not differ from that of a worker-owned firm, as both wages and dividends (either for workers or investors) should be equal for both types.

[62] The 'Illyrian model' used by Ward (1958) was set to replicate the Yugoslav model which had emerged during the Cold War period in communist Yugoslavia. In Yugoslavia, the state owned the means of production whilst control and management of the firm was delegated to the workers of each firm. This model worked in a market system where the state remained considerably active in economic affairs. The Illyrian model however, rejects state intervention, and would go on to mirror the model that Vanek would eventually develop, which has already been critiqued in Chapter 7)

[63] See Ireland and Law (1982:75-77).

[64] If a worker-owned firm has embraced a 'direct ownership' model with capital contributions, any redundancies the firm makes will require a debit of the firm's capital account to compensate the leaving workers with the capital they invested upon joining. This means that there is a cost to laying off each worker. Smith (1984) notes that various studies have identified how firms with this arrangement "will not reduce employment at all in response to a price increase", nullifying the Ward effect. See Ireland and Law (1982:21-23) for an explanation of labour reduction compensation more generally – reaching the same conclusions.

[65] See Ireland and Law (1982:142-152)

[66] As capitalist firms are likely to increase output rather than decrease it (in response to output price increases), foreign capitalist firms are likely to flood their imported products into the cooperative economy, should the domestic worker-owned firms reduce output. This could lead to a bounce back in prices to their original level, especially as aggregate demand decreases due to the higher rates of unemployment as a result of the Ward effect. As the negative supply curve would suggest, falling prices for output would lead worker-owned firms to increase employment and output back to the original level. The worker-owned firms would also recoup their market share from the foreign capitalist firms, who are likely to reduce their supply of imported products to the domestic economy. As a result, the hypothetical Ward effect is also a self-readjusting mechanism when free trade between cooperative and capitalist nations is permitted.

[67] The reader should note that this research includes survey responses from businesses with varying degrees of worker ownership.

Endnote

Below is a simple mathematical equation demonstrating the Ward effect for a hypothetical 'product X', adapted from Meade (1972:406).

Price (Px) = £1
Marginal Product (MP) = 1
Output (Qx) = 100
Capital (K) = 50
Labour = 100

From this we can say that:

Value of marginal product (PxMP) = £1
Value of total product (PxQ) = £100
Value of total profit (PxQ – K) = £50

From this we can calculate income per head (IPH), by taking the value of total profit and dividing it by the number of workers:

IMP = (PxQ – K) / L (total revenue – total cost / workers)
Income per head = (£100 - £50) / 50 = £1

In this scenario, IPH = MP. Now let us assume that the price of product X increases from £1 to £1.10 and everything else remains constant.

From this we can say that:

Value of marginal product (PxMP) = £1.10
Value of total product (PxQ) = £110
Value of total profit (PxQ – K) = £50

IMP = (PxQ – K) / L (total revenue – total cost / workers)
Income per head = (£110 - £50) / 50 = £1.2

In this instance, income per head has increased from £1 to £1.2, but as MP < IPH (£1.1 < £1.2), income per head can be increased further still by cutting labour and output.

As only labour and output can be altered in the short run (capital and marginal product remains fixed), the firm can continue to marginally increase income per head by reducing labour and output. This is how the Ward effect is said to function. The simplicity of this model in theory and the impracticality of this model in reality renders it largely useless.

	Price (Px)	Marginal product (MP)	Output (Qx)	Capital (K)	Labour (L)	Income per head (IPH)	Value of marginal product (PxMP)	
Scenario 1	£1.00	1	100	£50.00	50	£1.00	£1.00	MP = IPH
Scenario 2	£1.10	1	100	£50.00	50	£1.20	£1.10	MP < IPH
Scenario 3	£1.10	1	99	£50.00	49	£1.20	£1.10	MP < IPH
Scenario 4	£1.10	1	98	£50.00	48	£1.20	£1.10	MP < IPH
Scenario 5	£1.10	1	97	£50.00	47	£1.21	£1.10	MP < IPH
Scenario 6	£1.10	1	96	£50.00	46	£1.21	£1.10	MP < IPH
Scenario 7	£1.10	1	95	£50.00	45	£1.21	£1.10	MP < IPH
Scenario 8	£1.10	1	94	£50.00	44	£1.21	£1.10	MP < IPH
Scenario 9	£1.10	1	93	£50.00	43	£1.22	£1.10	MP < IPH
Scenario 10	£1.10	1	92	£50.00	42	£1.22	£1.10	MP < IPH

Chapter 9: The National Framework

The topics explored so far have helped us to imagine how a worker-owned firm might operate differently to a conventional capitalist firm in multiple scenarios. This chapter begins to pull all these pieces together in order to form what we might call a 'national framework'. By that, I mean the main differences between a conventional capitalist economy and a hypothetical cooperative economy, where worker-owned firms make up the majority of businesses. This chapter does not wish to intrude on the conversation regarding the state sector, what its role is and how large it should be. We must leave this perpetual debate to others. Although the title of this work is called 'The Cooperative State', this needn't imply that the state as an actor within the economy should be any more interventionist or any less so. The purpose of the cooperative state is simply to bring about a transition from capitalist to cooperative ownership of the means of production, and to sustain it as such. Other policies and methods that supplement this aim should and will be discussed, but the purpose of the cooperative state as a concept must remain true to this simple definition. Consequently, we can assume that in our initial comparison the size of the state sector should not change significantly moving from a capitalist to cooperative economy.

The chapter is also not concerned with the process of transitioning from a capitalist to cooperative economy, that is the *raison d'être* of chapters 11, 12 and 13 (13 most specifically). This chapter only seeks to compare the likely differences of a well-established capitalist economy to a well-established cooperative economy with a roughly identical sized state sector. Some may rightfully question the relevance of a comparison on a national scale considering the huge influence global issues have on developed economies. Chapter 10 will seek to seek to uncover some of the global ramifications for a cooperative economy and state by developing an 'international framework'. Developing a simple national framework is the first step to achieving this end, and is thus where we shall start.

The framework will draw upon the many concepts and assumptions made in all preceding chapters, and will amplify them onto the national level. The findings to be revealed will not be particularly surprising given that a lot of ground has already been covered, but nonetheless, the findings offer a stark contrast to many of the issues we find in contemporary capitalist economies. It will also allow us to better understand the new roles and responsibilities our cooperative state must undertake, we will also make some space to talk of additional social and political ramifications where appropriate.

Spending

Perhaps the first thing a student of macroeconomics is likely to learn is the relationship between spending and saving. As we know, when a commodity is demanded by a consumer, an enterprise will likely seek to produce and sell that commodity using various inputs, along with the employment of labour and the investment of capital. The more a commodity is demanded, the more it should be produced, and thus the more inputs, labour and capital are demanded. In a market economy, spending is what spurs on growth and economic development. The opposite of spending is saving. Saving does not induce growth in the same way that spending does, but where savings do not create growth necessarily, they are essential if growth is to be realised. Savings are required for investment, and growth cannot be facilitated without investment. But how do individuals decide how much to spend and how much to save? For every additional £1 a worker earns, they must decide what proportion of it they must spend, and what they must save. For a subsistence worker the answer is pretty obvious, they only earn enough money from employment to support their basic upkeep. There is little if any scope for saving. For every extra £1 earned, £1 is spent. Only when the worker begins to earn more than their subsistence do they start to consider saving it. A wealthy investor on the other hand may be more inclined to save a greater proportion of every additional £1 they earn, this is because they may already have a large enough income to cover their typical spending habits, and saving money can earn them interest. The more they save today, the more they can spend in future.

The decisions different people make about what to do with this extra £1 is called the 'marginal propensity to spend' and the 'marginal propensity to save'. If the marginal propensity to spend is 0.8 this means that for every extra £1 someone earns, they are to spend 80p of it. Mathematically, this means the rest is left for saving, so the marginal propensity to save is 0.2, or 20p. An individual's propensity to spend or save will differ greatly for a variety of reasons. Those who like to 'live in the moment' may prefer to spend a greater proportion of their income rather than save, whilst risk averse individuals are more likely to save it 'for a rainy day' than spend it. Higher interest rates on savings are likely to incentivise more people to save, whilst special deals, cheap credit or 'near future' price rises are likely to incentivise more people to spend.

So what does all this have to do with a cooperative economy? The answer to this is quite straightforward. At first glance, it would appear that worker ownership on a mass scale is likely to make workers better off compared to investors. As workers now own the companies they work for, they are to receive the profits their companies make. In a capitalist economy, companies are owned either by individuals who may also manage the business, or shareholders who have purchased shares to receive an income. This all depends on what type of capitalist company the firm is. Collectively we will call these individuals 'investors', as they have invested their own money into the enterprise and are distinct from the company's workers, even if they themselves work for the company they totally or partially own. Under a cooperative economy, these investors will no longer be able to own the companies they invest in. The transfer of profits from investors to workers will clearly make workers better off at the expense of investors. The question we must now ask is how this transferred money will be used differently, will more of it be saved or spent?

First of all, we must assume that the level of profit generated by all companies is identical in both systems. Although there are legitimate reasons to believe a worker-owned firm may produce higher rates of profit due to the incentive dynamic, for the meantime we will assume profits are identical. Using the concept of the marginal propensity to spend and save can provide some initial answers before diving in a little deeper. If we make the assumption that under conventional capitalism the majority of workers earn a subsistence wage, and that the majority of firms are owned by individual business owners who earn much higher levels of income, the results are relatively obvious. For every extra £1 a worker gains, the marginal propensity to spend is likely to be very high, 0.9 for example, and the marginal propensity to save is likely to be very low, 0.1 for example. This is because the workers' income is relatively low, and any additional income is likely to be spent on goods and services related to their subsistence, such as higher quality food and clothing, home improvements, leisure activities, etc. The incentive to save is likely to be very weak[68]. For a wealthy business owner the opposite is true. As we have assumed, for those with higher amounts of wealth, most of their living expenses are already accounted for. It makes more sense to save any extra income in order to gain a return on it and perhaps spend it in future. In this case, the marginal propensity to spend is say 0.1 for example, and the marginal propensity to save is 0.9. This means that if company profits were to be distributed to investors (as is currently the case in conventional capitalist economies), the majority of that money is likely to be saved.

> Moving money from the bottom to the top lowers consumption because higher-income individuals consume a smaller proportion of their income than do lower-income individuals (those at the top save 15 to 25 percent of their income, those at the bottom spend all of their income)[69].
>
> Stiglitz (2012:84)

If profits were instead distributed to a company's workers, the majority of that money is likely to be spent. This means that under a cooperative economy, under the assumptions we have set, profits are more likely to be spent than saved. This in turn would lead to higher demand for goods and services, as workers are now purchasing more than they did before. This would lead to higher growth and higher employment, as higher demand means that more output needs to be produced and more employees are needed to produce that output. On the flip side, it could be argued that as less money is being saved, there is less money available to invest in the capital necessary for companies to grow, an issue we will explore a little later. This basic concept demonstrates some of the preliminary changes we might see under a cooperative economy.

We must now proceed to abandon some of the assumptions we have made and look at things from a more realistic perspective. First of all we must abandon the assumption that most workers earn a subsistence wage. The amount of money required for subsistence changes between and within countries, so calculating this figure can be very complex. We must also not forget that due to recent changes in the labour market – favouring more flexible working arrangements – some may be earning below what is required for subsistence and may require state assistance in the form of welfare for example. In addition, a sizeable portion of workers could still earn over the rate of subsistence but could still consider themselves to be 'struggling' or 'just about managing'. With that being said, some figures can help us to understand what the average UK worker is earning and what it can buy them. The Living Wage Foundation has calculated that (as of 2016) a worker must earn £8.45 per hour to earn enough to live off, multiplied by 37.5 (the average amount of hours UK workers work for), and the weekly living wage comes to £317[70]. The Office for National Statistics (ONS) has calculated that (as of 2016), the average worker earns £507[71]. We can thus assume that the average UK worker typically earns above the rate of subsistence, but not to an extent where their marginal propensity to save is larger than wealthy business owners, to who we shall now turn to.

We must now also remove the assumption that most businesses are owned by individuals who are exorbitantly rich. Just like that of workers, the fortunes of business owners greatly differ, mainly down to the size and ownership type of the enterprise. Let us begin with larger firms – those with shares which are publicly listed on the stock exchange more specifically. Figures from the ONS indicate that those outside the UK owned 54 per cent of the value of total listed shares at the end of 2014[72]. They go on to state that "UK individuals owned an estimated 12 per cent of quoted UK shares by value at the end of 2014, an increase from the historic low of 10 per cent in 2010 and 2012"[73]. There was, however, no indication as to the wealth or status of the individuals who owned this 12 per cent. In Chapter 1 we briefly explored how for larger firms, CEOs and other top executives are often rewarded shares as an additional bonus to top up wages. Those individuals would most likely fit into these figures. We know that the richest sections of society tend to own the majority of capital more generally. "The wealthiest 10 per cent of households own 45 per cent of the nation's wealth, while the least wealthy half of all households own just 9 per cent." (Lawrence and Mason, 2017:2). It would therefore be no stretch of the imagination to assume that the majority of UK shares owned by UK individuals would be those who fit into this wealthiest 10 per cent bracket. Moving on, we know that 9 per cent of the value of shares at the end of 2014 were owned by unit trusts, which manage a portfolio of different types of investments that are bought by small investors. Again, there is no indication regarding the wealth of such investors. Other financial institutions and insurance companies hold 7 per cent and 6 per cent respectively[74].

Pension funds are also of particular interest, as they aim invest on the behalf of workers who contribute towards a pension. The dividends accrued from these shares go onto benefit workers once they retire. Workplace pensions in the UK for example include contributions from employee wages, along with a contribution from their employers, and a smaller top-up from the government. These funds are then invested via pension providers in, among other things, company shares. It is argued therefore that employees indirectly gain from company performance. However, the final figure prospective pensioners are to receive in no way reflects the effort applied individually throughout their working lives, nor is it likely to reflect the performance of the firm itself. This system is also likely to favour the rich, who pour more into their pensions and thus receive a bigger gain. This approach clearly flies in the face of greater economic equality, and certainly has no input in resolving the dual-contradiction. It is disappointing that this flawed system of private sector led redistribution would seem to be the most effective route to sharing the rewards of capitalist firms within our current economic context. The reader may also be interested to know that pension funds only owned 3 per cent of the value of shares at the end of 2014[75], and has been on a downward trajectory for some time. Again, this hardly demonstrates a move towards greater economic equality. Of course, the figures used above only account for UK shares – pension funds and small savers may hold a greater sum of foreign shares, but this of course exacerbates the dual-contradiction in other countries.

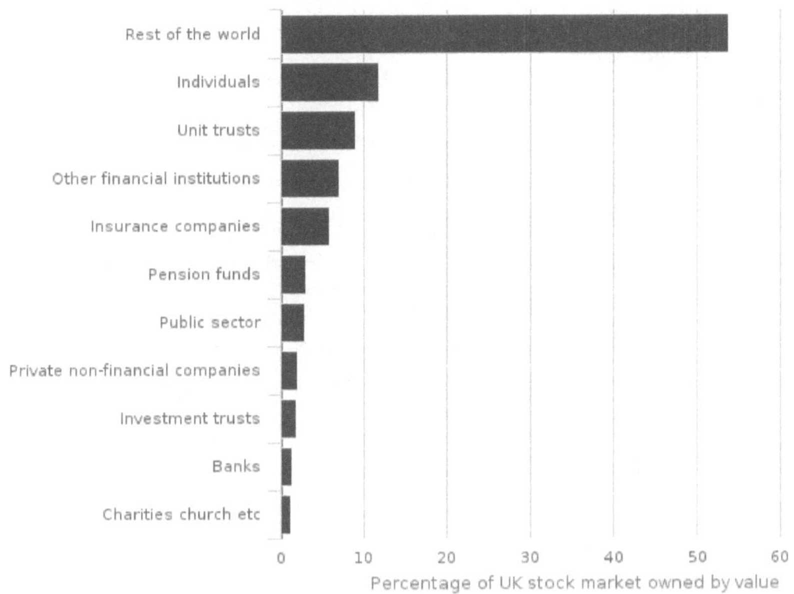

Beneficial ownership of quoted shares in **UK** domiciled companies 2014. Source: ONS, https://www.ons.gov.uk/economy/investmentspensionsandtrusts/bulletins/ownershipofukquotedshares/2015-09-02

Where larger businesses tend to be owned by a large set of shareholders, small to medium sized businesses tend to be owned by individuals or small groups of individuals. This distinction between ownership spread among a single or few individuals, or spread among a vast number of shareholders will lead to different outcomes in the coming analysis. So how do British firms vary in size and success? The Department for Business, Innovation and Skills states that "small businesses accounted for 99.3 per cent of all private sector businesses at the start of 2016 and 99.9 per cent were small or medium-sized (SMEs)"[76]. By this, we must logically assume that larger businesses make up just 0.1 per cent of UK businesses. Of the SMEs, "there were 3.3 million sole proprietorships (60 per cent of the total), 1.8 million companies (32 per cent), and 421,000 ordinary partnerships (8 per cent)."[77]. We can consider sole proprietorships to be 'worker-owned firms', as the firm is owned and managed by one person who is also the sole employee of the business. They continue by stating that "the combined annual turnover of SMEs was £1.8 trillion, 47 per cent of all private sector turnover in the UK"[78]. Again, it must be assumed that larger companies make up 53 per cent of UK private sector turnover. Lastly, where SMEs employ 60 per cent of those in the private sector, larger companies make up 40 per cent. As such, the majority of businesses (which are not sole proprietorships) are businesses which are likely owned by a single owner or a small group of owners, but at the same time, the most profitable business are the largest, which are mostly owned by shareholders.

If a small to medium sized enterprise is owned by a single individual, that individual will receive all of the profit that company makes. As this is a single sum, and not shared among many shareholders, it can be assumed that a great deal of that money will be saved rather than spent. If these profits were instead distributed to a larger number of workers, regardless of their incomes, more of this money is likely to be spent than saved. But why is this the case? This is due to what we can call the 'diminishing marginal utility of income'. This concept works similar to the marginal propensity to spend and save. We already know that the poor are more likely to spend extra income whilst the wealthy are more likely to save it, but rather than looking at just £1, what happens if we keep giving the poor person and the rich person additional £1s? The diminishing marginal utility of income assumes that the more money you earn, the less utility (satisfaction) you gain from it, and as such the more money you earn the less likely you are to spend it.

Let us use a hypothetical example to illustrate this. A business owner runs a company which employs 10 people, all of which earn £20,000 a year. The business owner is one of these 10 workers, and thus also earns £20,000, so before profits are taken into account, the business owner earns as much as the employees. At the end of the year it becomes apparent that the company has earned £10,000 in profits. As the business owner owns the business, they are entitled to the total sum of £10,000. As this is a large addition to their income, the owner decides to spend half of it and save half of it (a marginal propensity to spend of 0.5, and marginal propensity to save of 0.5). Now let us assume that the firm is owned equally by all 10 workers, the former business owner now owns only a tenth of the business, but still earns £20,000 before profits. At the end of the year the company still makes profits of £10,000, but rather than this being distributed to just one individual, it is shared between all ten. All workers receive a bonus of £1,000. So will these ten workers decide to spend half of it and save half of it like the individual business owner would have? The answer is probably not. The diminishing marginal utility of income implies that the smaller the income gained (£1,000 in this case), the more utility is gained from spending it. On the other hand, the higher the income (£10,000), the lesser utility is gained, because the beneficiary can already afford more of what they need and want.

This process can be seen graphically in Figure 9 – the higher the income received, the lesser utility is gained. Although the company in our example makes the same amount of profit in both scenarios, because it is split between more business owners, the total £10,000 is more likely to be spent than saved. For each of the ten individuals there may be a marginal propensity to spend of 0.8 and a marginal propensity to save of 0.2.

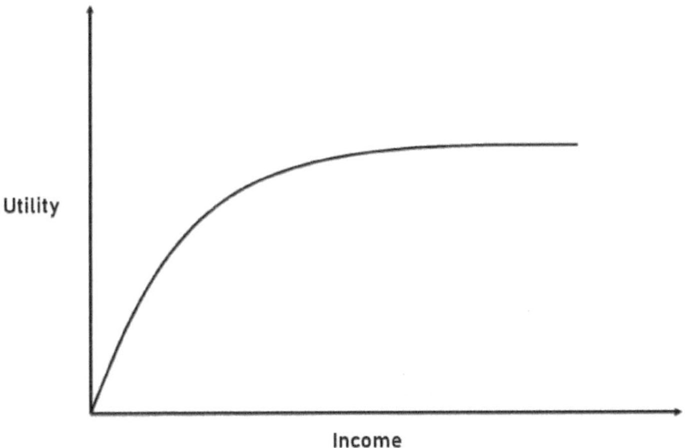

Figure 9

If this pattern of higher spending is replicated across a cooperative economy, our hypothetical assumption that cooperative economies are likely to induce more growth should hold true. The question now arises regarding larger corporations with a vast number of shareholders. As we have seen, although large companies only represent 0.1 per cent of all UK businesses, they make up 53 per cent of UK private sector turnover and employ 40 per cent of workers. Whether the profits made by these firm are more likely to be spent or saved under worker ownership depends on the number and the type of investors that own the shares. If a company has more shareholders than employees, then under worker ownership, the profits distributed to the workers may be more likely to be saved than spent, as the profits are being distributed to a smaller group of beneficiaries than before. This of course, depends on who owns the shares and what their marginal utility of income is. If there are more shareholders than employees, but the shareholders are highly wealthy and the workers are not, although, once again, the profits are being distributed to a smaller group, because these workers have a lower income compared to the shareholders, more of the profits will be spent as these workers gain more utility from spending them than the shareholders. In reality, many shares today are owned by wealthy investment funds and are rewarded to wealthy fund managers and

CEOs. Distributing profits from shareholders and individual business owners to workers is thus almost certainly likely to increase aggregate demand.

Non-Economic Benefits

Allowing workers to earn the profits they produce has more than simple economic benefits. Shifting one of the main flows of income from a wealthy minority to a poorer majority, will have a significant impact towards lowering economic and social inequality. Reversing one of the main causes of income inequality can have other secondary effects. As noted back in Chapter 1, works such as *The Spirit Level* by Wilkinson and Pickett (2009) have found that inequality has links to other adverse economic and social outcomes. For the very poorest, worker ownership might lead to a significant increase in their income, to a point above subsistence. Steady long term employment which is well paid and offers a good rate of profit can be the difference between living on the edge and having a good standard of living. Individuals with basic security are also more likely to act rationally in the marketplace. A society where workers and consumers feel unstable and whose lives feel not within their own control can lead to harmful and potentially dangerous decisions. Worker ownership can help to alleviate this, for as long as this is coupled with worker management. Davies (2011) discusses how the higher levels of employee wellbeing observed under employee ownership (compared to capitalist ownership) is most likely due to the higher levels of engagement, transparency and a focus on dialogue between worker-members. Davies (2011:19) goes onto say that for employee-owned firms, "the most important contributor to workplace wellbeing is the sense of working collaboratively towards well-understood, long-term goals." Economic democracy is a way of giving control back to employees, giving them a sense of security not just regarding incomes but also of other non-financial factors relating to their employment.

Worker ownership is no panacea. Western labour markets must still confront multiple challenges, from the displacement of work from automation, the growing flexibility of labour, and the displacement of peoples stemming from climate change and conflict. Coupled with other radical progressive policies, worker ownership can be an important first step towards building a secure working life for many who feel left behind by the pressures of a globalised society and marketplace. We should not be too surprised if a boost in income from worker ownership also correlates with healthier living (both physically and mentally), lower crime rates and better trust in community life and institutions. We know that increasing inequality worsens these indicators, so decreasing inequality, through worker ownership, should in theory relieve some of these pressures. Workplace democracy could also lead to more confidence in the political system. Embracing democracy on a day to day level in peoples working lives could translate into more participation in the political sphere. As Gamson and Levin (1984:219) rightly note "[I]n fact, it has been argued that political democracy must necessarily be seriously constrained in effectiveness in the absence of economic or workplace democracy". This is a positive we cannot stress enough, particularly at times when democratic principles come under strain. Resolving the dual-contradiction and improving income for workers should therefore not just be a mechanism for simply boosting blind consumerism, it should be about providing improved financial security, along with the social, cultural and political benefits that security can reap.

Saving

A cooperative economy where workers have a higher marginal propensity to spend can expect to see higher aggregate demand as a result. One question remains however: if more is being spent, what happens to savings? If less is being saved does this mean investment will become more expensive, as there are less funds available to lend? Under conventional economic wisdom this concept would appear to hold weight. As there is less money around for saving (less supply for investment capital), and because there is now higher growth due to increased national spending (more demand for investment capital), investment must therefore be more expensive. As we explored back in Chapter 7, the cost of borrowing to invest is regulated by interest rates. If investment capital becomes harder to come by, interest rates will be higher, making borrowing more expensive and saving more lucrative. There is much reason to doubt however, that such a situation would emerge should spending in a cooperative economy be higher. There are two main reasons for this. Firstly, there are the international dimensions. Although more money is now being spent rather than saved, additional finance capital can be procured from foreign investors. The fact that 54 per cent of UK shares are currently owned by foreign investors demonstrates this fact. The second reason is more complex and requires more elaboration.

All contemporary capitalist economies work under what is known as a 'fractional reserve banking system'. This basically means that the total amount of domestic money available for investment is not equal to the total amount of domestic savings. Under fractional reserve banking, private banks are able to create credit electronically with little hindrance. This means that banks can lend investment capital to borrowers without requiring additional funds from its savers. The group Positive Money in the UK have been most vocal on this issue[79]. This system ensures that the amount of money in circulation is determined more by the banks willingness to lend rather than the actual needs of the economy at large[80]. In the boom times, banks increase lending, increasing the likelihood of overheating the economy and causing a financial bubble. The 2008 Financial Crisis lays testament to what happens when credit growth is unlimited and riskier and riskier asset investments are taken. However, when the boom is finally met with a bust, banks lose confidence and investment dries up, at just the time when investment is needed to kick-start the economy. These are the realities of a fractional reserve banking system – investment and the growth it facilitates is not necessarily bound by changes in savings, but is instead bound by the confidence of banks. Consequently, although this type of banking system is highly volatile, under a cooperative economy with a fractional reserve system, both spending and domestic investment can rise in tandem.

To avoid the many negative aspects of fractional reserve banking, a cooperative state may decide to outlaw the process whereby private banks can create electronic money, by replacing the existing system with a sovereign money system. A sovereign money system would ensure that only the central bank (which is owned by and accountable to the government) can create new electronic money. Under this arrangement, banks act as intermediaries between savers and borrowers. Banks must borrow the money deposited to them by their savers and lend that money out to borrowers. In order to make a profit, they charge the borrowers a higher rate of interest than what they pay their savers. As a result of all this, banks cannot create new money but must instead use the money already created by the central bank. This would mean that, unlike fractional reserve banking, the amount of money available to lend is related to how much has been saved. One may therefore argue, that a cooperative economy utilising a sovereign money system would witness additional demand due to higher spending, and may experience a lack of savings available to meet that demand. This need not be the case however. Van Lerven *et al* (2015) explain how additional demand for credit, as a result of increased demand, can be met with an increase in the money supply from the central bank. As such, rather than banks being able to increase the money supply at whim, the central bank can increase the money supply to complement the demands of the economy in general. The central bank can do this by lending newly created money to the private banks, which can then be lent out to businesses. "If demand for loans far exceeded the willingness or ability of savers to lend, the Bank of England can allow banks to borrow newly created money directly from the Bank of England." (Van Lerven *et al*, 2015:8). For a firm looking to borrow money to invest, there should be no more difficulty or ease in procuring investment capital under this system than under fractional reserve banking. In reality, the borrower will notice little change.

For entrepreneurs and businesses, whether the money they borrow is newly created by a bank or previously existed in the hands of a saver makes no difference to the usefulness of the borrowed funds. What is important to entrepreneurs is that they can borrow money when needed.

Van Lerven et al (2015:8)

This means that an increase in demand for credit can be met with an increase in supply, should worker ownership succeed in increasing aggregate demand. As a result, whichever type of banking system is used, an increase in spending and decrease in saving should not lead to a lack of investment capital available for firms to invest and grow.

Of course, banks are not the only means of procuring investment capital. There are other important differences a cooperative economy would observe on the issue of investment. It goes without saying that an economy made up of worker-owned firms has no immediate need for a stock market, at least for domestic firms. Instead of a stock market, a cooperative state is likely to push for a better functioning bond market to take its place. As we have discussed before, stocks and shares are likely to be replaced with bonds for worker-owned firms who seek to fund large investments. Although investors no longer have a role of owning or controlling the firms they invest in, they do instead have an alternative type of financial product to invest and gain a financial return from. A cooperative state is not an anti-investor state, private investors are an essential component of any cooperative economy and must be treated as such. Bonds and debentures hold a (more or less) fixed and stable rate of return which stocks and shares do not provide. Also, unlike stocks or shares, investors are better able to identify which investments are likely to be more risky and which are likely to be safer. On the stock market, all bets are off, as all investors are exposed to a potential crash in the value of their stocks. Although worker-owned firms can still go bust, investors have the confidence in knowing that there may be means of being compensated a part of their investment. With stocks and shares, there is no justice in the fact that an investor could lose all their stake due to some irrational market reaction. Bonds, especially when performance indexed, offer scope for riskier investors, but they also offer a basic degree of security. This security easily trumps the benefits procured from owning a piece of the company. As research from the previous chapter has shown, worker-owned firms tend to fare better during economic downturns and are generally less prone to volatile reactions, this makes them perfect vehicles for long-term stable investment. In a world of growing financial insecurity, worker ownership complemented with an expanded bond market should be welcomed alternative.

Government Spending and Tax

The higher marginal propensity to spend that would be observed in a cooperative economy also has consequences for government revenue and spending; a cooperative state should expect to see potentially higher rates of tax revenue collected compared to a conventional capitalist economy. Let us discuss how this could be the case. Most economists[81] would profess that the majority of governments rely upon taxation to pay for the public spending their citizens rely upon. Governments receive income from multiple types of taxation, such as taxes on workers' incomes, taxes on goods and services sold (VAT) and taxes on company profits like corporation tax for example. Even if these tax rates remain fixed, the amount of revenue the government receives depends on how much money is being spent and saved across the economy. For example, if spending were to increase, the government would expect to see higher rates of tax revenue. The reason for this is simple. As more goods and services are being purchased, more VAT is being paid. As company profits go up (as more of their goods and services are being sold), the amount paid in corporation tax goes up. Over time, more workers will be needed to increase the production and sale of additional goods and services, meaning more income tax being paid. As such, the more money that is spent across the economy, the more the government expects to collect in tax revenue.

We could also say that as more spending across the economy leads to lower unemployment, the amount the government needs to spend decreases, as they are no longer paying social security to those unemployed individuals who have now found employment. As a result, if worker ownership across an economy leads to more spending, as we have argued, the more the cooperative state should expect to collect in tax revenue. Consider the following case study from Summers *et al* (2014) comparing two similar firms: a conventional capitalist firm (Marks and Spencer) and an employee-owned firm (the John Lewis Partnership)

The most recent figures from employee-owned John Lewis Partnership and from Marks and Spencer are revealing. They are very similar in size (JLP £9.5 billion sales, M&S £10 billion; JLP 84,000 people, M&S 81,000 [note that the employee-owned company has, typically, created more jobs for the same turnover]) JLP distributed £210 million to the employees, which went out with no transaction cost, the same percent of salary to every employee. This made a difference to 84,000 or so families, who paid their tax and spent the cash on ordinary things, lifting the local economy in every area where there is a store. By contrast, M&S paid out £268 million, which went overwhelmingly to City institutions, many of whom have sophisticated ways of avoiding paying tax; it will have incurred very significant transactions costs in the form of fees to the people who run these institutions; and it will largely have been 'invested' in hedge funds, derivative contracts and similarly unproductive instruments. The effect on the local economy will have been pretty well zero, as also on child poverty. Since this is a low-paid industry, that is a relevant point: the JLP effect was positive on child poverty, but not M&S. Almost certainly less tax was paid from the larger distribution from M&S than was paid on the lower sum from JLP.

Summers et al (2014:1-2)

As we know, the investor-owners of conventional capitalist firms are less likely to spend the profits they earn, as they have a lower marginal propensity to spend. Of the money they do spend, they are also less likely to spend that money in the domestic economy. This is because, as we have seen, investor-owners do not necessarily have to live in the same country as where their investment is located. A shareholder of a British firm could live in Japan, and spend any profits they make from the British firm in Japan, to the benefit of the Japanese economy and treasury. For worker-owners, they do have to live in the same country as their investment, as their investment is the company they work for. Under worker ownership, profits are thus more likely to be spent and taxed locally. Of course, there are leakages in this process, not every pound and penny earned by the worker-owners will be spent locally. If worker-owners use their profits to purchase imported goods, it will be the foreign firms who sell more, produce more and employ more. This will mean higher tax revenue for the government in the foreign firms' country of origin. We must remember, however, that some additional spending in the domestic economy is better than no extra spending at all. In addition, as the profits made by domestic firms and their worker-owners will be taxed by the domestic cooperative state, they will not be syphoned off to jet-setting oligarchs and foreign tax-havens. A cooperative state should therefore expect to see less tax avoidance and tax evasion. As one would expect, these distasteful practices will never be resolved entirely, but as with the argument on local spending, some reduction in tax avoidance and evasion is better than none at all.

Productivity and Innovation

The discussion must now move onto a different matter, that of productivity, innovation and the progression of technological development. To recall earlier discussions, the concept of the dual-contradiction is made up of two constituent parts, inequality stemming from the distribution of profits, and a lack of incentive for employees to apply more effort than the minimum expected. Under worker ownership, the inequality element of the dual contradiction has been more or less resolved – workers now gain the surpluses they produce or enable. This, as we have seen, is likely to boost growth as the profits these workers earn is more likely to be spent than saved. But the story does not stop there. The second element of the dual-contradiction has also been resolved, meaning that workers now have an incentive to apply as much effort as possible in order to maximise their income. The analysis made earlier was built on the assumption that worker-owned firms and conventional firms had identical rates of profit, we must now surrender this assumption.

This change will have considerable effects on the world of work. Although some conventional capitalist firms offer incentives to a number of their employees, we do not see a situation where all workers in all firms have an incentive to apply maximum effort. This means that for many capitalist firms, output is much lower than it could otherwise be. In addition to this, as workers of a conventional capitalist firm have no immediate incentive to respect the fixed capital and other inputs of production, they may be less willing to use these resources as efficiently as possible. Being wasteful might just be easier, again, there is no inherent incentive to prevent this. All of this changes under worker ownership. Once workers own the firm, along with its fixed capital and other inputs, they will have an incentive to minimise costs in order to maximise income per head. This drive to minimise costs and maximise income will undoubtedly lead to a greater efficiency of resource usage, along with a general desire to increase total output. This is not just the case in theory, in reality too there are signs of this positive effect on productivity. Doucouliagos (1995) examines the effect on productivity from various types of worker participation, from milder forms of participation in capitalist firms to those of full worker ownership and management. The abstract of his work neatly confirms what we would expect:

> [P]rofit sharing, worker ownership, and worker participation in decision making are all positively associated with productivity. All the observed correlations are stronger among labour-managed firms (firms owned and controlled by workers) than among participatory capitalist firms (firms

adopting one or more participation schemes involving employees, such as ESOPs or quality circles).

Doucouliagos (1995:58)

Similar results have also been found when comparing French worker cooperatives (known as SCOPs) with conventional firms in their own industries.

> We find worker cooperatives to be as productive or possibly more productive overall than conventional firms in most industries. However, the two types of firms use different technologies. These differences are consistent with the existence of incentive and information effects associated with full employee ownership that are embodied in the inputs and result in different output elasticities. In some industries, conventional firms would produce more if they used the cooperatives' technologies, whereas SCOPs always produce at least as much with their own technology as with conventional firms'. These findings suggest that in several industries French worker cooperatives produce in such a way that they use their current inputs better than conventional firms, which could produce more at their current levels of inputs if they produced in the same way as worker cooperatives.

Fakhfakh, Pérotin and Gago (2011:20)

When studying existing worker-owned firms in Italy, Smith (1994) implies that industrial cooperatives hold an organisational comparative advantage over conventional capitalist firms.

> The use of internally generated production knowledge as an innovation strategy is robustly associated with better cooperative firm performance, as measured by either profitability or income per member.

Smith (1994:319)

For worker cooperatives, observations that the workers make in the course of their daily work, whether in the context of building craft products, working on an assembly line, or service work, may be more likely to be mentioned, recorded, and built upon by the cooperative. In this way the cooperative can introduce improvements and new methods of production and organization with the more direct line of communication that their management structure facilitates. This is clearly a comparative advantage of cooperatives over conventional firms.

Smith and Rothbaum (2013:9)

As implied back in Chapter 5, worker ownership provides the incentive to apply maximum effort, but it is worker management and control that allows those proposed innovations to be discussed, planned and realised. Firms which are most able to gage the ideas of their worker-members are most likely to succeed. It is important at this stage to make a distinction between large and small innovations. Large scale innovations are usually new ideas for new products or entirely new ways of producing new or existing products. Small scale innovations are usually in the form of adjusting existing products and methods of production. This could mean finding ways to use fewer resources, whether that be materials, working hours, etc. It could also mean maintaining the existing amount of resources but applying them differently for more productive results. New thoughts and ideas will not lead to breakthroughs every time, but taking the time to discuss them and having the mechanisms of realising them can become a true asset to the firm. Workers who are accustomed to their workplaces and methods know them better than anyone, and now they have an incentive to make their methods of production more efficient. These incentives could lead to the development of whole new products or markets altogether, this would certainly be the most positive outcome, especially if income per head and employment can be increased.

The development of new products, methods and inventions is usually left in the hands of the entrepreneur, or the R&D departments of existing firms. Letting workers become entrepreneurs in their own enterprise is an additional source of innovation that should be welcomed. On a nationwide scale, all of the minor and major innovations and efficiencies added up could lead to a significant reduction in the cost of inputs as resources are used more productively. It would not be controversial to assume that a reduction in input costs could translate to a reduction in output costs in competitive markets. A free market working within a cooperative economy could thus see lower prices for at least the same quality products. Of course, the move from conventional capitalism to worker ownership could affect prices in other ways, but this is one example where prices might be put on a positive downward trajectory.

Smith (1994:307) goes onto imply that worker-owned firms are less incentivised to introduce labour saving technology, and thus specialise on high quality niche products that are more labour intensive. Regarding the point that worker-owned firms tend to stick to particular labour intensive markets, Pérotin (2016) states the following:

Worker co-ops are larger than other firms and not necessarily less capital intensive, although they may be created more often than other firms in less capital intensive industries, all else being equal. They are present in most industries and differences in industry distributions with conventional firms vary from one country to another.

Pérotin (2016:20)

Pérotin's (2016) research stems from a mix of large datasets comparing worker-owned firms across countries, and comparing them to conventional capitalist firms. As such, there is nothing to suggest that worker-owned firms are restricted to a particular trade, industry or size. The worker ownership model should apply to any sector and market that conventional capitalist firms currently operate in. There is also nothing to suggest that worker-owned firms should be hesitant of introducing labour-saving technologies. As was discussed in Chapter 6, a worker-owned firm could invest in labour-saving technology but reduce the hours worked by each employee rather than laying off a portion of the workforce. Workers would be paid the same salary but with the prospect of higher dividends and a reduction in working time, freeing up more time for other pursuits. This way all workers can benefit from the additional income per head the more productive technology has enabled[82]. Worker-owned firms will constantly rebalance the size of their workforce and fixed capital in operation to adjust to any new technologies or new efficient productive methods. As the free market dictates, those who are unable to make the necessary changes to production methods or their product range will fall behind those that make the risky and difficult decisions.

For as long as the market dynamic is in action, there is nothing to suggest that moving from conventional capitalism to worker ownership will slow the pace of technological progression nationwide. As we have seen, there is a greater chance that employee ownership could allow innovation to flourish more widely. The organisational comparative advantage Smith (1994) discusses proves that if anything, innovation and technological progression should advance at greater pace within a cooperative economy. The agglomeration of minor innovations in product design and production processes has the potential to bring down prices in competitive markets as firms become more efficient and productive at what they do. As Pérotin's (2016) research has concluded, worker-owned firms do not necessarily stick to niche markets like some form of inherent limitation, but are in fact present in a variety of different markets in a variety of different sizes. There is nothing to suggest that worker ownership cannot function in any sector we currently find conventional capitalist firms operating in.

Employment and Inflation

Topics such as employment and prices have already been briefly discussed in this chapter, but there are particular changes in moving from conventional capitalism to worker ownership that affect these two relationships. As we know, employment is not an end in itself, it is a means of maintaining subsistence at the very minimum and of gaining disposable income above that minimum. Wages and prices have an incontrovertible link. Under conventional capitalism, as labour is a form of input, increased wages will either have to be paid for with smaller dividend payments to shareholders, or higher prices for the products the company sells. If we assume that the firm does not wish to alter shareholder dividends or decrease output, the only way to pay for higher wages is by putting up prices. On the flip side, lower wage costs means that firms can potentially reduce their price to become more competitive. From the analysis made back in Chapter 6, we can see no logical reason to suggest levels of employment in a cooperative economy should be any different compared to an identical capitalist economy. Although the incentive to employ has altered slightly, the overall levels of employment should not be all that different. From our analysis in this chapter so far, we have postulated that higher rates of spending in the economy will have the likely potential to induce more economic demand, growth and employment in the macroeconomy, whilst more efficient firms can produce at potentially lower costs and pass that onto the consumer through lower prices.

The next part of the analysis depends on wage 'stickiness' – how easily wages can go up or down. In conventional capitalist economies, it is very difficult for companies to reduce the wages of their staff. This is especially the case when trade unions are operating and when minimum wage laws are enacted. Wages are flexible upwards, but tend to be rigid downwards. The reason for this is simple, workers will not tolerate a reduction in their standards of living, especially if shareholder dividends are protected at the expense of wages. This can become particularly problematic in cases where firms need to reduce their labour costs, in time of recession when demand is weaker for example. The result of this usually means unemployment. If firms cannot negotiate a lower wage for their workers they will have to reduce the workforce in order to decrease production. The alternative is to increase prices and risk becoming uncompetitive. It is therefore unsurprising that when an economy enters recession, or worse, a depression, we often see a large increase in unemployment but with wage-rates for those who remain employed staying roughly the same.

The pressure to reduce wages comes from a number of sources, but during a recession it comes from the need to cut costs as a lack of demand pushes down prices to a level where supplying current levels of output becomes unprofitable. Marginal cost now exceeds marginal revenue, as the revenue from selling the firm's output shrinks as supply exceeds demand. As firms decide to lay off workers as a response to the downturn, the unemployed are likely to struggle in their search for new employment and will inevitably receive some form of state welfare to maintain subsistence. It goes without saying that high levels of unemployment will lead to even less spending in the economy, as the unemployed receive less income through state welfare compared to those who remained employed. This works only to exacerbate the situation, as it reduces demand further, leading to further job cuts and so the spiral continues. It is therefore argued that during times of recession and when wages are sticky downwards, unemployment and economic contraction are likely to worsen further. Sticky wages are however only an issue in the short-run when firms have to make quick decisions as a result of a sudden shock in the economy. Recent trends in the labour market show a greater move towards flexible labour, where workers' hours are not guaranteed and basic employment rights do not apply. This means workers not being guaranteed the minimum wage in some cases, whilst others may earn the minimum wage at the hourly rate, but are not offered sufficient hours to maintain subsistence. This all means lower wages through the backdoor, not necessarily for existing employees but new employees taking less generous contracts. This is a more recent development, and there are some promising signs that these recent trends may be reversed. For short term shocks however, the problem of wage stickiness applies.

The answer to how a cooperative economy would fare against similar circumstances has already been alluded to in Chapter 8. Pencavel *et al* (2006) and Burdín and Dean (2009) note that during times of recession, worker cooperatives are more likely to reduce workers hours and salaries rather than issue redundancies. There is a coercive incentive for worker to keep their own employment and a moral incentive to keep employment levels maintained overall. In addition, workers are perhaps less hostile towards pay cuts compared to conventional firms. For such conventional firms, labour costs must be reduced in order to maintain a suitable level of profit for its investors. There is no incentive for workers to agree to voluntarily reduce their pay in order to maintain the profits of their masters. This is why the firm resorts to redundancies, as it is seemingly preferable to make a small number of workers redundant rather than decreasing the morale of all workers by cutting their pay.

Under worker ownership however, the firm can adjust to lower demand by collectively reducing hours worked or salaries earned in order to avoid this. They are essentially reducing labour costs in order to maintain their own future incomes rather than the profits of investors. On a macroeconomic scale this means that during an economic shock, rather than unemployment increasing and economic contraction worsening, instead wages are likely to be reduced slightly whilst employment remains stable.

Growth is still likely to take a further hit in the cooperative case, as lower wages means less disposable income for worker-members. This sacrifice, however, is certainly preferable over wide scale unemployment and the much larger effect on growth this will have. The ability of worker-owned firms to be able to adjust their labour costs to changing economic circumstances is a unique quality rarely found in any other business type. For many firms, labour is the largest input cost. Having the ability to adjust this with the consent of those affected – for better or for worse – is surely another competitive advantage worker-owned firms have over their conventional capitalist counterparts.

One particular case where wages alter on a regular basis is due to changes in the cost of living. Consider an example where inflation has increased relative to wages. If on a macroeconomic level, capitalist firms decide to respond to inflation by increasing wages, paid for by raising its prices, the workers will not technically be receiving a wage increase, as everything those workers purchase with their wages has now become more. This is called a wage-price spiral, where prices are constantly increasing to pay for higher wages, and wages are constantly increasing to pay for higher prices. The only way to stop the spiral is for either workers to accept a lower wage or for firms to accept higher labour costs and become potentially unprofitable. The sticky wage mechanism makes this even more difficult to crack. Under a cooperative economy such inflationary spirals are still likely to occur. If inflation suddenly increases, workers may decide to increase their prices in order to maintain their wage rates, and so the spiral begins. There is one additional factor that must also be considered. Workers in a worker-owned firm not only receive wages, they also receive a dividend which is paid out at regular intervals, most likely annually. Meade (1972) gives a good summary of Vanek's analysis.

> But Professor Vanek argues that at the same time it may be much easier in a
> Co-operative system to avoid a continuing upward inflation of money prices,
> since there can in a Co-operative economy ex hypothesi be no simple
> straightforward wage-cost inflation. Workers take what money earnings are left

over after the firm has conducted its operations; they do not set money wage
rates on which employers construct their cost prices.

Meade (1972:414)

Knowing which rate to increase wages by is simple when incomes are pre-determined for the year. If inflation is running at 2 per cent it makes sense to increase wages by 2 per cent in order to keep the value of your earnings equal. Dividends throw all this into the air. As we have previously mentioned, there is an interdependent relationship between wages and dividends. Workers can choose a higher wage at the expense of lower dividends, or can choose lower wages but with higher dividends. Both options should ideally give workers the same figure. However, workers cannot know with any great certainty how high their dividend payments will be at the end of the year, as this depends on how financially successful the company is that year. Forecasting total income per head thus becomes more difficult, especially compared to workers in capitalist firms, whose wages are fixed and stable for at least that year. Also, if workers are earning above subsistence and competitors keep their prices stable, we may see no initial desire for worker-owned firms to rise prices in response to higher inflation. The incentive to do so will only become apparent if competitors begin to rise their prices or if workers' total incomes are below what they were last year with inflation taken into account. All of this makes inflationary spirals more difficult to take hold, not impossible by any means, but certainly less simple.

The ability of workers to be able to adjust their wages, and democratically determine the future of their firm more generally, means a reduced role for trade unions. Trade unions are traditionally seen as a way of matching the bargaining power of employers when it comes to issues such as wage determination, job retention and working conditions. They are firmly apart of the mechanism which prevent wages from lowering during times of recession. Unions also aim to increase wages for existing members, even if this means potentially preventing the firm from being able to afford to employ more workers. Despite the many advantages of trade unions in a conventional capitalist economy, for a worker-owned firm there is clearly no need for worker-members to join a trade union, at least in their current form, as the role of employees and employer have now combined. The obsolescence of trade unions in their current capacity should not necessarily mean an end to trade unions in any instance. Indeed there is scope for unions to change their purpose and remain relevant in a cooperative economy. Unions could take up an advisory role, offering guidance on how to deal with internal disputes and legal issues, or to advise upon how to improve accountability and managerial methods. Rather than dealing with disputes between employer and employee, unions could tailor their services for inter-worker disputes within a particular firm should existing structures to deal with these issues breaks down. As we noted back in Chapter 5, smaller worker-owned firms may not have the capacity or resources to deal with internal disputes, this would be perfect opportunity for trade unions to fill the void. Of course, the role of trade unions is unlikely to change for the public sector within a cooperative state, where there is still a distinct separation between employee and employer.

Concluding Remarks

The macroeconomics of employee ownership on a national scale clearly shows some distinct differences compared to the conventional capitalist model we have all become accustomed to. It is important to remain clear that the assumptions made in this chapter are not set in stone, they are all based on relatively well-known concepts within both modern and traditional economic theory. The results we find are quite impressive. The pre-distribution of profits from investors to workers will undoubtedly affect spending habits. If the theory holds true, in that those with smaller incomes tend to spend (rather than save) additional income more so than the rich, then we would expect to see a shift towards higher aggregate demand in the economy. Higher demand leads to higher growth, higher employment and a larger tax base. Although less of the distributed profits are being saved away, we should not expect to see a reduction in investment due to the nature of contemporary banking methods, the use of alternative financial products like bonds and the ease of capital movement between countries. In fact, we should actually expect to see investment levels remain fairly similar between capitalist and cooperative systems regardless of whether the demand for capital is high or low. The incentive dynamic shows how workers are more willing to engage with the research and development processes of the firm, especially when it comes to the fostering of small-scale innovations in the production and delivery process. A cooperative economy should be a more innovative and engaging economy. A cooperative economy should also see less volatility when it comes to unemployment, as workers adjust working hours and wages to account for changes in the economy.

Economics, we must not forget, is a social science. Changes in the economy can rarely be predicted with any real certainty, and when predictions do come true, it is often with a heavy and hearty dosage of luck, coincidence and other unexplainable causes. Although we may know the likely theoretical effects of the changes we make to our economic system, it remains impossible to know all the likely effects and consequences in reality. Jumping to conclusions that transitioning to a cooperative economy will boost growth and innovation and stabilise employment may be justified in an economy where everything remains constant. In reality, other things are likely to change around us at an immeasurable rate. A transition from conventional capitalism to worker ownership will see little if any improvements to growth, wages and employment if coupled with a recession, war, major environmental collapse or some other disruptive force. Indeed, this chapter has assumed that economic growth is a benefit. Considering the vast ecological destruction and irreversible impacts of climate change that are likely to befall the planet, this assumption should be taken with an earthy pinch of salt. Perhaps as Kate Raworth (2017) suggests in *Doughnut Economics,* we should be agnostic about growth and instead focus on the real-world factors that affect people's daily lives. Raworth's (2017) appraisal of employee ownership demonstrates that this business model is not at odds with the 'doughnut' approach of tackling inequality within our ecological boundaries. Whether we take the ignorance of conventional economic thinking or the enlightening insights of contemporary economic thought, worker ownership scores well with both. Not all policy proposals in the field of economics enjoy this privilege; the point now is to decide whether we want to make that idea a reality.

---

[68] For those struggling to get by, any extra income may actually be saved rather than spent. This money could be used to pay off an unexpected bill for example. Although this money is being saved it is likely to be spent in the short run (within the space of year), and so this will still count as spending rather than saving. Savings are usually considered money saved for the medium to long run, of at least a year.

[69] Stiglitz references the following: Karen E. Dynan, Jonathan Skinner, and Stephen P. Zeldes, "*Do the Rich Save More?*," Journal of Political Economy 112, no. 2 (2004): 397–444.

[70] See http://www.livingwage.org.uk/what-living-wage-annual-salary

[71] See https://www.ons.gov.uk/employmentandlabourmarket/peopleinwork/earningsandworkinghours

[72] See https://www.ons.gov.uk/economy/investmentspensionsandtrusts/bulletins/ownershipofukquotedshares/2015-09-02

[73] See above

[74] See above

[75] See above

[76] See https://www.gov.uk/government/uploads/system/uploads/attachment_data/file/559219/bpe_2016_statistical_release.pdf

[77] See above

[78] See above

[79] See http://positivemoney.org/how-money-works/banking-101-video-course/

[80] Indeed, the only limits on the amount of money banks can create depends on banks being willing to lend to one another in the inter-bank lending market, and if not, then that all banks are roughly creating the same amount of money at the same time. A bank will only require additional savings to invest if the inter-bank lending market crashes or if they create too much money relative to other banks and those other banks refuse to lend to it.

[81] Other economists, such as 'modern money theorists', argue that a government which issues its own

currency will spend what it sees fit regardless of the tax revenue it receives. Tax, they argue, is simply a means of maintaining the money supply (controlling inflation) and ensuring there is demand for the very currency they issue (citizens can only pay tax in the currency the government issues). See L. Randall Wray's (2010) *Modern Money Theory: A Primer on Macroeconomics for Sovereign Monetary Systems*.

82 If this were to be replicated across the economy, one may begin to see the emergence of a 'post-work' society, where highly advanced technologies are capable of producing goods and services with little human effort. This does pose one important question. A post-work society would require consumers with the adequate incomes needed to purchase these auto-produced goods and services. If said consumers do not work, or do not work enough, how could they afford to purchase these commodities? In this circumstance, an entirely new economic system would be required. This is, however, purely speculative, and a discussion for another time.

Chapter 10: The International Framework

In this section we get to discuss the concept of the cooperative economy in the realm of international economics. This will build upon the reasoning and conclusions proclaimed in the previous chapter, but with the addition of including another interesting fact that must be considered: the fact that any cooperative economy must compete in a world of capitalist economies. By the word 'compete' we are not of course referring to some derogatory cultural or physical conflict between nations. Instead we mean commercial competition between the worker-owned firms of a cooperative economy and the investor-owned firms of the foreign capitalist economies, which in themselves take multiple forms. This means examining the global movement of goods, services, capital, people, technology and ideas, among many other things. Nation-states are increasingly using economic policy as a foreign policy instrument, as such the discussion on international economics is not solely focused on economic matters, geopolitical priorities must also be considered.

International Trade and Labour

Examining international trade and labour together, rather than separately, may seem to be rather unconventional at first. We must, however, be mindful that these two factors have a very important link, the protection of jobs is often used as an excuse for reining-in free trade. Let us first examine the benefits of free trade in normal capitalist economies. It is most widely recognised that nations export commodities where they have an abundance of a particular input. Say for example, a nation that has a large and successful dairy industry is more likely to export milk, cheese and other dairy made products. Whereas nations tend to import goods where there is a scarcity of inputs. For example a country which has yet to industrialise is more likely to import manufactured goods, such as cars. Of course 'inputs' can mean a variety of things, such as raw materials, land, labour, etc. A country with an abundance of skilled labour is likely to export goods that require high skilled labour to make them. A country with little arable land is more likely to import food products, as there is little capacity for producing such commodities internally.

If a nation has an abundance of something, we call it an 'advantage'. We can then split these advantages into two types; comparative advantages and competitive advantages. Comparative advantages are abundances of natural factors, such as arable land, fossil fuels, a tropical climate, a colder climate. For example, countries with a hotter climate are more likely to export tropical fruits, and import goods from colder climates, such as grains for example. Competitive advantages however are man-made advantages, high skilled labour for example. Countries that invest in skills and training are more likely to go onto trade goods that require those skills. Countries with a well-established car industry are more likely to export those cars, as other nations do not have the capacity to produce cars as efficiency or to the same quality. As a result of these factors, it is argued that countries should stick to producing what they hold a comparative and competitive advantage in, and not try to emulate the advantages of other countries. A closed economy (one which does not trade internationally) has no choice but to produce everything that country needs whether they are efficient at producing it or not. An open economy on the other hand (one which does trade internationally) can focus on producing solely on what they are efficient at producing, and import the goods they cannot produce efficiently. As we have discussed before, when goods can be produced more efficiently, it means lower prices for the consumer. Therefore, if every country focuses on what they are most efficient at producing, the prices of all commodities will decrease; this is the main argument in favour of free trade.

> If a foreign country can supply us with a commodity cheaper than we ourselves can make it, better buy it of them with some part of the produce of our own industry employed in a way in which we have some advantage.

Smith (1776:350)

So what is the alternative to free trade? The most extreme option is to become a closed economy where there is no international trade, but as we have found this means a country producing commodities they are not efficient at producing, leading to higher prices for consumers. A softer approach is to introduce barriers to trade, there are policies that make it (artificially) harder to import foreign goods or to make those goods more expensive. Deterring consumers from buying foreign goods can influence customers to stick to domestic products that would otherwise be more expensive. These barriers can include everything from import tariffs (taxes on imported goods), import licenses, import quotas, increased regulation and paperwork for importers, for example.

So why deter imports? If imports enable lower prices for consumers, what's the catch? The catch primarily comes down to jobs. If foreign companies start to produce and sell commodities for a cheaper price compared to domestic firms, those domestic firms are unlikely to compete. If they cannot compete, the firm goes bust. If this happens on a major scale, across an industry which a large portion of the population depends upon for employment, there are likely to be significant challenges. Large scale unemployment, reduced tax revenue and a swelling of government spending for the unemployed are among a few of these likely consequences. The foreign competition may even stem from a domestic firm. For example a domestic car manufacturer may relocate to a foreign nation where there are lower labour costs[83], and where they can then sell those cars for cheaper in the domestic economy. If this were the case, the remaining car manufacturers in the domestic economy may not be able to compete, having to lay off their workers and cease production, or perhaps take a decision to move abroad themselves. As a result, rather than finding new markets to develop a comparative/competitive advantage in, uncompetitive firms can lobby for governments to add barriers to trade to artificially increase the prices of imports. By doing this, the prices of inefficient domestic firms will be cheaper than the prices of the more efficient firms overseas. This means a number of jobs are saved, but all consumers have to pay a higher price for the same commodity. This endpoint is known as a dead weight loss, as more lose out from tariffs than win. This is without mentioning that if the government of our domestic economy adds tariffs onto the products of a particular foreign economy, the government of that foreign country may retaliate by introducing tariffs on the exports of our domestic economy, leading to fewer sales and fewer jobs in the sectors which export. Again, more lose out than gain.

> In every country it always is and must be the interest of the great body of the people to buy whatever they want of those who sell it cheapest. ... it is the interest of the merchants and manufacturers of every country to secure to themselves the monopoly of the home market. Hence, in Great Britain, and in most other European countries, the extraordinary duties upon almost all goods imported by alien merchants. Hence the high duties and prohibitions upon all those foreign manufactures which can come into competition with our own.
>
> Smith (1776:380)

This is the conventional theory. We must, however, look at all things 'capitalist' from the perspective of the dual-contradiction. We must also look at the realities of free trade and how it differs from the theory. Firstly, for uncompetitive domestic firms, simply shifting from an industry where they no longer hold a comparative/competitive advantage to a new industry where they can gain these advantages, is for the most part, easier said than done. Where an entire sector is no longer competitive, this transformation becomes even harder. There have been many cases across the developed world where well paid manufacturing jobs have left and relocated to countries where labour costs are cheaper. In many cases, those communities which lost those jobs have since never recovered. The loss of income and the degeneration of communities creates a difficult environment for new industries to be established and nourished, let alone establish an international competitive advantage. We must also remind ourselves that the primary purpose of a conventional capitalist firm is not naturally to maximise employment, but instead to maximise shareholder value for its investor-owners. Of course, no one should argue that protecting dying industries from the inevitable is a productive way forward. A firm that does not or cannot produce goods or services consumers want to buy, whether it be capitalist owned or worker-owned, should not expect to survive in a fully functioning market economy. This is not particularly controversial. There is however, a case for questioning whether companies are seeking the right or best competitive advantages. Or more specifically, whether a worker-owned firm holds the potential for alternative comparative/competitive advantages that lead to different outcomes compared to the capitalist type.

Where a cooperative economy functions as an open economy, which it should, the market dynamic and principal balance must also be intact. By this we mean that worker-owned firms are able to produce goods and services that can be sold abroad, and secondly, that these goods and services are competitive, both in terms of other domestic competitors or competition from foreign companies. Of course, the foreign competitors are most likely to be conventional capitalist firms. Worker-owned firms must therefore compete both with other worker-owned firms, capitalist firms or any other type of firm that exhibits the dual-contradiction. How these different types of firm operate in an international marketplace stems from the profit principle: the difference between wishing to maximise total profit for the company or wishing to maximise income per head for the workers. Most of the consequences of this distinction have already been discussed in chapters 6, 7 and 8. We will discuss the situation of labour, capital and output for an open cooperative economy operating in a globalised marketplace later on. There is however, one other important distinction regarding the profit principle and how this relates to trade and employment more generally. This distinction is quite a simple one: worker-owned firms are less likely to relocate abroad. The main purpose of a worker-owned firm is to maximise income per head for its workers and to maintain levels of employment. It therefore would make little sense for the workers to make themselves redundant and essentially donate the company and all of its assets to a group of workers in a foreign country. Such a situation taking hold is wildly unrealistic, especially as worker-members require a subsistence income. A conventional capitalist firm –

which seeks to maximise total profits for its investor-owners – has a remunerative incentive to lay-off its workforce and relocate abroad if the labour costs are cheaper and higher rates of profit can be achieved. For worker ownership this could not be the case. Indeed, worker-owned firms may decide to expand abroad to take advantage of cheaper labour costs, but they would not make themselves redundant in order to do so.

Our cooperative state must ensure that any domestic worker-owned firm that establishes divisions abroad must also ensure that any foreign workers employed hold the same membership rights as domestic employees. The domestic workers of a worker-owned firm should not be able to establish a sweatshop-styled operation in a foreign country and exploit the workers in a similar manner exhibited by many conventional capitalist firms. The workers in a foreign division must be worker-members in the same respect as the domestic workers. If both domestic and foreign workers have the same voting rights in the firms, which of course they should, both can remain accountable to each other. The foreign workers should not allow themselves to be exploited by the domestic workers, and any surpluses should be distributed fairly and reflective of effort applied. A cooperative state should also encourage domestic firms to examine their supply chains more generally. A worker-owned firm purchasing inputs that were produced on wholly unethical grounds, such as child labour practises or deforestation for example, cannot be tolerated. Similar to their own affairs, firms must find a principal balance when searching for suppliers, a balance between applying ethical principles and maintaining competitiveness. Although worker-owned firms may wish to purchase inputs from other worker-owned firms abroad, they need to ensure that such a move is competitive and affordable. On the flip side, firms need to remain competitive, but this is no blank cheque to violate the company's principles.

If we return to a hypothetical example where a worker-owned firm decides to expand abroad in order to take advantage of lower labour costs, where does this leave the domestic workers? This would of course depend on what the new foreign workers would be doing. If both domestic and foreign workers were undertaking the same or very similar roles, an inevitable issue is likely to emerge over the medium to long run. Under the capitalist business model, the domestic workers would likely be made redundant, as the foreign workers can undertake these roles for cheaper. Under worker ownership however, workers must take a gamble. If the workers need to expand abroad to take advantage of lower labour costs to remain competitive, the new workers abroad could vote to dismiss the original workers if they outnumber them and have determined that there is no longer a financial case for retaining the original workers. If the income per head of the foreign workers would rise as a result on this, the remunerative incentive is there to do so. Alternatively, the original workers may instead decide to avoid this altogether by not expanding abroad, and instead decide to continue production domestically. However, this option runs the risk of the firm no longer remaining competitive. Either way, the original workers lose their jobs. Both unfavourable outcomes are due to the same problem: it is no longer competitive for the domestic workers to continue to operate the way they do. Something must change. The principal balance compels worker-owned firms to remain competitive, even if this means making difficult choices. This pressure to remain competitive nudges worker-owned firms into finding new competitive advantages. Rather than simply being dismissed and left to fend for themselves, as often observed under conventional capitalism, domestic workers can use the infrastructure of their firm to make their current production more efficient and productive, or can invest in new products in new markets. If there is still a worthwhile opportunity to expand into countries with lower labour costs, this can still go ahead. The only difference being the original workers need to change their purpose within the firm, thereby remaining essential to its survival and future. The original workers may decide to outsource the more labour intensive aspects of production overseas, whilst investing in the more capital intensive aspects of production at home. The domestic workers may decide to specialise in the more technical or specialist aspects of production. This could mean retraining, gaining entirely new skills altogether, or simply modernising existing skills. It will all depend on the context.

Erdal (2011) discusses the case of Tullis Russell, a firm formally owned by his family which converted to employee ownership in 1994. Tullis Russell is a coating, laminating and converting company based in the UK. The firm originally produced decal paper in the UK, but during the 1990s and 2000s British mills began to close as South Korea gained a competitive advantage in this industry. Erdal (2011) discusses how the company decided to shift its decal paper milling operations from its original British plant in Stoke-on-Trent to new operation in Korea.

> When one of the Korean decal paper producers went bankrupt in 2002, the Tullis Russell team of decal business managers convinced the board that they should acquire the Korean company. It was clear to everyone that the Stoke-on-Trent plant would be affected, probably drastically. ... There was a long discussion. But the situation did not come as a surprise to the employees ... The employees in Stoke could see what was happening around them – they had witnessed the gradual closure of almost all their major customers. And they were involved in the plans to develop new products: they were already

experimenting with coating different types of paper for different industries. With this full understanding of the strategic position of the business, they joined colleagues in voting 100 per cent in favour of the acquisition.

Erdal (2011:80-81)

The Stoke plant would eventually close, but due to the success of their experiments with new products, new investments were made in the remaining UK plant in nearby Bollington. As a result, many of the former Stoke workers were retrained for new jobs. Redundancies did occur, but the overall viability of the firm was protected and employment remained for many of the original workers. This case study shows a capability for the worker-owned firm to adapt to changing economic climates whilst prioritising the needs of its employee-owners. What the firm does not do however, is simply abandon its original workers and leave their communities to economic and social ruin. Instead, the firm gives provides the original workers with a fighting chance to change and adapt. Not all will succeed in taking this gamble, but it is certainly an improvement over the alternative arrangements frequently undertaken by conventional capitalist firms. By the same token, we should not feel guilt in offshoring production to nations with lower labour costs. Let us not forget, worker ownership increases workers' incomes and wellbeing wherever they are. The prospect of workers in foreign capitalist economies being given the opportunity to work for a worker-owned firm – which could considerably increase their incomes – is likely to be received more positively compared to the arrival of a corporate capitalist firm with an exploitative disposition. Employee ownership is a win-win for both sides. The foreign workers receive dividends on top of their wages and domestic workers remained employed with a newfound relevance to the firm's future.

Worker ownership across international boundaries is also likely to contribute towards fairer gains of free trade. When domestic capitalist firms relocate abroad, there is no benefit to the workers they leave behind. It is unlikely these workers will be shareholders of these relocating firms. Even if they are, they may find themselves needing to sell those shares in preparing for the financial hardships of unemployment. On the other side of the equation, when a foreign capitalist company arrives, so does the dual-contradiction, along with the added insult to injury as profits are typically syphoned off to the firm's country of origin, or perhaps even a foreign tax-haven. The perception of being cheated is amplified when capitalism goes global. Jobs are lost in the domestic economy, and an intensified variant of the dual-contradiction arrives in the foreign economy. This need not be the case. Worker ownership links work with reward, regardless of which side of an international border a worker happens to find themselves on. With the profit principle in motion, any relocation or expansion of a worker-owned firm abroad must be either to sustain or increase the income per head of the original workers. In addition, the new foreign workers are only likely to take employment at these firms if they expect to witness their standard of living improving as a result, especially if they are surrounded by conventional capitalist firms who may seek to exploit them. Worker ownership can be a key instrument of withering away the perception that globalisation creates more losers than winners. As with the free market more generally, it is not free trade itself that creates inequality, it's how free trade functions, who benefits from it and who does not.

International Labour and Migration

For the domestic labour market, the main international effect of transitioning to a cooperative economy will be the effect on immigration. Although we have discussed the supply and demand elements of labour before, we have yet to discuss what happens when the supply of labour increases or decreases relative to demand. I have saved this discussion for now, as it has an unmistakable relevance to our discussion on international processes. In the short to medium run, the main cause of a decrease in labour supply would be emigration - workers leaving the domestic economy to live and possibly work abroad. On the other hand the main cause of an excess of supply would be immigration - foreign workers entering the domestic economy in search of work. If you subtract the total emigration figure by the immigration figure you are left with the 'net migration' figure. Net migration tells you if more people are entering or leaving a particular territory, and from here we can see how this affects labour supply[84].

The supply of foreign workers depends on migration policy, which we shall assume is relatively open and flexible. This assumption is based on the earlier assumption that a cooperative economy should embrace free trade, along with the observation that many modern trade agreements include provisions to loosen migration rules between the signatories. The demand for foreign workers will depend on whether there are candidates for jobs with the right skills available domestically. If not, worker-owned firms will require foreign worker-members to join up. This is no different to the demands faced by capitalist firms. There is, however, one notable distinction when moving towards worker ownership. Now that workers earn dividends on top of their wages, there may be an added incentive for foreign workers in capitalist countries to immigrate to the cooperative state in order to reap the benefits of worker ownership. This incentive, if combined with flexible migration policy, could lead to higher levels of immigration which could artificially increase labour supply relative to demand.

If there are more suitable candidates to choose from as a result of higher immigration, worker-owned firms are no longer required to offer higher wage rates to new members. It could be proclaimed that lower labour costs may be irrelevant, as whatever a prospective worker loses in reduced wages offered by the firm, they gain back in dividends. This of course depends on how dividends are distributed. If dividends are distributed as a percentage of wages, the lower the wage the lower the dividend, meaning more profit is left to distribute to the remaining workers with higher salaries and thus higher dividends[85]. The same is true in reverse. A lack of suitable workers, due to high levels of emigration for example, is likely to firms offering new workers a higher wage. Higher wages will impact on the income per head of the remaining workers, perhaps removing the incentive to employ in the first place. It is therefore in the interest of all workers that supply and demand of labour should not vary too much from the ordinary. If migration is too high, it may push down wages for new workers, whether they be domestic or migrant workers. On the flip side, if migration is too low and the working population starts to shrink, this may either remove the incentives to employ or significantly lower income per head for the remaining workers. Firms need a suitable number of suitable candidates to apply for employment opportunities, preferably at a wage that suits both the new worker and the existing workers. A balance must be found.

Freedom of movement between nations should be a fundamental obligation of an open globalised economy. The incentives that draw foreign workers to cooperative economies must be perceived with caution. In modern times, immigration has become a politically emotive issue. However, it requires sound mind and rational thinking. The idea of worker ownership and the concept of the cooperative economy must be exported wherever possible, as this will prevent brain drains and prevent an artificial exodus of those rightfully seeking a better standard of living. There is a case for restricting immigration if there is a strong likelihood that open migration policy will lead to an excess of labour supply[86]. As we would not expect to tolerate the dumping of goods and services to lower prices below the cost of production, we therefore should also not tolerate an over-supply of labour to disrupt the labour market to a damaging extent. As we know, markets are not perfect, they must be monitored and nudged every so often. The same is true of labour markets. Freedom of movement must be permitted to allow for an effective labour market, but we should not be hostile towards implementing restrictions when there is evidence of an excess of supply.

Freedom of movement may be more practical between cooperative economies where the standard of living is similar in both countries.

There are social and cultural elements of immigration we have not touched upon. The desire to increase immigration can transform communities for the better, although this can materialise at a pace some find uncomfortable. Many populist movements seek to restrict immigration, but ignore the economic consequences and potential social benefits. Worker ownership gives workers control of the company they work for. If their company requires immigrants to fill job gaps, they are now more likely to favour immigration. Under conventional capitalism, where workers are not in control, higher immigration may be perceived as a threat to jobs and living standards. Worker ownership now puts migration into greater economic perspective. Giving workers control of their workplaces and engaging them the realities of running a business is likely to lead to better political choices and outcomes. Internationally, this may help to put a more rational, realistic and hopefully humane face on the effects of migration.

International Capital

Like goods, services and to some extent labour, capital is freely able to enter and exit the majority of economies across the globe. Foreign money is invested in everything from housing, to gold, to stocks and shares, currencies, etc. As we explored in the previous chapter, the majority of shares (by measure of value) in UK listed companies are owned by foreign bodies and individuals. Of course, what we are most interested in is the relationship between foreign investment and worker ownership. In our cooperative economy, it will not be possible for foreign investors, or domestic investors for that matter, to buy shares of worker-owned firms. Like domestic investors, they are still able to invest in worker-owned firms but this cannot intrude upon ownership rights and the management and control of the enterprise. In Chapter 7 we detailed the opportunity of expanding the use of bond markets to replace the role and function of stock markets. In this scenario, foreign investors could purchase the bonds released by worker-owned firms, but cannot expect a stake in ownership or control.

Any cooperative state must ensure investment does not become more difficult to facilitate. Different means of investment could put off some investors who are unfamiliar with worker ownership or corporate bonds. However, there are certain incentives that foreign investors may have to invest in a worker-owned firm rather than a conventional capitalist firm. Bonds, as we know, offer a fixed or semi-flexible rate of return guaranteed to investors. This may be preferred over investing in stocks, which have the inherent potential to lose all of their value, meaning investors lose all their capital. Bonds are a more stable and certain means of investment. Secondly, investors may find more appeal in companies where the workers have a direct incentive to make that company as successful and profitable as possible. The same cannot be said for conventional capitalist firms. Investors are more likely to invest their capital in companies, and more importantly people, they trust. Profits and rates of return are important, but having a real human connection and relationship with those who work within the firm is just as imperative. All in all, we should expect to see little change in the quantity of foreign investment in a cooperative economy compared to a capitalist economy. The losses in investment from those who are apprehensive about investing in a company with alternative ownership and management arrangements should, at a minimum, be cancelled out by those who see the direct benefits of investing in such firms. We should not expect to see too much variation. Nonetheless, our cooperative state must embrace and attract foreign direct investment to ensure that worker-owned firms have ample opportunities to find investors and access the necessary investment they need to grow and prosper.

Worker Ownership in a Capitalist World

Any foreign company setting themselves up in our cooperative economy must comply with the rules of worker ownership. If a foreign company is to be established internally within the cooperative economy, worker ownership must still be in effect. There are multiple alternative arrangements foreign firms can take to establish themselves in a cooperative economy without holding direct ownership or management. The most obvious arrangement would be to introduce a form of franchising. A franchise is simply the right to be able to use a company's brand and business model. A classic example of this would be fast-food franchises such as McDonald's, who are responsible for producing their products but are not responsible for selling them. McDonald's restaurants are owned by franchisees: independent investor-owners who invest their own money to set up a store, use McDonalds' branding and business model, and sell their products. The franchisee then provides an agreed share of the proceeds to the franchisor. This is already a common method for companies seeking to enter foreign markets.

For a foreign enterprise to establish themselves within a cooperative economy, they must establish a worker-owned enterprise under their name. The worker-owners of this new firm still own and manage their enterprise, as would any other worker-owned firm, however they are not totally separate and independent of the foreign capitalist firm. The worker-owned subsidiary/franchise may have to negotiate certain terms with the foreign firm, for example on the quantity of goods and services to be produced, the cost of production, the sell price, etc. On the upside this gives workers access to patents, popular brand names and experienced advice on how to produce or sell. Having to negotiate with a larger company with higher bargaining power is not ideal, but it does provide tangible benefits workers may not receive if they started an independent firm on their own. The workers could also decide not to continue their franchise with the larger firm if subsequent negotiations are unsuccessful, meaning the worker-owned firm can run independently or perhaps choose a different franchisor. In addition, foreign firms may wish to enter the cooperative economy without necessarily establishing a new subsidiary. Rather than getting involved in the start-up of new ventures abroad, companies wishing to expand abroad into a cooperative economy could simply offer contracts to existing worker-owned firms who can produce or sell the foreign firm's products. Highly developed economies already accommodate diverse supply chains, where the multiple components of a final saleable product are produced across the globe and produced by many different companies. It is rare in modern times to observe large companies which produce and assemble all of their inputs themselves. Worker-owned firms bidding and winning the contracts of capitalist firms is not a new phenomenon. Mondragon for example has previously accepted a contract to manufacture car components for large foreign capitalist corporations.

Franchising and contracting may appear to be somewhat inferior alternatives compared to conventional ownership and control by the parent company, but this of course ignores the benefits of worker ownership. Foreign firms tapping into worker ownership should expect to see better results, through higher quality, productivity and innovation. The workers now have an incentive to know and understand the products foreign companies wish to obtain or sell. There is an added element of care and interest the foreign firm would struggle to find elsewhere. In an ideal world, these foreign firms would also be worker-owned, but in a highly globalised capitalist marketplace, worker-owned firms must accept that the dual-contradiction is to remain undisturbed in some form or another within the foreign firms they deal with.

Although these alternative ownership and management arrangements may at first appear odd to a foreign capitalist firm unfamiliar with worker ownership, there is still great scope for foreign enterprises to invest and expand in a cooperative economy. Indeed, as discussed with investment earlier, our cooperative state should encourage foreign firms to set themselves up and take advantage of the benefits worker ownership has to offer. If anything, it may entice these firms to experiment with types of worker ownership back home. Although we have advocated for full worker ownership and control, any movement towards greater worker ownership in foreign nations, particularly where this may otherwise be more difficult to achieve, should always be welcomed when applicable and sustainable.

Concluding Remarks

The effects of a single economy switching from capitalist to worker ownership is unlikely to change all that much in the greater/global scheme of things. The effects on our hypothetical cooperative economy however reveals some interesting developments. Having control of the company gives workers greater protection against some of the more disruptive elements of globalisation. Worker-owned firms are more likely to anchor themselves in their local and regional economies, where workers are less likely to pack their bags and shift their whole operation abroad. Foreign expansion should be welcomed, as this can benefit both the domestic and foreign workers as well as exporting the ideals of worker-ownership abroad. The workers of employee-owned firms which begin to face tight competition from more competitive firms abroad are given a longer opportunity to experiment in new markets, or find a new place to become competitive within an existing market. The 'cut and run' approach of the conventional capitalist firm leaves their workers, or former workers, unable to develop new skills, to find new markets, or to develop new competitive advantages. Other impacts of worker ownership from globalisation include greater flows of migrants seeking to take advantage of higher incomes and improved wellbeing. As we have acknowledged, some form of freedom of movement is essential for the supply and demand of labour in a globalised economy. However, this should not justify an excess of labour that distorts the economy. All else being equal, levels of financial investment, and flows of international trade in goods and services, should not alter greatly as a result of switching to worker ownership on a national scale.

---

[83] One might rightfully ask how some countries have cheaper labour costs than others. This is largely because the means of subsistence (food for example) in these countries is comparatively cheaper. This is because they are likely to have the comparative or competitive advantages that allow them to produce the means of subsistence for much cheaper. As we have noted multiple times, the wages employees receive are often linked to the value of the basic necessities of life.

[84] Labour supply can also be affected by what happens domestically. For example if there is another 'baby boom' where the birth rate suddenly increases, this is likely to increase the supply of labour in future, perhaps in 18 years or so when they are ready to join the labour market and start work for the first time. For the most part however, large and sudden shifts in labour supply are most likely to come from migration.

[85] This practice could not be sustainable if the majority of workers were on a lower wage, as they would simply vote against it. However this practise is a real possibility for a minority of newer

workers.

86 Immigration can be managed through various methods. Governments could simply set national limits on net migration, perhaps giving preference to those with job approvals or certain desired skills. Alternatively, governments could allow local communities to set local/regional quotas, ensuring that there is scope for additional migrants in areas with insufficient labour supply whilst limiting settlement in areas with an excessive supply of labour. The practicality of this system however, remains an important question – what would stop migrants moving between regions upon arrival?

Chapter 11: Why Now?

Policy-makers across the political spectrum are acknowledging the potential of employee ownership in public and private sectors. But sentiment alone will not realise that potential. ... Like any business model, employee ownership is most likely to flourish if the right architecture is in place.

Lampel et al (2010:3)

As the reader may have rightfully speculated, this is not the first time an author has advocated for worker ownership on a grand scale such as this. This beggars two questions: if a cooperative economy is such a worthy proposal, why has it never emerged before and; why should it emerge now? If worker-owned firms are a superior business model, why are they currently so uncommon? All of these are relevant and respectable questions to ask, and all require a solid credible answer. Of course, nothing in human affairs is caused by one factor alone, this is certainly the case in economics and politics too. As such we shall examine the multitude of reasons why conventional capitalist firms have outnumbered and outmatched worker-owned firms so frequently throughout history. What we are primarily concerned with is why worker ownership has not emerged to dominate capitalist economies in the past, and with this knowledge, use it to explain how a cooperative economy may be able to emerge in future. We will deal firstly with the former.

A Historical Struggle

The First Cooperatives

The 'worker-owned firm' as a business model emerged not long after the birth of industrial capitalism. The Industrial Revolution was a major social and demographic shift, migrating those in rural communities towards the industrial towns and cities. The rise of the machine and steam technology were pivotal catalysts in this process. However, despite the advancement in technology, working conditions and standards of living deteriorated for many of the working poor. Chapter 10 of Marx's (1867) *Capital* serves as a good reminder of the tragedies of early capitalism. Documentation of child labourers having to work 20 hours a day being a prime example. Cooperatives (consumer and worker-owned firms) were an early experiment to counter the detrimental aspects of the industrial capitalist firm without moving backwards technologically. Many hail Robert Owen, Dr William King and Charles Fourier as the fathers of the cooperative movement, but research suggests that firms based on cooperative principles occurred a little earlier. G.D.H Cole's (1944) research into the early days of the cooperative movement makes for interesting reading. Indeed, the first case Cole (1944) explores of the earliest forms of cooperative are particularly telling of the struggles the movement was yet to befall throughout its complex history.

> Its beginnings in Great Britain go back to the middle of the eighteenth century; and its originators, as far as we know, were the workmen employed by the Government in the dockyards of Woolwich and Chatham, who, as early as 1760, had founded corn mills on a Co-operative basis as a move against the high prices charged by the corn-millers who held the local monopoly. These early Societies speedily found themselves in conflict with the private bakers as well as with the millers; and when, in 1760, the Woolwich Mill was burnt down, the local bakers were accused of arson a charge which they rebutted in a statement sworn before the Mayor. To this burning we owe our knowledge of this early Co-operative mill, and also of the mill at Chatham; for we are informed that "the late Accident of burning down the Shipwrights' Mill at Woolwich has put the Shipwright Bakers here [at Chatham] upon their Guard, and all necessary precautions are taken to preserve their Mill from the like Fate, and especially to prevent any malicious Design." The dockyard shipwrights, then, were the pioneers; and Co-operation, as far as we know, began with flour-milling and baking.
>
> Cole (1944:12-13)

This capitalist monopoly of mills was also accused of adding chalk to its flour to cut costs (Thornley, 1981). This was one of the primary reasons the cooperative was established, perhaps as an early form of consumer protection. The sabotage and destruction of these early societies meant they left little historical impact on the cooperative movement. It also demonstrates an early example of how monopoly power can flex its muscles and deal with competition in a destructive manner.

Due to these isolated experiments failing at an early stage, the cooperative movement at the time of the early Industrial Revolution could hardly be considered a 'movement'. One of the first common-known pioneers of the cooperative movement was Robert Owen, a British industrialist who was more successful in implementing his radical ideas to achieve social change during a period of vast industrialisation. Owen's main premise was that giving workers a better working environment can bring them out of desperation and increase productivity. Owen's renowned social experiment was at New Lanark, a small community where workers lived and worked together, and where social provisions such as education and healthcare became universal (Harrison, 1969). Although Owen was a keen advocate of consumer cooperatives, in reality New Lanark, as well as the failed experiment in New Harmony, USA, were little more than isolated communities where workers both produced and sold their products to one another. Of more historical significance was the cooperative established by the Rochdale Pioneers, a group of 28 individuals who started their own consumer cooperative store in 1844. Cole states that "The Rochdale Pioneers themselves set out originally to create, not a mere shop for mutual trading, but a Co-operative Utopia" (1944). The Rochdale Society of Equitable Pioneers (RSEP) was to much extent the first successful consumers' cooperative, whose main importance to the movement was to show that cooperatives could function successfully in a wider society, rather than being confined to isolation like the communities designed by Owen. The reasoning behind Rochdale's symbolism, according to Fairbairn (1994), was due to the heavy presence of Owenites that were already established in Rochdale during this time. The early successes of RSEP helped to manifest a greater cooperative movement, which would eventually form into the Co-operative Wholesale Society, now known as the Co-operative Group.

The First Worker Cooperative?

It is important to remind ourselves that so far our historical analysis has yet to mention worker ownership as a specific business model. Consumer cooperatives were generally the preferred alternative business model to conventional capitalism and state socialism. Historical documentation of the first worker-owned firms are much harder to come by. This is unsurprising however, as worker ownership as a concept has likely changed and evolved over time. There were likely to have been firms in pre-capitalist economies that were started by a small group of individuals who shared the profits and had an equal say in the business. It is unlikely that this concept has only emerged over the last couple of centuries, as state and consumer ownership has.

It is perhaps of more relevance to track the history of worker cooperatives rather than worker-owned firms more generally, as this is where worker management and democratic forms of control on a larger scale began to emerge. This particular form of business model also emerged during the Industrial Revolution and the birth of 'wage labour' – the purchasing of labour-power for productive purposes (hiring an employee). Prior to industrialisation, the working classes had specific skills, such as shoemaking, butchery, baking, etc. They were generally self-employed or in small groups, catering towards local markets and local demand. With industrialisation came the need not for specific crafted skills, but simply the ability to man machinery and conduct tediously basic and often dangerous tasks. Cottage industry and individual craftsmanship were becoming replaced by large industrial firms who employed hundreds of employees. For many, this would be the first time they had ever been employed. This particular point in time is perhaps the best to begin looking into the history of worker ownership, not because this is where it was conceived, but because this is the period where worker ownership was likely to have emerged on a larger industrial scale, large enough to implement the cooperative ideals.

The wider cooperative movement, and worker cooperatives specifically, were born out of two revolutions, the Industrial Revolution as we have mentioned, but also during the time of the Second French Revolution. Mellor *et al* (1988) states how this period witnessed the birth of the worker cooperative model as something similar to what we observe today. Growing industrial strife in 1833 France led to a number of workers setting up their own workshops to compete with the capitalist firms they had just left, almost as a type of strike tactic. Worker takeovers would come and go as the revolutions did, after 1848 and the Paris Commune of 1871. Mellor *et al* (1988:17) states "The cooperative workshops formed in France during the 1830s were echoed in Britain", the first cooperative manufacturing community, producing brushes, appearing in London in 1830 (Holyoake, 1875-9). This is when worker ownership first became a distinct alternative to capitalist ownership, but not as a step backwards into the age of the artisan shopkeepers or as some form of technophobic backlash. The development of the wider cooperative movement gave worker-owned firms an opportunity to embrace the cooperative principles of democracy, equal ownership and free speech.

Marshall (1890) in his *Principles of Economics* discusses many of the benefits worker ownership boasts.

> [T]hey have fairly good means of judging whether the higher work of engineering the business is conducted honestly and efficiently, and they have the best possible opportunities for detecting any laxity or incompetence in its detailed administration. And lastly they render unnecessary some of the minor work of superintendence that is required in other establishments

> Marshall (1890:177)

Despite this, Marshall (1890) goes on to highlight some of the difficulties experienced at the time. He argues that a lack of trust between shop-floor workers and upper management became a major challenge. The rationale seems simple enough. Workers were likely to have been envious of the higher wages earned by the managers, either leading to quarrels or lower wages for the managers. It is because of this, Marshall (1890:177) argues "managers of a co-operative society seldom have the alertness, the inventiveness and the ready versatility", especially compared to the managers of capitalist firms. This being said, no empirical examples are given of when such circumstances have befallen any particular firm.

This is not the case in all early commentaries of worker ownership however. The first worker co-operatives highlighted in Potter's (1904) critique of worker ownership were those established by the Christian Socialists in the early 1850s. Again, these were unequivocal failures primarily due to quarrelling and disputes.

> Within a few years all the London and south country associations of producers [cooperatives], promoted or aided by the Christian Socialists, had either dissolved without trace, or degenerated into the profit-making undertakings of small masters.
>
> Potter (1904:124, comment and bracket added)

The best examples of worker-owned firms that employed a large number of employees and embraced cooperative principles emerged out of the early successes of the consumer cooperative movement. Early debates concerning ownership took place within the Co-operative Wholesale Society (CWS, a consumer cooperative, which considered establishing productive firms of their own to supply their shops.

> In essence, the debate was over who should control such produce cooperatives and how any surplus should be distributed. The choice was between control resting with shareholding, which could be open to all, shareholding restricted to the cooperative societies, shareholding restricted to the workers in the enterprise, or a mixture of the latter two.
>
> Mellor et al (1988:18)

These were more labour intensive enterprises where worker ownership most likely appeared to be the best method of carrying through the cooperative principles into the realm of production. These early worker-owned firms were known as 'producer cooperatives', as these cooperatives were solely designed to produce rather than to sell products to the consumer cooperatives' member-owners. Mellor *et al* (1988:19) claims how a number of worker-owned firms had formed at a similar time to the CWS' producer cooperatives, but these were "little more than conventional companies ... they used cooperation as little more than a cover for dubious profit-sharing schemes and anti-union policies". Thornley (1981:24) notes how from 1855 onwards "the cooperative ideal was drowned in the more modest ambitions among the working class to have a stake in their firms". Profit sharing schemes and were becoming more popular, although short-lived. Companies of this nature had put doubt into the worker cooperative model as a means of upholding the core cooperative ideals.

Worker cooperatives in coal mining and engineering began to emerge, primarily as a response to industrial disputes or the buy-out of failed capitalist firms. These experiments, despite much encouragement from various actors, were also prone to fail. Infighting, inexperienced management and other structural faults ensured that any success was short lived. Cole's (1944) analysis of engineering producer cooperatives around the time of 1873 lays testament to this. In this scenario poor management led to good quality products, but set at prices which were too low, leading to financial difficulty and worker disputes. This case too would go onto taint the worker cooperative model as ineffective, which consequently dried up lending for other producer cooperatives.

Potter (1904:147) sums up her analysis of the failed producer cooperatives by describing the movement as an "indescribable industrial phantom, which, unlike the texture of real existence, becomes more and more imperceptible with the application of the magnifying glass". Clearly she was unimpressed. Potter (1904) proclaims that the inability to procure financial capital, commercial inexperience and a lack of discipline are the main reasons why worker ownership simply could not work. Throughout this research we have carefully laid out the theoretical concepts and processes that would prevent all three of these issues taking shape. As Oakeshott (1980:47) puts it, "historically most workers' co-ops have suffered from various specific but theoretically avoidable handicaps". As we shall see a little later, modern developments show how these handicaps are even less likely to take shape today. One suspects that Potter's opinions are more driven by ideology than empirical fact[87]. Admittedly, the worker cooperatives of this period were mostly failures, but to object to worker ownership outright today due to the failures of the past is unjustifiable. Potter herself notes that many of the failures of the worker-owned firms were due to a misunderstanding of the fundamental changes of industrialisation, those being "increasing returns from the use of large capitals, the elaborate discipline of the factory system, the skilled intelligence needful for securing a market under stress of competition" (Potter, 1904:167). This quote is more interesting, as it would imply that the failures of the worker cooperatives were not only due to internal factors, but also due to external (political, economic and social) factors as well. John Stuart Mill (1848), who was more favourable toward worker ownership, claims that the failure of early worker cooperatives was primarily down to the environments they found themselves in.

> The vitality of these associations must indeed be great, to have enabled about twenty of them to survive not only the anti-socialist reaction, which for the time discredited all attempts to enable workpeople to be their own employers—not only the tracasseries of the police, and the hostile policy of the government since the usurpation—but in addition to these obstacles, all the difficulties arising from the trying condition of financial and commercial affairs from 1854 to 1858.
>
> Mill (1848:201)

Context is key. Even with internal stability, the actions and reactions of those matters external of the firm can be as influential, if not more so, in determining the firm's future. The Long Depression which started in 1873 also contributed in further disrupting the cooperative movement; by 1882 there were reportedly only 20 producer cooperatives left (Cole, 1944). The failure of the majority of worker-owned firms in this very early period was most likely down to a combination of internal and external factors. External factors are difficult to mitigate and predict, therefore establishing internal stability – averting mismanagement or perpetual quarrelling – is an essential first step. Like any form of democracy, it must be a constant process of trial and error. A preferred democratic model cannot simply be 'cut and pasted' from one firm to another, it must be nurtured and flexible towards new challenges and circumstances. This constant process of trial and error for worker-owned firms is the reason why we see more successful examples today than during the times of Potter and others.

The worker cooperative model would not witness the levels of academic interest it experienced in the 19th century until the 1970s. The failures of the producer cooperative movement in the 19th century were certainly to blame for this, for the reasons we have already discussed. The yearning for an alternative to capitalist ownership came from other sources. Firstly, trade unions were becoming more popular and effective in their role. Secondly, the consumer cooperative movement was growing, especially with the rise of the Co-operative Wholesale Society, later renamed to simply 'The Co-operative'. Lastly, the state socialist model, either moderated within a mixed economy or universal through central planning, became of most academic interest, especially after the Russian Revolution of 1917 which brought about the first so called 'socialist' state. The beginning of the 1970s altered academic interest once again. By this time, the state socialist model was exposed for its inefficiencies. State owned and managed firms experienced the inevitable lack of incentives from both the workers on the shop-floor and the managers. At least under the capitalist model the managers (who also tended to be the owners) had an incentive to maximise efficiency and profitability. The consumer cooperative movement was still popular at this stage, but it did not have the momentum or appeal to replace conventional capitalism that it once did. The story of the trade union movement during this time is also not particularly positive. Regardless of many of its intentions, it became a symbol of the failures of the state socialist model in many regards. In the UK, political militancy and a swath of strikes during the late 1960s, the 1970s and 1980s had made the trade union movement deeply unpopular with a significant proportion of the population. It was because of this that the worker ownership model began to attract academic, and in some cases, political interest.

During the period between the end of the 19th century and the mid to late 20th century, several examples of successful worker-owned firms were beginning to emerge. The John Lewis Partnership, which was originally established using a conventional capitalist business model, transitioned to employee ownership in 1929 and quickly became a nationally significant brand later that century. John Lewis would go on to incorporate Waitrose into the partnership in 1937, later to become a major British supermarket brand. In 1951 Ernest Bader – whose intellectual heritage stemmed from the Christian Socialist movement of the previous century – transferred the ownership of his chemical company to the Scott-Bader Commonwealth. The transfer of ownership to a common trustee company was a gift to his workforce. The company remains worker-owned to this day. Successful examples were also taking fold in Europe. The Mondragon Corporation in Spain, which begin in the 1950s, had proved how worker ownership could function successfully in a market system and within a local community. The cooperative movement also gained renewed support in post-war Italy and France. These examples demonstrate how worker ownership can be effective when external hostility is mitigated and internal disputes are prevented through solid constitutions and procedures. They showed how the failures of the 19th century were the exceptions, not the rule. Learning the lessons of these failures gave worker ownership a second chance in the eyes of the academics. This second chance was somewhat short-lived, especially in the eyes of the critics. During his time as the UK Secretary of State for Industry, Tony Benn used the worker cooperative model to save three failing (largely unionised) companies. The firms were financially bailed out by using government grants in order to prevent the unemployment that would inevitably follow should the companies go bust. These companies were Kirby Manufacturing, the Scottish Daily News and Meriden, which made Triumph motorcycles. All three were relatively uncompetitive, struggling in the marketplace. They were also heavily dependent on state subsidies, which ironically were too costly to support a dying company but insufficient to invest in its potential competitiveness.

> Central government assistance to these firms became associated with 'lame ducks', sometimes blackening the image of co-operatives in the public eye and among organisations which could offer the help. ... They were all grossly undercapitalised and had little chance of long term survival without a major injection of finance.
>
> Thornley (1981:111)

Mellor *et al* (1988) points how many of the workers were unsympathetic to the cooperative model, whilst the hard-line trade unionists saw it as a deflection from their preferred outcome, that of 'true' (state) socialism. An uncompetitive firm uncertain and, at times, hostile towards its own ownership model is no recipe for success. These firms were doomed to fail, like that of their 19th century predecessors. If worker buyouts were ever to be trialled, surely it would make more sense to do so with a successful and profitable company. Transitioning a failing capitalist company into a failing worker-owned company does not solve the fundamental fact that the firm is failing. In addition, using public funds to finance a buyout can only be justified if there is a credible plan to bring the firm back into profitability. Government grants that are applied to simply keep dying firms alive is no efficient use of public resources. Instead, the grants should either have been prevented outright, or increased if the prospect of potential future profitability presented itself. With that being said, ultimately this well documented case study would become another string in the bow of the critics of worker ownership. The fall of communism and the spread of the capitalist ideals across the world, particularly in the Far East, produced little appetite for alternatives at that time. This would, of course, change after the pending financial meltdown.

Worker ownership and the worker cooperative movement has experienced a notable increase in political interest since the financial crisis of 2007/8, but little has materially changed. One positive development is that those institutions, organisations and individuals who represent the cooperative movement have become much more vocal in promoting the model. The most recent research on worker ownership in the UK comes from the Employee

Ownership Association and Co-operatives UK, who have analysed the cooperative sector more generally and have developed a range of facts and figures on worker ownership in the UK. Data from 2017 shows that 118,000 workers and freelancers in the UK are members of a worker cooperative. The turnover of employee-owned firms stood at £10.7bn in 2017, £10.5bn in 2016 and 2015, £9.7bn in 2014 and £9.1bn in 2013[88], an estimated 4 per cent of UK GDP annually[89]. Most of these figures are swallowed up by the John Lewis Partnership, but nonetheless demonstrates that the worker ownership sector in the UK is of significant size and is steadily growing. Globally we find that as of 2015, the number of employees worldwide that own their businesses co-operatively is estimated to be 10,841,500[90].

> Worker co-operatives represent a very small proportion of all firms in most countries. However, they are more numerous than is usually thought. At least 25,000 can be found in Italy, about 17,000 (employing some 210,000 people) in Spain, 2,600 (employing 51,000 people) in France and about 500 to 600 in the UK.
>
> Pérotin (2016:5)

These figures show that employee ownership can function successfully and sustainably in the real world, but as a business model, it has not experienced the propulsion necessary to become the dominant business model at an international or national level. Worker ownership does have stronger standings in regional economies, such as in Italy for example. "30 % of the GDP of the Emilia Romagna region in Italy is produced by worker cooperatives – this alone equates to about 2.65 % of the GDP of Italy" (Erdal, 2012:942). Using a variety of datasets from across the world (many of which have been mentioned throughout this work also), Pérotin (2016) has been able to draw the following conclusions on the state of the modern global worker cooperative sector:

- Worker co-operatives are larger than conventional businesses and not necessarily less capital intensive
- Worker co-operatives survive at least as long as other businesses and have more stable employment
- Worker cooperatives are more productive than conventional businesses, with staff working "better and smarter" and production organised more efficiently

- Worker co-operatives retain a larger share of their profits than other business models

- Executive and non-executive pay differentials are much narrower in worker co-operatives than other firms

Pérotin (2016:3)

Academic interest has also grown from the more radical and progressive schools of thought. With more and more academics looking for an alternative to conventional capitalism, more and more are turning to worker ownership as a potential remedy. Most proponents have not given a detailed account of how employee ownership on a national scale would work or how it would look, but the interest is indeed there. Examples of preliminary interest include authors such as Alperovitz (2005), Wilkinson and Pickett (2009), Wright (2010), Mason (2015). So how can worker ownership become a success now and avoid the mishaps of the 19th century and the Benn Cooperatives in the 1970s? That is the next phase of our 'why now?' question.

Setting the Mould

Worker-owned firms are far more able to sustain themselves today than in the past. That being said, as a business model, they do not currently have the energy and propulsion to become the most common type of business in modern economies. In this section we will begin to discover what preconditions are needed for a cooperative economy to emerge and how far we are to achieving those preconditions today. Thankfully, a lot of this work has already been done. Vanek briefly examines the various "institutional, legal and attitudinal preconditions" (1971:91-92) that are required for a particular economic model to emerge, aggregating these preconditions into a concept defined as 'the mould' (Vanek, 1971:97)[91]. Vanek (1971) asks the question as to why the capitalist business model emerged as the dominant driver of the Industrial Revolution. If we can answer this question, we may be able to understand how this model was favoured over worker ownership, as well as understanding how worker ownership could emerge as the dominant business model in future. Vanek states:

> From the social point of view, the class stratification which capitalism implied was at that time perfectly natural and accepted state of affairs. And so was ownership of enormous assets by single individuals.

Vanek (1971:91)

Pre-capitalist society had all of the necessary institutional, legal and attitudinal preconditions to allow capitalism to take fold. As Vanek (1971) points out, a hierarchical society based on socio-economic classes was entrenched. This had been the case during feudalism also, where a small group of landowners controlled large agricultural estates, whilst the workers worked for their subsistence and paid rents to the estate-holders. Switching farmland to factory, estate-holder to capitalist, and land-worker to factory-worker was in theory, a relatively simple social transition. With technology advancing it became more profitable for the estate-owners to invest their capital in industry. The potential for higher wages and non-seasonal employment encouraged the working classes to move from the countryside to the towns and cities, and so urbanisation began. Capitalism was a natural next step from feudalism, spurred by technological change and engrained social hierarchies.

Whilst social attitudes adapted to this new economic model, the institutional and legal preconditions allowed the capitalist model to turn from niche to norm. Ownership of property meant control of property, which would be inherited down the generations. This passing down of wealth from one generation to another was the norm prior to the dominance of capitalism, and remains the case to this day. Workers wishing to form a cooperative would not have had the financial capital to start such an endeavour, especially at a time where the majority of industrial investments depended on self-financing from wealthy individuals[92]. A worker-owned firm during this period would most likely need to borrow all of its financial capital. This would have been highly difficult to procure, essentially due to the perception of excessive risk for the lender. The practice of risk-spreading hedged investments that we observe today was not an available option during this time. Pre-capitalist laws were also present for wage-labour, whereby the capital owner, whether it be estate-holder or factory owner, could freely hire and fire a worker at whim. The worker could not lay a claim to the products they had made using the capitalists' means of production. As Vanek (1971:91-2) goes onto say "all the institutional, legal and attitudinal preconditions of capitalism existed well before the technological and economic forces actually produced it". Of course what many of the working classes found upon their arrival to the industrial towns and cities was often more destitute than what they had just left. The social hierarchies and distribution of power ensured that property rights for the investor-owners remained impenetrable. With the working classes unable to procure the capital required to start enterprises of their own, capitalism became an economic model fixated on the needs of a small minority of people who had access to capital.

It would have been infinitely more surprising if in the days of industrial revolution there had emerged a firm based on industrial democracy, or any other type and form of organisation other than capitalism.

Vanek (1971:92)

The odds have been stacked against worker ownership from the outset, but there are signs that things are starting to change. Capitalism has unquestionably changed since its early industrial beginnings. Workers now enjoy more rights at work, can typically expect to earn more than bare subsistence and have a greater chance of becoming managers or owners of companies themselves. This situation, as we have revealed, is still not superior to worker ownership. We know the transition to capitalism was relatively smooth, whilst early cooperative experiments ended in failure. So are the necessary preconditions for a cooperative economy present today?

A Cooperative Mould

Vanek (1971) fails to mention which types of institutional, legal and attitudinal preconditions a cooperative mould would require. It is up to us to fill in the gaps. Attitudes are essential, as they help to shape where political support is given, how workers or investors should be treated and help to amend or sustain the laws and institutions that make up any political and economic system. There are already traces of what could become a cooperative mould in our own economies. As we know, laws are in place to allow worker cooperatives to start-up and compete in the marketplace. Some institutions, such as Co-operatives UK for example, are also available to encourage and support new and existing cooperatives. The reason worker-owned firms are not more prevalent is because simply letting something superior exist is not enough to allow it to flourish and take hold.

The Desire for Change and a Lack of Alternatives

The internal factors that beset the worker cooperatives of the past are less likely to take hold today. The lessons of the 19th century have been learnt. Any worker-owned firm intending to sustain itself requires the procedures to prevent workplace disputes and ensure effective management takes hold. We have already set out in Chapter 5 what sort of procedures these would look like, most of which would be enshrined in some sort of company constitution. For the experiments of the 19th century there was no tried and tested template to follow, they were simply taking a trial and error approach. Further to this, no opportunity to humanise or indeed replace the conventional capitalist model other than through worker ownership has emerged in recent years.

The levels of dominance from the trade union movement seen in the 1970/80s is unlikely to be repeated today, mainly due to the marginalisation of trade unions that occurred during and since that period. Trade unions, as important as they have been in many respects, are unlikely to re-emerge as a force for economic change. Compared to worker ownership, trade unions are a means of giving employees a voice without giving them responsibility. Not to mention that union membership is voluntary, it will never capture all of the workforce, all of whom have an equal stake in the survival of the business. The appetite for greater trade unionism may seem appealing in an age of growing workplace insecurity and precarious employment, but it does not solve the dual-contradiction, nor does it offer a convincing alternative that could be applied universally.

The same can be said for state ownership. Although there are some reasonable cases for further nationalisation of natural monopolies (those industries where market competition could not apply), the levels of support for state ownership of all sectors is highly unpopular due to its past failures, and rightly so. Thornley (1981:12) states that worker cooperatives "have never existed in large numbers. ... To begin with, their socialist aims make it very hard for them to survive in the market". The spectre of state socialism may still linger over worker ownership by some of those who still defend the injustices and inefficiencies of conventional capitalism. For these people, mostly academics and political commentators, worker ownership and state socialism may be one and the same, which is obviously not the case. The state-socialist model advocated by many academics before the end of the Cold War has undoubtedly failed. Those seeking an alternative to conventional capitalism have few places to look. If the anti-market and anti-free trade voices of today's anti-capitalist movement can be prevented from re-emerging, worker ownership is likely to be successful not just as a political ambition, but as a sound structural alternative. This is essential to prevent those who wrongly see the market system as the primary enemy and target for change.

For the lowest paid, fighting for an increase in the minimum wage might appear to be the best method, but this fails to establish a longer term solution for all workers and is by no means a more radical or effective means of modifying conventional capitalism and solving the dual-contradiction. There is no realistic or superior alternative to the conventional capitalist model than through effective worker ownership. The desire for some form of alternative is clear, we see this (in early 21st century terms) through Brexit, the election of Donald Trump in the US, SYRIZA in Greece and Jeremy Corbyn as Labour leader in the UK. The reader will perhaps not struggle to think of other recent examples of how a justified yearning for economic change has resulted in populist successes which have failed to materialise the change desired. Worker ownership could easily fill this void of political and economic discontent we have witnessed. But where is this desire for change coming from? History, again, holds some of the answers.

Education and Democracy

Mill (1848) claims that education is key to achieving greater freedoms and liberties for the working classes. The example he applies is the move away from slavery and towards democracy.

> Of the working men, at least in the more advanced countries of Europe, it may be pronounced certain that the patriarchal or paternal system of government is one to which they will not again be subject. That question was decided when they were taught to read, and allowed access to newspapers and political tracts.
>
> Mill (1848:194)

The more educated the working classes become, the more independence they demand from their political and economic masters. Mill (1848) sets this out as a slowly evolving movement for the working classes, from one of dependence and protection from the higher classes towards self-governance. The more educated the wider population becomes, the more intolerable dependence seems to be, with this process materialising in the end of slavery, the right to vote or the right to a social security system. In current times we see a situation where more and more of the working and middle classes are becoming highly trained in academic and advanced technical skills. As such, they are more likely to demand a greater share of the value they help to produce. There is nothing to suggest that worker ownership will not be the materialisation of the next stage of this trend Mill (1848) describes. Of course, there have always been criticisms of capitalism and a desire to change it, regardless of the levels of educational attainment. However, education enables a greater proportion of the working population to think critically, uncover feasible alternatives and postulate a realistic means of bringing about those alternatives. We have seen throughout the history of capitalism that it has rightfully been subject to plenty of opposition, but perhaps not enough proposition. The alternatives that have been trialled have rarely succeeded. This is perhaps why the state socialist, trade unionist and indeed worker cooperative experiments of the past have been so unsuccessful. Vanek (1971) also points this out from the context of the early Industrial Revolution.

> Second, there is the quite significant fact that any productive organisation, capitalist or otherwise, needed then as now a certain minimum of highly qualified technical and organisational cadres. And for the vast majority of those eligible, then as now, it was certainly not well looked upon to join a "socialist" or other producers' cooperative.

Vanek (1971:97)

The working classes did not have the means of making worker ownership work without the technical and organisation skills that were so necessary. There is also a positive relationship between education and democratic decision making. Democracy only works when the majority of participants make the decision which is most rational and logical for themselves. Education allows this to happen, it allows participants to calculate and judge which option is best. Without it, the wrong decisions can be made, or the right decision is made for the wrong reasons. The need for rational decision making is as important in political life as it is for economic affairs. Workers need the skills to make the right decisions needed to sustain the firm, whether it be the pivotal decisions determining the future of the firm, or the smaller issues that will impact co-workers on a day to day basis. This is something Father Arizmendi acknowledged when setting up Mondragon.

> He [Arizmendi] recognised that employees are generally socialised into passive roles, and, if employee ownership is to work, one of the great educational tasks is for employees to develop the knowledge, skills and confidence to become active participants.

Erdal (2011:30-31, comment and bracket added)

The adoption of worker ownership and management on a wider scale is more likely to be effective now than it ever has been, as highly educated employees have the skills to rationalise, analyse and make sound judgement. We must also add that the workers of today are accustomed to democratic decision making on a political level. This means a move towards economic democracy should be simpler compared to the times of the Industrial Revolution, when political decision-making was gifted to the privileged few rather than a right for the deserving many.

Challenging the Owners

We have noted earlier that academic interest in worker ownership is growing as its supporters are becoming more vocal. This has enabled the worker ownership model to be broadcasted to a greater number of people. This is also beginning to challenge the status quo regarding ownership and control. The largest enabler to the birth and delivery of capitalism was the laws and customs concerning ownership of capital. Even with the class system heavily diluted and greater freedoms and democracy in place, without changing the attitudes and laws concerning ownership of the means of production, worker ownership will remain as a marginalised niche of minimal economic significance. There is some evidence to suggest that the norms of ownership are being challenged. We have seen in the case of John Lewis and the Bader Commonwealth, that there is an appetite for some business owners to pass their companies onto their employees. Employee buyouts are slowly becoming more popular. Business owners often prefer selling on their company to their workers rather than competitors or other outsiders. It allows the workers to carry on the legacy of the firm, protecting its culture and identity. For larger multinational corporations, where ownership is diluted amongst many shareholders, this appetite for worker ownership is much rarer. There is also the perception that transitioning to employee ownership is complex and laborious, leading to misjudgements on the viability of a worker ownership buyout. The entrenched traditional approach to succession planning has ensured that the worker buyout option remains largely unknown to many business owners. The advice given by many professional advisers has led to the perception that worker buyouts are infrequent, niche and only appropriate for certain types of business. However, in reality this option has the potential to be a simple and effective route to transition, leading to an optimum outcome for both the current business owners and the prospective worker-owners. Consequently, these outdated perceptions need to change. That being said, employee buyouts are slowly becoming more popular, signalling a positive albeit sluggish change in attitudes.

Along with worker buyouts, there is also more opportunity for the working classes to start their own business, certainly more so compared to the start of the Industrial Revolution. Financial capital can be borrowed from a variety of sources to start a small enterprise, to employ, to produce, to sell. The ability to start a worker-owned firm from a financial perspective is still no easy task. Worker-owners are still unlikely to have the funds themselves to start an enterprise. The variety of financial instruments now available means that borrowing to invest is much easier than it was during the early stages of capitalism. There is nothing to stop a worker-owned start-up making use of this. All of this means that a worker-owned firm could be developed. Obviously, no effort has been made to encourage a widespread emergence of worker ownership throughout our economy. This means more needs to be done on an attitudinal, institutional and legal basis. Mayfield, Purnell and Davies (2012) discuss the success of John Lewis and the worker ownership model more generally, but also reach the question as to why the sector is not larger or indeed dominant. The reason they come to is a sort of 'chicken and egg' situation, where the necessary ingredients new and existing cooperatives need to develop are not present, but they are not present because the sector is so small. If an adequate number of worker-owned firms were present in the wider economy, there would be sufficient demand for the ingredients worker-owned firms need. So what are these necessities they refer to? Mayfield, Purnell and Davies (2012) discuss how alternative ownership models can often put off investors, leaving them short of the necessary financial capital to start-up or expand. Dickstein (1991) notes how conventional lenders often struggle to evaluate them in terms of risk. The Nuttall Review also found this to be the case in their inquiries.

> This review heard evidence for example that it was not easy to find someone to talk to at a bank or other financial institution about financing an employee buy out. Analysts may not include employee ownership models in the diagnostic tools used to assess investment propositions.
>
> Nuttall (2012:51)

If worker ownership were to become the norm, financial investors would have no choice but to accustom themselves to the intricacies of worker-owned businesses. There are many other services worker-owned firms will require to succeed.

> One of the reasons it is difficult to set up an employee-owned business is that there aren't many lawyers or accountants who you can talk to who know much about this area. If you talk to most in those professions about this subject they look at you as if you are odd or from a different planet ... [I]f you go to a lawyer or an accountant at the moment, or for that matter if you study an MBA, you are told that the purpose of a company is to maximise returns to its owners, which are its shareholders, and that these people have no interest in a

company beyond that. And it is partly that which has to change – that rigid
orthodoxy about what companies are.

Mayfield, Purnell and Davies (2012:220)

This chicken and egg dilemma will need to be resolved if a cooperative economy based on worker ownership at its very heart is ever likely to succeed. A capability to form a worker cooperative will only get you so far. Even in a firm with no internal disputes, with effective constitutions, with first-rate management and high customer demand, if the external necessities (the lawyers, accountants, investors, etc.) are not present, the firm will likely fail. The Nuttall Review into employee ownership found a lack of knowledge on the matter more generally, stating "[T]his review concluded that a lack of awareness of the concept and benefits of employee ownerships limits interest in and demand for this model." (Nuttall, 2012:32). This not only has a detrimental effect on existing worker-owned firms, but also puts off new firms from starting. Along with a lack of support and resources from government, Nuttall eludes to why this may be the case.

> An overwhelming message received during this review is that awareness of employee ownership is extremely low among all involved in business. Lack of awareness was cited repeatedly as a fundamental obstacle.

Nuttall (2012:30)

> Respondents gave examples of how they were held back by a lack of awareness amongst the wide range of groups businesses need to support them. Many could not find advisers who were sufficiently knowledgeable about employee ownership to advise on it. ... Others had problems in accessing bank lending due to the lack of familiarity with this business model. Also, general understanding of employee ownership in business schools or higher education is low.

Nuttall (2012:31)

None of these factors should be particularly surprising. What is clear is that the era of hostility, indifference and unfamiliarity needs to come to a swift end – this is the justification and purpose of the cooperative state.

<h1 style="text-align:center">The Pangloss Theorem</h1>

Despite everything holding back the possibility of a cooperative economy, there are those who claim that because worker-owned businesses have not been able to overcome the difficulties they face, they are somehow inferior compared to conventional capitalist firms as a result. We can call this idea the Pangloss Theorem. Dr Pangloss is a fictional philosopher featured in Voltaire's (1759) *Candide*, who claims to his students that they live in the best of all possible worlds. So the theory goes, if there is a better way of doing something, it would have been implemented already. As a result, we must live in a state of being which reflects the best possible way of doing all the things we can control. Voltaire ultimately uses the character of Pangloss to ridicule this overly optimistic and simplistic world view. George (2007) adapts this theory to the worker-owned firm and why it has not become the dominant business model in modern economies.

> In this context the [Pangloss] theorem simply states that there is no need to 'promote' self-management, because it would emerge naturally in a 'free' economy if it genuinely offered benefits to workers superior to those available elsewhere. After all, in such an economy, there is nothing to stop workers from forming a cooperative if they wished, so the fact that they rarely do so simply reveals a preference for orthodox forms of economic organisation.

George (2007:539)

As we have uncovered, there are multiple reasons why worker-owned firms have been unable to become dominant in modern economies. The ability to degenerate (either into a capitalist firm or to sell off the firm to reinvest capital) and the bankruptcy of firms as a part the business cycle, has led to a reduction of the worker-owned sector at various times throughout the last couple of centuries. The birth of new worker-owned firms is largely prohibited by the difficulty to procure capital. All of this is occurring in an environment where the support structures conventional capitalist firms enjoy are not available for worker-owned firms, further exacerbating the failure of existing worker-owned firms and exacerbating the inability of new ones to form. None of this sounds like the sort of 'free economy' the Pangloss theorem needs to stand as a legitimate objection to worker ownership. As we have seen, there is now a better environment for worker-owned firms to be established, which has resulted in a larger worker-owned sector. Basic support structures are starting to emerge, workers are more educated and more aware of the economic alternatives, and the ability to procure capital is starting to improve in some respects. That being said, this 'better environment' has certainly not extended to the extent that would allow worker-owned firms to flourish and dominate. Expecting worker-owned firms to emerge and compete in a modern economy geared towards serving conventional capitalist firms is not too dissimilar from expecting a football team to compete in Rugby Union and somehow win. Indeed, such an outcome could occur, but by and large each sport requires its own rules, standards and support structure in the same way worker-owned firms and conventional capitalist firms require their own 'moulds'.

> [T]oday, more than ever, economists tend to assume that anything of benefit to the community is sure to come about as a matter of course at some point in time and that anything failing to assert itself unaided can barely be advantageous for society as a whole.
>
> Jossa (2015:266).

In reality, there is no 'free economy'. All economies rely on the attitudes, laws and institutions which build and sustain them. Each system requires a 'mould' as Vanek (1971) would proclaim. "Simply expecting accountants and lawyers to promote this model has, over many years, proved ineffective in growing the sector. It requires legislation." (Summers *et al*, 2014:3). Consequently, applying the Pangloss theorem to argue against the development of worker-owned firms is illogical and somewhat ignorant of the realities of political economy and differing economic systems. The logic of Pangloss is perhaps as flawed here as it was in the words of Voltaire!

Concluding Remarks

The desire for economic change is present. As our societies become more educated and technologically advanced, the appetite for greater political and economic independence grows. The successes of current worker-owned firms and the future potential they hold for all workers is clear and consistent. On an attitudinal basis, convincing the electorate of the benefits of employee ownership should be no difficult task if carried out effectively and honestly. People have the skills and democratic experience to make worker ownership work. As we know, this probably hasn't always been the case. The potential is there, but the necessities to succeed are not – this must change. The pre-conditions needed for capitalism to take hold were already present, all it needed was the technology to take it forward. A cooperative economy must rely more on social and political change rather than technological change. Front and foremost it requires the desire of employees to want to take the responsibility that comes with employee ownership. That is why a cooperative economy is not inevitable, even if some of the preconditions required for a cooperative economy have emerged over recent years. A convincing manifesto for change is needed, one that positively combines the progressive attitudes and desires for economic reform with the legal and institutional policies to match it. Attitudes towards the ownership of the means of production need to change. There is already some appetite to do so, but we must go much further. Once this has been achieved the necessities and ingredients that worker-owned firms need to start-up and expand will be present. From there onwards, a cooperative economy can be established, and with the right laws and institutions in place, it can be sustained. This comfortably leads us to our penultimate chapter, the one that outlines a blueprint for a cooperative economy, put forward by a cooperative state.

---

[87] Potter (1904:155) objected to the idea of worker-owners of a cooperative becoming profit-seekers, stating "an industrial organization which substitutes for one profit-maker many profit-makers, is not a step forward in the moralization of trade". Potter would go onto uncritically support Stalin, the Soviet Union and central planning more generally.

[88] See Co-operatives UK, Economy 2017, https://www.uk.coop/sites/default/files/2020-10/Annual%20report_Online.pdf

[89] See Employee Ownership Association, http://employeeownership.co.uk/what-is-employee-ownership/

[90] See Co-operatives UK, https://www.uk.coop/newsroom/global-co-operative-employee-ownership-figures-close-11-million

[91] Vanek's theory of the mould is similar to Marx's theory of the base and superstructure, perhaps acting as a combination of these two concepts.

[92] See Vanek (1971:98)

Chapter 12: The Cooperative Manifesto

[I]f we are to regain control of capitalism, we must bet everything on democracy.

Piketty (2014:573)

This chapter will essentially function as a manifesto. A manifesto is only as good as the context it applies to. The challenges and opportunities that have been outlined in the preceding chapters serve to give the reader an understanding of why certain proposals have been included in this manifesto and others have not. This chapter will be split into three sections. Firstly, there will be a brief list outlining all of the general issues worker-owned firms have faced historically and today[93]. This will remind the reader of the context, which is so key. The second section will proceed to address these main issues one by one, with clear proposals and solutions. These proposals intend to be both radical and progressive, all of which will serve to bring about a cooperative economy that can be sustained. These will therefore make up the core reforms. Lastly, additional reforms will be discussed that offer solutions to the other problems that have been mentioned throughout this work but are no means strictly related to worker ownership.

What is Holding Back a Cooperative Economy?

All of the primary reasons preventing the emergence of a cooperative economy have been discussed in some form or another in the preceding chapters, especially the last. The points below offer a brief reminder.

Access to capital is limited: It is difficult for ordinary working people to own a share of a company when they are likely to be earning on or just above subsistence. This prevents the growth of worker-owned firms. In conventional capitalist firms, the majority of capital is typically owned by a wealthy minority. A cooperative economy would need to redistribute capital ownership amongst those who produce and work for capital: the employees.

Alternative ownership structures limit access to financial capital: Unlike conventional capitalist firms, worker-owned firms cannot trade away shares in the firm in exchange for investment capital. Money for investment must come either from retained earnings (internal) or must be borrowed (external). The alternative ownership structure has also turned off potential investors, who are more likely to invest in a model they have come to know and trust.

Degeneration: In the past, some worker-owned firms have been able to degenerate into conventional capitalist firms, either through entire sell-offs or new employees being brought on without being given a share of ownership.

Poor management: Some worker-owned enterprises in the past have been besieged with poor management practices and worker disputes. This has often been due to a lack of knowledge on how to manage a firm with different internal structures and how issues should be dealt with. If left untreated, this can lead to poor decision making, bad work ethics and even company collapse.

Misconceptions: Worker ownership has previously been associated with state socialism, central planning, communism, anarchism, militant trade unionism and a whole host of other, often contradictory, ideologies and models. This has prevented it from moving toward the political mainstream.

Education and attitudes: We are all brought up to accept that companies are owned by shareholders, often a single individual in many cases, who employs workers for a set wage. The idea of worker ownership, and income based on effort rather than a set wage, is to most people an alien concept. It is not normally something we are aware of or consider when we first start employment. We are all accustomed to the conventional capitalist model and education providers (for right or wrong) prepare us for this.

The chicken and the egg: As there are few employee-owned firms in any one economy, there is consequently little demand for the organisations, institutions and specialist firms available in an economy to assist worker-owned firms in reaching their fullest potential. As there are too few of these specialists, there are likely to be fewer worker-owned firms, who would otherwise be dependent on these resources. Such specialists could include lawyers, accountants, lenders, etc.

Core Reforms

A cooperative manifesto that aims to bring about an economy comprised of mostly worker-owned firms must be bold enough and radical enough to accept that fundamental and potentially uncomfortable change is required. Simply acknowledging the benefits of worker ownership whilst doing nothing to promote it, in the hope that things will change by themselves, is not an option. If nothing is committed, nothing will change. We have seen periods over the last few centuries where academic and popular interest in worker ownership has increased and then lost favour, only to become temporarily popular again a few decades later. This cooperative manifesto aims to stop this cycle and create the necessary mould for worker ownership to be universal and sustainable.

Transferring Ownership

The first and arguably most radical proposal of the manifesto, is to accept that the ownership of all private enterprises within a national economy should be owned and managed by their employees. This is necessary to resolve the dual-contradiction, thereby increasing productivity and increasing the share of national income going to workers, so that work (more or less) equals reward. A mandated transfer of (equal) ownership, either to the workforce directly or informally through a trust, of all firms must be complemented by a legal requirement for all new enterprises to be worker-owned as well. This ensures that workers in all instances are ultimately sovereign. Ownership of a firm by investors, consumers, the state (where state ownership is not usually expected[94]) or any other external actor should not be permitted. This would set a legal precedent, abolishing structural wage exploitation and ensuring that all firms are accountable to their dependants. This would also mean prohibiting partial employee ownership; ensuring that all workers are equal co-owners and that the workers own the whole company in its entirety.

This policy would also require that the so called 'bogus self-employed', who only work for one company, should in fact be considered employees of that company. Trying to use self-employment as a means of reducing employee numbers and the benefits that come from employment (including worker ownership in this case too) is incompatible with the principles of a cooperative economy and should not be tolerated. Worker-owned firms are still able to employ workers from outside of the company to fulfil a particular service. For example, a company could hire a gardener to maintain its grounds. If the gardener was employed every day, they should be a worker-member of the firm, as any other. If the gardener were to treat the grounds once a month, whilst treating the grounds of various other clients throughout the remainder of the month, they would instead be considered to be a contractor, either self-employed or perhaps a part of a gardening firm, itself being employee-owned. The cooperative state should specify when a worker should be regarded as an employee or as a contractor, as the former implies ownership of the firm whilst the latter does not. The main difference is quite simple, an employee works for the same firm over a consistent period of time. A contractor works for multiple companies, usually as a one-off or temporary period of time. In cases where this distinction is not clear cut, the cooperative state should allow the courts to decide, setting a precedent in case law.

As discussed in earlier chapters, different forms of employee ownership can be applied, including ownership via a trust and direct ownership through capital contributions. We have already discussed the issues with capital contributions and this should also be dealt with here. Capital contributions should only be used where sustainable and appropriate. For example, this may be appropriate for federations of worker-owned firms, where capital can be hedged between them, like Mondragon for example. As such, if a company ceases trading, or if all the employees leave, then there needs to be at least sufficient reserves to pay back the contributions. That or capital contributions can be allowed until a point where unsustainable or unattainable financial reserves are required for repayments. It is because of the issues surrounding capital contributions that ownership through a trust appeared to be the most effective. There should however, remain room to experiment with other forms of employee ownership[95], for as long as ownership is absolute and employees retain full control. Differing means of managing the firm can also be trialled. As time goes by and employee ownership becomes mainstream, it will become apparent which forms of employee ownership and management are optimal for certain types of firm. The process of how ownership will be transferred is the topic of the next chapter.

Degeneration

Laws need to be in place to prevent remunerative incentives to degenerate. Degeneration can take many forms. The ability to degenerate into a conventional capitalist firm is prohibited under the assumptions made above. This means the company cannot be sold off to investors or creditors. It also means that employees cannot be separated into those that are worker-owners and those who work for the firm but are not owners. Employee ownership must be binding and applicable to all employees. Selling a worker-owned firm can occur without degeneration. For example, the employees could decide to merge or sell the business to another worker-owned firm. In this case, the company has changed hands, but the firm remains employee-owned and fully functional. Alternatively, the employees could transfer ownership of their firm, but still remain worker-owned, by selling it off to a cooperative federation like Mondragon[96]. In this instance, the original workers now own a share of all the other firms (who have bought the original firm), but all of the other workers now also own a share of the original business. This means ownership can be transferred without breaching the principle of full employee ownership and management.

Degeneration can also take place whereby the employees collectively decide to wind down the business, sell of its assets and make a profit as a result. This should be discouraged, especially for profitable firms with the potential to employ many more people in future. In Chapter 7 it was discussed how this could be prevented, with laws to be introduced that deter liquidation purely for one-time gains. In Spain the revenue of financial gains made from selling off a company's assets are appropriated by the state. In a cooperative state this could either be replicated or replaced with a mandatory contribution to charity. Alternatively, a phoenix tax could be established where revenues made by degenerating firms can be taxed and given to cooperative development funds. These agencies then use the funds specifically to issue loans to start-up businesses. Each of these policies sets to remove the remunerative incentive to sell-up for purely financial gain. Assets should only be sold off as a last resort, for example when the company is no longer profitable or in unsustainable debt. For smaller companies who do not own any assets of significant value, they should be allowed to sell off any remaining stock without facing any additional tax impediment or other liabilities.

Contracts and Constitutions

In conventional firms we often see a contract being presented to the employee from the employer at the beginning of employment. The contract lays out the responsibilities of the worker. In a cooperative state this should be reformed to take into account the responsibilities each employee has not just as a worker but also as an owner. Companies should have some form of constitution laying out the code of practice for the firm. This should act as a form of contract whereby the firm guarantees democratic accountability with equal and fair judgement of each worker-owner. This is to prevent worker disputes and offer a means of resolving conflict when it does occur. For smaller firms with only a handful of workers, a template constitution should be made available, as lengthy and complex constitutions are not applicable in these cases. As proposed before, the cooperative principles could be applied to a universal (template) constitution which smaller firms could use as a baseline. Gamson and Levin's (1984) 'Formal Code of Social Statutes' discussed in Chapter 5 may also have some relevance here. With this in place, the confusions and mismanagements of the early experimental worker cooperatives should not be replicated in our cooperative economy.

Mechanisms of Support

Cooperative Development Agencies (CDAs) or reformed trade unions should be available to support worker-owned firms, especially smaller firms, to assist them with drafting their constitutions and help to deal with any internal predicaments if and when they arise. As discussed in Chapter 5, these actors have the added benefit of being perceived as a more neutral, trusted and professional means of resolving issues. Forced transfer of ownership from investor-owners to worker-owners breaks the chicken and egg dilemma, by artificially increasing the supply of clients and thus increasing the demand for support providers. With this cooperative mould in place, more private sector providers should be at the ready to supply the demand of worker-owned business support that will be required. The state sponsored mechanisms of support should therefore reflect the gaps in the market left by the private sector.

Education

Reforming education is necessary to prepare the worker-owners of tomorrow with the necessary skills needed for worker ownership. Under conventional capitalism, workers must obey the wishes of their employer and other hierarchies they are presented with. "In fact, schools tend to be impersonal, bureaucratic, and hierarchical, like the typical workplace." (Gamson and Levin, 1984:224). Rather than just teaching students to simply obey, they must be trained to understand the complexities of democratic management. This means understanding how to listen, think rationally, negotiate, confront opponents diplomatically and embrace unfavourable decisions agreed upon by the majority of workers. This may also have a positive impact on democracy at the political level (voting in elections), but more importantly, it prepares prospective workers for a workplace based on collaboration and understanding rather than the primitive art of simply obeying one's superior.

Teaching future and existing workers the ins and outs of democracy is also more likely to sustain worker ownership as an economic system. As with universal suffrage, once the majority of working people have the freedom to determine their own destiny, and have the tools to make their wishes a reality, they will be more hesitant in relinquishing those freedoms. In a cooperative economy we must assume that there will be those who wish to revert back to investor-ownership for selfish remunerative reasons. With the right skills to ensure worker ownership is a success, any suggestion towards going back to conventional capitalist ownership will be seen as barbaric as the calls to revert to political dictatorship.

Reforming Finance

A cooperative economy requires an efficient capital market, meeting the supply of capital funds from investors to the demand of worker-owned firms for investment capital. Investors can no longer expect their investment to be linked to equity of the firm. As a result, a worker-owned firm must expect their external finance to be a form of debt. A cooperative state should therefore facilitate the necessary reforms to allow worker-owned firms to easily access capital markets. As with other support providers, lenders are more likely to invest in worker-owned firms now that they have become the predominant type of firm in the economy; they are no longer an obscure oddity deemed to be too risky simply because they are not understood. Banks and other financial institutions within a cooperative economy must also be worker-owned, if our manifesto's first principle is to be adhered to. A cooperative economy will no longer require a stock market, at least for domestic firms. Instead, this means establishing a liberalised, standardised and digitised private bond market to maximise liquidity. Replacing a stock market with a bond market should not impact the supply of finance capital to any significant extent.

> Just as in private companies, new business investment in the vast majority of quoted companies is funded from retained profits and borrowing. Instead new shares are generally issued not to build businesses, but to expand through acquisitions. And acquisitions have been shown to be as likely to destroy value as increase it.

Erdal (2011:58)

With an expanded bond market in place, there must be scope to trial different types of bond to offer a variety of financial instruments to that market. Legislation to permit and regulate performance-index bonds (where the interest rates cannot be artificially reduced/increased by the firm/investors) should be brought forward, to ensure there are multiple financial options that suit the needs of firms and investors. Tax incentives could be offered to replicate the Mondragon/Italian model, whereby worker owed firms have the opportunity to put a fixed percentage of their earnings into a cooperative development fund, which it and other new and existing firms can procure investment capital from. These funds can be subsidiary banks like Mondragon, or perhaps linked to a specific location or sector. We noted in Chapter 7 that there should be no considerable change in the supply and demand of investment capital in a cooperative economy all else being equal. With the right reforms in place, this hypothesis should remain true. If however, the supply of investment capital consistently falls short of demand, this would constitute market failure, and the cooperative state would be expected to intervene and correct it.

Self-Exploitation

Contracts and constitutions should ensure that worker-owners understand their responsibilities to the company whilst the company understands its responsibilities to each of its workers. There must also be laws in place to prevent self-exploitation. This can take the form of working for a wage rate which is below what is needed for subsistence. It could also mean regulating against employees working too many hours or taking on too much responsibility. Workers may feel the need to do this to maximise the profitability of the firm, but it is, after all, most important that the health and safety of the worker comes first. As such, there is still a need for minimum wage legislation to ensure that worker-members still earn enough on a weekly/monthly basis. Laws like the working time directive should also remain in place to maintain rights at work. Trade unions would need to reform their purpose to protect individual workers in cases where self-exploitation or unfair treatment from co-workers is taking place. Productivity and workplace satisfaction is highest when workers can manage their responsibilities and see the fruits of their labour.

A Cooperative Labour Market

Although worker-owned firms are more likely to retain their employees during tough economic times, there is still a requirement for the cooperative state to enact policies aimed at keeping unemployment to a minimum. A cooperative labour exchange similar to what was suggested by Wolff (2012), could be applied here. These 'WSDE boards' have been discussed already in Chapter 6, but in principle they work similar to a Job Centre but without the additional (and often controversial) responsibility of issuing welfare payments. It would serve primarily as a form of intermediary between firms with excess supply of workers and firms with excess demand of workers. As practised by Mondragon, firms could directly sign up to a system whereby those companies which need to reduce their workforce can advertise their surplus labour to a company which is looking to expand its workforce. This partnership approach could work for firms in similar industries[97] or where workers utilise similar skill sets. This may not be practical for all workers but as an approach it is far more considerate than simply laying off a worker-member who then becomes exposed to the social and economic ills of unemployment. In an ideal world, this process of worker transfers would be carried out without the period of unemployment that often follows redundancy. In reality there would likely be a period of temporary unemployment to retrain, which could be provided either by education providers (in partnership with the cooperative labour exchange) or provided by the in-taking firm itself.

When unemployment increases to the point where there is more supply than demand, there could be a case of funding the unemployed to form their own worker-owned firm, if practical and sustainable. The funds gained from a phoenix tax could be used to fund new ventures, alongside the business support offered by business and employment cooperatives (BECs). A BEC is a type of shared workspace where members are given a small income and the ability and resources to start their own enterprise. If the enterprise takes off, the member no longer receives income from the cooperative but instead pays it back a portion of their income from their new business. Where the cooperative labour exchange assists workers to find jobs in existing firms, the primary focus of the BEC is to assist worker with starting their own enterprises, whether it be self-employment or the beginning of a new worker cooperative.

Promoting Entrepreneurialism

All new firms are born out of an idea, of one individual or a group of partners. Any cooperative state must ensure that worker ownership complements this entrepreneurial spirit. This means linking entrepreneurs to potential worker-partners, as they may not have the resources or experience to easily access the labour market in the same manner as large and existing firms. This is another potential role for the cooperative employment board discussed earlier, especially if this is not delivered through conventional recruitment agencies. Laws must remain in place to protect the ideas and innovations of the entrepreneur, whilst ensuring they receive the just rewards for taking the initial risk of setting up the business and investing in their idea or innovation[98]. The entrepreneur would be unable to realise the full potential of their idea without the employees to make it a reality, whilst the employees would not have their job unless for the risks taken by the entrepreneur. There must be sufficient legislation in place to protect a fair and just balance so that work (including risk) equals reward for all parties.

Competition Law

Legislation ensuring that free markets remain open and fair must be strengthened; there is no excuse for monopolies in the private sector. Monopolies increase prices for the consumer and hold back on innovation. A cooperative state should help to spur investment and technological innovation when appropriate, especially where this is lacking from the private sector. Regulatory bodies must be given meaningful powers to ensure that monopolisation, collusion, market failures and barriers to entry can be deterred as best as possible.

Worker Ownership Abroad

Worker-owned firms expanding abroad must offer the same membership and ownership rights as domestic worker-owners. Although foreign states will have their own laws and regulations, there should be no domestic mechanism to deny worker-members abroad the same rights as domestic worker-members. A successful cooperative economy which exports its principles overseas is more likely to increase the support for worker ownership abroad. This can only be a good thing.

Additional Reforms

Worker ownership on its own will not solve all of the economic and social issues we face. Worker ownership resolves the dual-contradiction, a major economic issue that befalls all capitalist economies in one way or another. Other contradictions, pressures and crises must be dealt with, often with solutions as radical as those we have proposed. These will primarily focus on inequality. Tackling inequality is essential, especially in preparation for dealing with the other major issues humanity faces, such as climate change, environmental degradation and increasing resource scarcity. The following policies are not prerequisites or necessities of a cooperative economy, but do offer interesting solutions to the other types of inequalities we find that are not caused by the dual-contradiction *per se.*

Taking on the Rentiers

The inequalities observed within the world of work stem from both the dual-contradiction and the labour market; which prioritises jobs and allocates incomes according to the scarcity of the required skills. A monopoly of capital by the wealthiest segments of society ensures that these inequalities are maintained generation to generation. By developing a cooperative economy, along with an education system that allows workers to gain which ever skill they wish to learn, these inequalities can be greatly diminished. Other existing forms of economic inequality also rely on some type of monopoly control of a particular asset. In the same way that most workers will be unable to fund a new business venture of their own, in the UK many residents of rented accommodation will be unable to purchase their own property. Rent remains a significant cost to many tenants. For the landlord, simply having the ability to purchase this asset gives them an ability to earn an income from little if any labour; work does not necessarily equal reward. This is also the case for small businesses, who lease commercial property without having the prospect of owning their own premises. If a cooperative state seeks to extend the scope of its anti-inequality agenda, it could tackle monopolistic practices and rent seeking activities. This is not just the case for residential and commercial property, but intellectual property, natural resources and other forms of rentier accumulation.

A cooperative state could resolve excessive property accumulation either by taking direct ownership of these assets or by creating a 'right to own'. For the former, this practice could be used to build local authority housing offering below-market rents to incentivise saving, acting as a stepping stone for future home ownership. This could work for commercial property too, with the added benefit of generating an income for local authorities or central government. For the latter, a right to own would guarantee tenants an opportunity to purchase the property they currently (privately) rent after occupying it for a certain amount of time. In this instance, rent is no longer 'dead money', but is instead partly used as an instrument to purchase the property they reside in. This policy would help reduce inequality by spreading ownership of assets amongst a greater portion of the population. Land and property is just one example. As technology progresses, other forms of monopolies and rentier activities will take shape, which a cooperative state should seek to resolve if it wishes to stay true to its founding principles.

Other Types of Cooperative

Although it has been advised throughout this work that firms are best owned and managed by their employees, this does not mean that other types of cooperatives should be disregarded from our cooperative economy. Quite the contrary, they should be encouraged, the only condition being that they should not exhibit the dual-contradiction. Consumer cooperatives can still operate without the dual-contradiction in play, for example in circumstances where workers are also consumers. Wikipedia, Amazon, Ebay, Facebook and other popular websites could be transformed into user-owned systems based on cooperative principles. These sorts of companies are known as platform cooperatives and already exist in multiple forms. Platform cooperatives are unique, as they embrace innovations in digital technology to create cost free methods of buying, selling or any other type of online activity. They offer an opportunity to the consumer cooperative movement that prevents the dual-contradiction and ensures cooperative principles can be extended into the digital realm.

Other types of cooperative should also be embraced. One particular example is the marketing (or retailing) cooperative model. This type of cooperative is created when several firms combine their purchasing power to purchase their inputs in bulk. Purchasing stock as a larger buying entity, rather than as an individual purchaser, will pass on savings to each member of the cooperative (each firm), which in turn could help to pass on savings to the consumer. This type of organisation is particularly popular in the agricultural sector, typically referred to as farming cooperatives. Benefits from pooling various firms together can also benefit each member in terms of output, rather than just inputs. Farms for example can pool together and form farm coops to increase their bargaining power when negotiating with purchasers of their product. For example, small dairy farmers are unlikely to get a competitive price for their product from a large (potentially monopsonistic) supermarket, when the supermarket could threaten to withdraw their purchase in favour of another supplier. If however, the dairy farmers combined to form a farm cooperative, they could negotiate a higher price which none of the participating members could have achieved alone. Supply and demand in the market is much more likely to reach the desired outcome when both seller and buyer have equal bargaining power.

Cooperatives are not necessarily restricted to the world of work and production. Housing cooperatives are an interesting example. In this case, the cooperative owns multiple residential units (whether they be houses or apartments) and allows prospective residents to purchase a share of the cooperative. In return, the new member takes up residency in one of the units. This model acts as an alternative to conventional rental or owned accommodation. It goes without saying that the cooperative principles could be applied to almost any organisation or group of people in some form or another.

State ownership, whether it be local, national or perhaps even international, is still justifiable in circumstances where the private sector will not or should not (for moral reasons) embark. Education, health and defence are the most obvious examples that come to mind. Keeping ownership and control tied to local communities should be a priority, even for publicly run assets and services. As already discussed, there is as a case for local government ownership of rentable assets in order to earn an additional income on top of tax revenue. Local government is not the only means of realising local ownership. Not for profit organisations such as community shops and pubs should be welcomed and encouraged, again, for as long as they do not embody the dual-contradiction. Voluntary groups establishing collective assets should be encouraged when there is demand. Cooperatives have the democratic appeal to spread across economic and social activities. A cooperative state should create the environments where such endeavours can be taken.

Basic Income

It is argued that globalisation and growing automation has radically increased the supply of workers relative to demand. This means work is becoming more menial and precarious, shrinking real incomes at the bottom of the income spectrum and multiplying incomes for those at the top. For the least fortunate, this economic reality can lead to longer term unemployment, or precarious employment which is not sufficient to maintain subsistence. If this happens on a greater scale, with little or no income for a significant segment of the population, there will be no demand to purchase the goods the automated firms are producing. In this scenario, where workers do not have the means of maintaining subsistence, this is likely to cause political instability.

Worker ownership does not necessary relieve this pressure. In Vanek's (1977:173-174) *Essays* he discusses the undesirability of a highly automated firm with only a few worker-owners. He postulates how these firms would only require a janitor and a director, both incredibly rich off the returns made by the highly automated mode of production. This would lead to wide scale unemployment where the vast majority of people cannot afford the goods being produced. Basic income has been proposed as a solution to the issue of insecure work and insecure income. Unsurprisingly, the concept of a universal basic income is becoming more and more popularised in political and economic discourse. Basic income is the idea that every citizen is given a regular sum of money from the government to cover basic needs. The income received would be universal, meaning that citizens cannot be disqualified from receiving it. It gives basic safeguards against poverty, homelessness and other social misfortunes. It also guarantees a basic level of demand for certain goods and services.

Paying for this welfare policy would indeed be expensive, but if coupled with a progressive tax system and the funds of existing obsolete welfare programs, the policy may be more affordable than initially thought. The incentives to work also alter. Those on a basic income now work to purchase the things they want rather than the things they need; the coercive incentive to work is replaced with a remunerative incentive to work. Workers without a basic income, struggling to make ends meet, are unlikely to be productive and healthy contributors to society. Basic income would relieve this stress, whilst making paid employment a more plausible route to achieving the luxuries we all strive toward, whether they be material, social or otherwise.

For a cooperative economy to embrace the basic income proposal, all three of the main incentives (remunerative, moral and coercive) must be in play for worker-owned firms to remain competitive and sustainable. If worker-owners become indifferent to the profitability of the firm as a result of receiving the basic income, then this could have serious consequences for an economy still dependent on labour for production. Evidence from Alaska would suggest that universal payments have no negative affect on employment, instead suggesting that aggregate employment increased to some degree (Jones and Marinescu, 2018). If this were to be the case in reality, there should be no serious negative consequences as a result of combining worker ownership and basic income.

Whichever welfare system a cooperative state embraces, workers should not be given welfare payments which perpetually bring them to the same level of income regardless of the amount of work applied. For example, say the government guaranteed workers a minimum of £5000 for a set period. If a worker earns £4,500 they would collect £500 from the state, or if a worker earns £1000 they would collect £4000. This damages the incentive element of worker ownership, as work does not equal reward. Polanyi's (1944) examination of the Speenhamland Laws of the 18th and 19th Centuries gives a good historical examination of this type of welfare system in practise. As a result, any state benefit should reward maximising effort, that or provide a blanket rate such as a universal basic income which is topped up from income from employment.

Employer of Last Resort

Basic income is not the only policy suggested to combat growing automation and the loss of jobs that could result. Another suggestion is for the government to act as an 'employer of last resort' guaranteeing every citizen a job if they are unable to find adequate employment in the conventional job market. Government jobs would have to be slightly below the minimum wage, as not to incentivise workers in the private sector to join the government scheme in search of better wages. In a cooperative economy, these government jobs would not pay a profit on top of the basic wage (inhibiting the dual-contradiction), acting as another incentive for workers to seek employment in the private sector where possible. These jobs should be the least desirable in terms of pay, but not by activity. They should help to retrain workers with the skills needed to help them find and sustain longer term employment elsewhere. This scheme would likely be administered by a cooperative employment board as discussed earlier. It could enable workers to establish a worker-owned firm of their own, if the jobs the government has created can be sustained if moved into the private sector. This policy would require knowledge of which jobs would actually be needed, as in, what work needs to be done that is not already being done by the private and public sectors. This will be determined by the economy and society in question. Whether such a proposal would be preferable to a basic income would depend more on which economic pressures become more problematic as technological change progresses. There may also be a case for both programs to be enacted, if necessary, appropriate and practically possible. As with basic income, this policy could come at a significant cost, requiring new progressive forms of taxation and income generating assets for local and national governments.

Citizens' Wealth Fund

Another means of reducing wealth inequality would be to create a Citizens' Wealth Fund. These funds, which are owned by governments, invest public monies into private assets and financial products, such as stocks and shares, bonds and property for example. This type of fund is not a particularly new concept, "there are now more than 70 government funds, in countries including Singapore, New Zealand, Ireland, France and the UAE, as well as in a nine US states." (Lawrence and Mason, 2017:11). Revenue to start up the fund could be obtained by implementing more progressive tax policies, targeting those with 'unearned' wealth, monopolistic firms earning supernormal rates of profit and getting tougher on tax evasion and avoidance. Unlike other costly proposals, this initiative would only need one large input of capital rather than requiring a long term cost commitment. The purpose of the fund would be to earn an income from what has been invested. The profits made by such a fund could help to finance a basic income, jobs guarantee program, or progressive government spending more generally.

---

[93] These 'general' issues are not country specific, but generally apply to the majority of developed countries globally.

[94] State ownership can be justified in instances whereby the profit principle is not morally appropriate and where moral incentives outweigh personal remunerative incentives.

[95] Although we have previously discredited Vanek's 'labour management' model regarding issues around ownership, Vanek's (1977:181) U-B ownership model could be trialled nonetheless.

[96] As Mondragon operates under a 'direct ownership' model, is it likely that should they purchase a worker-owned firm (to join their federation), those workers will receive an equal share of the market value of their firm once it has been sold. However, they will likely have to pay a capital contribution to remain employed by the federation.

[97] This could only realistically work when there is no likelihood of industrial sabotage between competitors.

[98] This is no excuse for a 'rentier economy' where patents give long term monopolies to their holders. This should instead allow innovators to benefit from their work and give some level of protection, whilst allowing competition to take hold.

Chapter 13: The Transition

> Eventually, and in perhaps a less remote future than may be supposed, we
> may, through the co-operative principle, see our way to a change in society,
> which would combine the freedom and independence of the individual with
> the moral, intellectual, and economical advantages of aggregate production

Mill (1848:202-203)

A cooperative economy can become a reality. It is not beyond human comprehension to develop such a system if there is the willing and inclination to do so. With a moral and economic justification, along with a solid manifesto for change, that reality becomes more possible. The manifesto in the previous chapter sets out the end goal: an economy where the majority of firms (all of those in the private sector) are owned and managed by their employees. One could perfectly favour this end goal, but argue against it on the grounds of the transition that would be required to bring about that cooperative economy. Indeed, it is both the role of the cooperative state to bring about a cooperative economy and then to sustain it. This final chapter explores the actions necessary to bring about a cooperative economy. This is mainly a political matter, one of governance and diplomacy. We will begin by examining the attitudinal change that will be required – winning over the hearts and minds of the voters, convincing them that this is electorally desirable and credible. As we know from Vanek's (1971) theory of 'the mould', attitudes are essential for systems change, even if legal and institutional change has already occurred. For if there is no faith or understanding of the cooperative model, all legal and institutional arrangements become unstable. Lastly, the issues of managing the transition will be dealt with, assuming that a cooperative state has been elected and has the means of effectively governing.

Winning the Hearts and Minds

Theories of transitioning away from a conventional capitalist economy to an alternative economic model have been developed before. Wright's (2010) *Envisioning Real Utopia's*, which includes a 'cooperative economy' as one of the potential alternatives to/of capitalism, is a good place to start. Wright (2010) proposes three distinct routes of transformation (transition) for the various alternatives he proposes, those routes are: ruptural, interstitial and symbiotic. We will apply the basic principles of Wright's (2010) three models to reveal how these different types of transformation could apply to a worker ownership transition on a national scale. This will also reveal a preferred method of transition which will be applied for the remainder of the chapter.

Ruptural Transformation

We will begin with arguably the most radical method of transformation, that of ruptural change. A ruptural approach to transition would primarily entail some form of revolution and a process of overthrowing existing institutions and norms and replacing them with entirely new structures. Marx and Engels' (1848) prophecy of the overthrow of capitalism could be seen as a theoretical example, whilst the 1917 revolution in Russia could be seen as a consequential empirical example. In this instance, a transition to state socialism was the end result, not worker ownership. In the case of worker ownership, of which is our main concern, the advocates of a cooperative economy would seek to overthrow the government of the day, and to replace that government with a cooperative state and enact the principles set out in the manifesto. In a democratic nation where free and fair elections are held, this means of transition is not appropriate and will likely lead to prolonged instability and a plethora of unintended consequences which will plague the transition process. In addition, it would also be somewhat hypocritical for those who advocate economic democracy to bring it about by evading and undermining political democracy and its existing processes. There is a case for this type of transformation if there is no democratic political mechanism that allows economic reform to take place. If the will of the people is to establish a cooperative economy, but there is no means of achieving that transition, then ruptural transformation is justifiable. Dictatorships seek to retain power, preventing alternative governments from forming with alternative policies, and so what is demanded by the majority of citizens cannot be delivered. In a free and fair democracy, there is a mechanism that allows economic reform to be delivered, thus making ruptural transformation unnecessary and undemocratic in this instance.

Wright (2010) supposes that ruptural change could also come about through democratic political means. In this instance, existing institutions and norms are still dismantled and replaced, but this is done through taking power democratically rather than through violence. The hypothetical example used by Wright (2010) is a radical socialist government coming to power and seeking to rewrite the rules of the economic system. The enormity of its task, however, will likely lead to a detrimental short-term economic impact. A democratically elected government intent on delivering comprehensive ruptural change in a short space of time (before the next election) will likely daze markets and stifle economic activity. This immediate economic impact may prevent the finalisation of the transition, as political opponents capitalise on the short-run economic disruptions whilst ignoring or discrediting the potential long-run advantages. A ruptural cooperative state would have to both remain in power for long enough to ride the storm and maintain democratic legitimacy. Although not impossible, this approach appears to be a risky and somewhat speculative way of delivering a sustainable cooperative economy.

Interstitial Transformation

Interstitial transformation is a process of change from within existing structures but separate of them, within the "niches, spaces and margins of capitalist society, often where they do not seem to pose any immediate threat to dominant classes and elites" (Wright, 2010:211). One could argue that worker-owned firms today would qualify as one of these niches. Where ruptural transformation acts as a sudden and forceful sweeping-away of existing structures, interstitial transformation occurs within structures with the aim of fundamentally changing them beyond recognition. It still seeks to challenge the status quo, but over time and without the voracity of ruptural transformations. Regarding a cooperativist form of interstitial transformation, Wright states that "marginalization of cooperatives in contemporary capitalism reflects the lack of a supportive social and economic infrastructure for cooperative activity in capitalist economies" (2010:168). The contents of Chapter 11 serve to remind us why and how this came about. We cannot rely on worker ownership to blossom and predominate an economy by itself, without the necessary support structures they depend upon. These support structures come and go as enthusiasm for worker ownership ebbs and wanes. Worker ownership has never emerged to the extent where it has challenged the conventional capitalist model, and as we have said before, simply sitting back and hoping change will occur by itself is a woeful attempt to resolve important social and economic issues.

There is another important aspect we must consider. The emergence of a cooperative mould is likely to pose an immediate threat to the dominant classes and elites who have something to lose from the proposed changes.

A skeptic might argue thus: If indeed these institutional arrangements constitute central components of a viable movement in the direction radical democratic egalitarian emancipatory ideals, then the creation of these institutions would be massively opposed by elites whose interests would be threatened by such changes. And so long as capitalism remains the dominant

component in the economic structure, those elites would have sufficient power
to block or subvert any serious movement along the pathways of social
empowerment.

Wright (2010:191)

A ruptural transformation would likely entail the overthrowing of the establishment, even potentially leading towards some form of physical confrontation. This extreme scenario would not occur under the interstitial method. Instead, change would occur 'under the feet' of the establishment, who may still be able to slow, stall and revert such change should it grow to the extent where it poses a risk to their interests. Those with a vested interest in sustaining the status quo, and preventing the wide scale emergence of an alternative model like worker ownership, will most likely utilise their resources to disrupt the process. Economic power and political power often seem indistinguishable, possibly due to the fact that those with the former also strive for the latter. To deny that those with wealth and economic power often actively seek, and typically gain, political power would not be an accurate interpretation of reality. This is both the case in democratic and dictatorial political systems. If something threatening were to emerge under the feet of those who wield such power, they are likely to use their economic and political assets to deter and challenge that threat. That is the purpose of achieving political influence to begin with, it acts as a form of insurance against the loss of existing wealth and the loss of the ability to gain further wealth. With an interstitial approach, they may need not challenge worker ownership at all, as the chicken and egg dilemma largely prohibits the ability of worker ownership to threaten the status quo to begin with. As a result, an interstitial approach to achieving a cooperative economy would appear to be largely ineffective, drawing only the hope of an eternally patient optimist.

Symbiotic Transformation

The concept of symbiotic transformation the last of the three types of transformation Wright (2010) articulates. This is a process of transformation from within existing institutions and being vastly dependent on them – using the democratic process for example. Such processes would involve working alongside the dominant classes and elites, with the aim of establishing coalitions and producing mutually beneficial results. This is different from ruptural transformation, as a symbiotic approach uses existing structures rather than establishing new ones. It also differs from the interstitial approach, in that it seeks to use existing structures to achieve economic reform rather than expecting economic change to occur by itself, without the necessary structural support. This type of transformation should "involve systematic forms of collaboration and mutually beneficial cooperation between opposing social forces" (Wright, 2010:253). In the case of worker ownership, this would mean the collaboration between those who favour worker ownership (the workers for example) and those who oppose it (the existing owners of companies for example). Although this approach could prevent hostility from those who might otherwise oppose worker ownership, there is one obvious disadvantage. This approach could lead to the watering down of the cooperative principles and policies required for creating and sustaining a cooperative economy. For example, the concept of a cooperative economy (where worker ownership is universal) could be bargained away, with loopholes and exceptions that allow the dual-contradiction to remain undisturbed in some cases. This cannot be allowed to happen. If all of the preconditions required to establish a cooperative mould are not present, the ability to create and sustain a cooperative economy will be greatly diminished. The chicken and egg dilemma cannot be solved with half a chicken or half an egg, either one or the other, or preferably both, must be brought about. This means universalising worker ownership across all existing and future firms and establishing the necessary support systems this type of firm requires. A means of transformation which threatens this necessity cannot be an effective means of transitioning to worker ownership.

A Hybrid Approach

It is important to state that different countries with different political systems will require a means of transformation which best suits their particular system. In the case of an economically developed and politically democratic country such as the UK, a hybrid approach to achieving a cooperative economy will be required. All of the methods examined so far have upsides and downsides, a hybrid approach can combine the upsides and minimise the downsides.

The preferred means of transition to worker ownership should be a 'targeted ruptural approach' which uses democratic processes. As was mentioned earlier, a ruptural transformation brought about democratically can be achieved, but as its purpose is to achieve a radical overhaul of the political and economic system, the elected government will likely try to change too much too soon. This is likely to cause instability, increasing the likelihood of this radical government being electorally defeated at the next election. A targeted ruptural approach however, would only seek to overthrow and replace particular elements of an economic (or political) system, rather than replacing the whole system altogether. The 'particular element' we have in mind is the transition to a cooperative economy, were all firms are owned and managed by their workers. Although this transition is indeed radical and transformative, it is unlikely to constitute a major reordering of political and economic life, as the 'general ruptural approach' discussed earlier potentially would. As such, this policy should be achievable for a democratically elected government, as economic disruption from a targeted transformation is limited.

As this type of ruptural transformation would be brought about democratically, this would require the advocates of a cooperative economy to actively contend with those individuals who have a vested interest in the status quo. This must be facilitated using the traditional and established methods of political democracy. Unlike the symbiotic approach, this does not mean cutting deals with the establishment and watering down the policies necessary for achieving economic democracy. Those with vested interests are therefore likely to engage with the threat posed to them by worker ownership, but they too must use the established structures to defend their position and attack the concept of a cooperative economy. For as long as this is a fair and even fight, the prospect of achieving a cooperative economy using this approach is indeed possible. If the fight is not fair and even, and the will of the people is ignored or heavily subdued, a ruptural transformation achieved through non-established routes and mechanisms is justifiable. For the majority of western nations, it is hoped this would not be the case.

This hybrid approach appears to be the most effective and justifiable method of producing a cooperative state in a democratic polity. Once a cooperative state is in place, it must work with all parties to ensure the transition period to economic democracy runs smoothly and effectively. The more who are disillusioned or feel cheated from the transition, the more difficult and needlessly complicated it will be.

Winning the Mandate

With a preferred method of transition in mind, the very first steps of enacting this method must be laid out. As the method in question is dependent on democratic consent, these first steps are reliant on the support of worker ownership from the workers themselves, as they ultimately represent the largest bloc of voters. Implementing worker ownership across a national economy without the support of the workers themselves is pointless. The policy needs popular support if it is to succeed. It is likely that not all workers will agree with the concept of worker ownership on ideological grounds, believing it to be inferior to the capitalist or state socialist model. Perhaps they may be hostile towards the accepting of responsibility (with the rest of their colleagues) for the firm's sustainability, instead favouring the capitalist model due to its lack of worker engagement with the management process along with the lower MAEL. If the policy of worker ownership is successfully driven forward but without the support of the workers, irrational decisions are likely to be taken during and after the transition phase. Workers may use their democratic powers within the firm to keep existing hierarchies and structures, so that the day-to-day managing of the firm remains the same as before. There is nothing necessarily wrong conserving particular arrangements, but if workers fail to take responsibility of the firm, relying on former owners/managers, this could put the stability of the firm at risk. Those at the top of the hierarchies must remain accountable to the whole workforce. Workers need to accept the responsibility they have of the firm and embrace the opportunities it provides. Due to the significant financial incentives worker ownership creates, it is unlikely that many firms will be plagued with this issue. The coercive incentive to remain employed remains the same, so workers must ensure that any ideological distastefulness of worker ownership does not put their employment at risk. In addition, those who are unsympathetic to worker ownership cannot simply leave and gain employment in a conventional capitalist firm, as this is not an option in a cooperative economy.

The idea that workers will not accept mandatory worker ownership has been used as an excuse for rejecting this policy before. When discussing mandatory buyouts, Oakeshott (1980:51) rejects Jay's (1977) approach to top-down cooperativisation of the economy, stating that structures will change but attitudes will remain the same. Only through a gradual transformation from the bottom-up, it is argued, can the necessary attitudes, needed to build what we would call a cooperative economy, be changed. Attitudes will change over time, but these proposals require initial support on the shop-floor if they are to succeed. Although this is true, a gradual transformation is not a necessary approach to achieving this. This is why any mandatory ownership transfer scheme must be brought about democratically. If we assume that the majority of the population work and vote, any vote in favour of worker ownership clearly demonstrates its appeal to the workforce. We need not wait for a gradual transformation when the appeal of worker ownership is already demonstrated. Support from the electorate is the key test of a policy's popularity.

As has already been stated, it would be contradictory to bring about economic democracy without using the conventional processes of political democracy. Building worker ownership on a consensual basis with the former business owners is always preferable to simply seizing their property. Either way, there must be popular support for worker ownership before it is implemented, otherwise, its success is not guaranteed. A vote on worker ownership could take two shapes. Firstly, a political party could include within its manifesto the desire to bring about a cooperative economy through the transition process we are setting out. If this party were to win power, they would have the mandate to begin this process, along with (as we have assumed) the consent of the majority of workers. This method does have its risks, as parties are likely to include multiple policies in their manifestos, and worker ownership – which could be very popular amongst the electorate – may be rejected, as the same party looks to bring forward a less favourable policy. The same could be true in reverse. Worker ownership could be deeply opposed by the majority of voters and workers, but as the party has other very favourable policies, it could still win that election and worker ownership may still go ahead. As a result, the policy of mandatory worker ownership should be centre stage of a party's election manifesto, the 'big ticket item' so to speak. The second method to achieving democratic consent is by holding a referendum. This method has one major benefit that the party/manifesto approach does not, that the political debate will be set exclusively towards this policy and will not be marred by other policies and debates, as they often are in the run up to an election. The downside of the referendum approach is, however, that the government/party in power may not support worker ownership even when the electorate do. A referendum should only take place if the transition process can be effectively brought forward by whoever is in government.

As the transition to worker ownership is reliant upon the acceptance of this transition process from the electorate, then worker ownership as an idea will be the subject of great debate. If this debate is to be reasoned and fair, with the audience (the electorate) acting rationally come election day, one might expect worker ownership to carry the day. Democratic consent relies upon having a sensible debate about whether worker ownership on such a grand scale is preferable to the status quo. The defenders of the status quo will be relentless in their opposition of worker ownership. The debate surrounding whether worker ownership as a business model can work effectively has already been won. As we examined back in Chapter 11, there are multiple examples of successful, profitable and innovative worker-owned firms across the globe.

Mondragon and John Lewis are two examples, both with differing managerial and ownership arrangement to suit their economic environment, but both adhering to the principles of worker ownership and control. The lessons from the early (failed) experiments have been learnt. If worker ownership is good enough for the workers of existing worker-owned firms, why would it not be good enough for all workers? We know worker-owned firms have the incentives in place to make them profitable, innovative and disciplined. We know that inclusive management practices, where roles and responsibilities are clearly set and where common goals are established, can lead to a more engaged and productive workforce. We know that democracy, with all its faults, has always been a better form of management than authoritarianism. There has been little evidence to revoke these claims and plenty of evidence to support it.

The argument that worker ownership can only be applied to certain types of firm has also been won. We know for example how worker cooperatives can be found in various markets, in various sizes with varying capital-labour ratios.

> Worker co-operatives have traditionally been viewed as small, specialised and undercapitalised organisations. It is commonly thought they thrive in unusual conditions and cannot possibly constitute a serious alternative to conventional firms. This view has long been shared by many economists studying labour-managed firms on the basis of economic theory and relatively limited empirical observation.
>
> Pérotin (2016:4)

Once the evidence has been examined, as Pérotin (2016) has done, we find how worker ownership can be applied to any industry and sector. There is no evidence to imply that worker ownership is incompatible with a certain industry, market or capital intensity. On the theory side of things, we have applied most of the economic theory of previous authors in this field with our own principles (the incentive dynamic, the market dynamic, the principal balance, etc) and have found worker ownership to be a generally superior business model compared to the conventional capitalist type.

The legitimate arguments against worker ownership are few and far between. For if one were to prove that the conventional capitalist model is best retained, they would first have to disprove the evidence that suggests worker ownership is superior and then supplement that argument with evidence to suggest the capitalist model is superior. In addition to this, they would also have to either resolve the dual-contradiction by other means, which (as we have proven in Chapter 3) is rather difficult without considering worker ownership, or deny the existence of the dual-contradiction altogether, which is also relatively difficult. The opponents would most likely devise new and sensational arguments against worker ownership, hoping that this will sway undecided voters. This cat and mouse approach to dissuading voters may pay off once, but it will not pay off forever.

It is important to set aside some space to talk about those who would be against worker ownership if this policy were to be put before the electorate. The most obvious actors are those who have something to lose from worker ownership, those who currently collect the surpluses that would otherwise be distributed to the worker-owners. Business owners and shareholders are likely to be against the policy of mandatory transition to worker ownership, as it would end a stream of future income. The owners of small businesses, who are likely to work for that business alongside their staff, are likely to be less hostile to worker ownership. As we have said before, worker ownership spreads the responsibilities and risks from one individual to all those working in the enterprise (a positive for the business owner), in exchange for an equal distribution of the surplus to all of those working in the enterprise (a negative for the business owner). As all workers now have an incentive to maximise their MAEL, total profit should increase, so that both the incomes of the workers and the former owner increase in tandem. Also, as all workers across the economy now have higher incomes as a result of worker ownership, there should now be higher demand for the goods and services on offer, boosting surpluses for the former owner and the rest of the staff further still. Here we have assumed that the former business owner wishes to remain employed by the firm post-transition, they could of course leave the firm and retire on the income gained from selling the business to the remaining workers. As a result, the hostility to worker ownership is less potent from these individuals, as they have the least to lose and potentially something to gain. The biggest losers from worker ownership are those who gain the surpluses of the firm but do not work for it, or have any other interaction other than receiving dividends. Although such individuals will still receive the value of their investment from selling their share to the workforce, there is no prospect of earning any future dividend income from the firm post-transition. At least with the smaller business owner there is scope for maintaining an income stream from being a joint worker-owner with the rest of the staff. For general shareholders, this is probably not the case.

In a society 'where owning shares is as common as having a car', again, there should be little hostility towards worker ownership. Although the working population will no longer receive an income from those shares, they will now have a share of the business they work for. The loss of income from shares will at the very least equal the income gained after becoming a worker-owner of the firm they work for. Their income should actually increase, as the remunerative incentives start to kick in. As we have seen, however, we do not live in this 'shareholder society', instead shares are owned mostly by foreign investors (as is the case in the UK), investment funds and wealthy individuals. These actors have the resources to shape the political landscape, and will likely constitute the main opposition to worker ownership on the wide scale we have advocated. They will use the surpluses they have earned in the past to ensure they remain entitled to the surpluses of the future, for them, it is an obvious investment, a risk worth taking. In societies where these actors are entrenched within their respective political systems, they will be a formidable foe. Their lobbying power could influence political parties to oppose worker ownership in order to protect the status quo. The media could also be used to change and cement attitudes (which are so vital) against the idea of worker ownership. As we have said, this will be a very difficult argument to pursue in the context of a fair and reasoned debate. If the debate has been skewed by the opposers of worker ownership, this will be a much harder political battle to fight. But lost battles do not mean a lost war. If the advocates of worker ownership remain persistent in their aims and consistent in their reasoning, the tides can eventually turn.

Managing the Transition

Once the electorate has given democratic consent for worker ownership to be mandatory across all private sector companies, the transition process will begin. This will require the government (a cooperative state) to deliver this transition phase of producing and sustaining a cooperative economy. As the manifesto in the previous chapter sets out, the change in ownership is not the only policy to deliver (although it is arguably the most important), and so the cooperative state must take this into account too[99]. This section will look at how our cooperative state will go about that transition period.

First and foremost, a 'Department for Economic Democracy', should be established as a single point of contact for employee ownership before, during and after the transition process. It should provide support for the companies transitioning, establishing a template for various types of worker-owned firm that is updated regularly to take into account the successes and failures of previous case studies. It should "develop simple employee ownership toolkits including 'off-the-shelf' templates, to cover legal, tax and other regulatory considerations" (Nuttall, 2012:60). Now the debates of the electoral process are over, the new DfED must be a means of building bridges between both sides of the argument, in order to effectively materialise the cooperative manifesto and the other preconditions needed to establish a cooperative mould. The transition process for each individual firm will work best when both the existing owners and the workers are on board and have a mutual understanding of how the transition will proceed. This mutual understanding will not materialise in every scenario, and so this must be prepared for also. The DfED will be the mouthpiece of the cooperative state on all matters regarding the transition. Governments have multiple services to provide and issues to address, so setting up a distinct government body with a clear strategy, vision and purpose is key. Of course, other departments will make contributions to this process where appropriate, but having a purpose-built body leading the process forward will ensure it remains transparent and effectual.

The Transfer of Ownership

As has been stated throughout this study, one of the greatest drawbacks of conventional capitalism is that the majority of people have no access to capital. Consequently, most individuals cannot own the means of production necessary to maintain at least their own subsistence, typically resulting in a rich and powerful minority of the population owning the majority of firms. A cooperative state would have to change this, by forcibly transferring ownership from one party to another, from the business owners to the staff. This, of course, must be achieved as a form of sale, whereby the business owners receive the value of their business in return for transferred ownership to the workers. A cooperative state should not seize property and donate it to the workforce. This form of ownership transfer should only be utilised in particular circumstances as a last resort, such as when business owners try to illegitimately frustrate or evade the process of ownership transfer. More on that issue later.

In the past, commentators have suggested that rather than forcing employee ownership on workers, there should be a 'right to request', as suggested in the Nuttall Review.

> Based on the existing statutory 'right to request' models in employment law, any Right to Request employee ownership would broadly involve a group of employees developing a proposal for employee ownership, discussing it with their employer, and the employees having an expectation that the employer should reasonably consider the proposal and respond to it. However, there would be no 'right to have' and therefore there must be an equivalent expectation that the employer can turn down the proposal.
>
> Nuttall (2012:40)

> This review favours drawing the grounds for turning down a request broadly. It could be that the timing is wrong. It may simply be that the owners of the company are not prepared to make shares available. The key is to ensure a reason is provided.
>
> Nuttall (2012:42)

If a right of request was made of all businesses, the vast majority business owners are likely to reject the idea. The reason for this is simple, as most business owners will believe that they can earn a higher financial return in the long run through retaining ownership rather than through selling their equity. Why cash out early on a winning bet? This great gamble – of giving employers an opportunity to dismiss a worker buyout proposal – should not be the means of promoting employee ownership or establishing a cooperative economy. This voluntary approach places the power straight into the hands of the business owner who is unlikely to part way with their share of the firm. There is also another reason why business owners may be less likely to sell their business. For many smaller businesses, there is typically one business owner who established the company themselves, taken all of the risk and taken all of the physical and mental baggage that often comes with it. Setting up and managing a business as an individual is no easy task. Consequently, being told you have to sell on your business is, understandably from the point of view of the business owner, a potentially crude and unfair request. This perspective must be respected; many business owners have exploited themselves rather than any employee. This is simply another injustice of the conventional capitalist model.

The intense burden many business owners frequently face is, from our perspective, just as crude and unfair. Under employee ownership, no one person is taking all the risk and being subject to all of the stress and responsibility, indeed this must be shared by all. More hands make light work. Business owners, whose company is being transferred to employee ownership, should be given an opportunity to remain employed in the company they have helped to build after it is sold. This has a benefit to them, as it distributes the risk and responsibility. In return, the business owner receives the value of their firm (during the process of ownership transfer) and gains an equal share of the future profits they and the rest of the employees make. Trying to justify the continuation of the capitalist model in this instance is particularly difficult. Employee ownership should be regarded as a win-win for both parties.

Of course, not all firms operating within a particular economy will be domestic. Foreign firms operating across multiple national boundaries are a common feature in our highly globalised economy. Transferring ownership in these instances can appear to be more complex, as the domestic government has the ability to force transfer of ownership for domestic firms, but does not have the jurisdiction to force firms based in other countries to do so. The cooperative state can resolve this quite simply. Foreign firms would have to sell off their domestic subsidiaries to their respective workforces. Under a franchise arrangement the new worker-owned firm can remain a part of the parent company's operations, but where full ownership and control is given to those employees residing in the country transitioning to a cooperative economy. With highly developed global supply chains emerging, it is becoming less likely that multinationals will set up new branches of their own firm overseas. They are more likely to allow external firms to take contracts for various stages of production, rather than produce everything internally. For example, a BMW car is not produced solely by

BMW, its clutches could be produced by a company in Japan, tires by a firm in the UK and assembled by yet another firm in China. This prevents the costly need for BMW having to set up new operations across the globe, along with all the risk this entails. The hypothetical Japanese company could be producing clutches for a variety of car manufacturers and so are not dependent on one firm. Franchising and contracting allows worker ownership to be implemented in a national economy without disrupting global supply chains.

Getting the Ball Rolling

As soon as the government assumes the role of a cooperative state, notifications should be made to all businesses, informing them of their duty to begin the process of transition their firm to worker ownership. Similar initiatives in the UK have been approached in this manner, including the introduction of the minimum wage and mandatory workplace pension schemes for example. All firms that employ should be given a deadline whereby they must inform the DfED of their intentions to begin the process of ownership transferral. This should include the method of transition and the end date they have forecast when the transfer of ownership is complete. The route each company takes will be determined by the workers in agreement with the firm's management, the latter presumably representing the current owners. Firms must establish an employee board, where the workforce decide the type and manner of transition which is most appropriate. This board can be set up by the workers themselves or set up by the company, either way it must be democratically accountable to the entire workforce. The board will act as the workers' representative during the transition. This board should also be given immediate voting rights on key company decisions affecting the transition and the future of the firm generally. The existing owners must not be given responsibility to control the transition process without worker engagement, as this may create opportunities where they can potentially start to asset-strip the company to extract as much value as possible, leaving the workers with an empty shell of a business. This sort of situation can be avoided where information and intentions are shared by both parties at the earliest possible opportunity. One would expect private sector companies specialising in business development to offer paid advice and support for businesses with the resources to do so. However, it is important that the DfED has all the support structures in place to engage with firms without the financial capacity to receive private assistance.

The Value of the Firm

If the firm is to be sold, from the investor-owners to the workers, it must be effectively valued. This is important as it provides the existing owners an idea of the total remuneration they will receive once the process has concluded, whilst providing the workers an agreed cost and timeline for the purchase period. The firm is essentially buying itself from external owners, so it must be generating the necessary income required to facilitate that purchase. This means calculating the value of the firm and the projected income over the forthcoming transition period. The valuation of the firm should be carried out according to industry standards; there must be no attempt to undervalue or overvalue the firm to any party's advantage. If attempts are made to deviate from the market value, the cooperative state should have the authority to rectify this, to compensate those who have been disadvantaged. If the firm is not likely to have the income necessary to allow worker ownership to take place, either due to a low profit margin or a temporary state of unprofitability, a long term approach must be taken, one that allows the purchase period to be stretched over a longer period of time. If a firm is genuinely unprofitable, either recently or historically, there must also be concessions. Of course, a firm which remains unprofitable for a longer period of time will eventually cease trading. Worker ownership should not be forced upon those firms in this position. It is assumed however, that the majority of firms will be in a position to successfully transfer ownership and remain profitable throughout and after the process. As Erdal (2011:41) rightfully notes, "business assets pay for themselves; nobody buys a business except in the expectation that it will pay back within a reasonable time the money invested in buying it, and significantly more. ... A successful company will pay for itself over time". A worker buyout of a perpetually unprofitable firm should only be considered if it is likely to make the firm profitable; we must not repeat the failures of the Benn cooperatives of the 1970s. There may be examples where businesses attempt to give a perception of unprofitability in order to evade or defer worker ownership. Where such practises can be evidenced, the DfED will have the authority to implement a transition process which will lead to a lower sale value for the existing owners. This should create a coercive incentive towards such behaviour, instead leading to an outcome which is mutually beneficial for both parties.

Methods of Transition

So what are the likely methods of transition that firms could utilise? This is likely to depend on the current ownership status of the firm. For private limited companies, the workers will be purchasing ownership from an individual or group of shareholders, whereas for public limited companies the shares could be owned by potentially thousands of shareholders.

In some scenarios, the workers may have the necessary savings to purchase the firm outright themselves. Shares could be purchased by the workers immediately, or the workers and existing owners could arrange for shares to be purchased over time at a set price and set date. The ability of the workers to buy shares using their own capital is an unlikely reality for the majority of workers, especially as capital is becoming more and more concentrated and monopolised by a wealthy minority. Instead, if workers wish to pay back the existing owners over time, the workers will hold an immediate debt burden of the total value of the firm.

> Since the EOT [employee-owned trust] does not have independent means, it has to fund the acquisition of the shares through one of three methods: external bank finance, a loan from the company, or by agreeing to pay the vendor (the original business owner) on deferred terms over a period. In all three, the EOT uses the future dividend earnings arising from its ownership of the company's shares as the basis for its initial acquisition. These future earnings are used to pay back an initial loan, or to provide deferred payments to the vendor.
>
> Lawrence and Mason (2017:17-18, bracket and comment added)

The best arrangement to transfer ownership from the existing owner/s to the workers over time is through an employee-owned trust. This is the 'indirect' type of ownership discussed in Chapter 4. Under this arrangement, the transfer of ownership can occur immediately, with the original shareholders conceding their ownership and control of the firm in exchange for a debt obligation by the firm to pay those shareholders the total current value of the firm over time. The shares are transferred from the original owners to a trust, where those shares can remain (as a form of indirect ownership) or the shares can be distributed to the workers individually if they decide to implement a direct ownership approach (like Mondragon).

Although a loan from a bank or some other financial institution may work best for many firms, the most attractive means of purchasing the firm would be to pay down the debt over time using the future surpluses generated by the firm. For private limited firms, the timescale of repayment can be negotiated with the existing owners. A monthly or annual repayment schedule can be formalised, similar to conventional loan agreements. For public limited companies, a mandatory switch of market shares to market bonds could take place. This approach involves converting existing shares into bonds, where the firm becomes the borrower and the original owners become the creditor. Whether these bonds could be freely exchanged on the open bond market should be agreed in advance by both parties. The principle of the bond (its value) should equal the share price of the typical value of the original stock. Any interest should ideally be set at a rate not too dissimilar to the typical dividends paid on the original stock. The principle and interest should not be linked to the share price or dividends received once the transition is announced or is about to begin, as this could artificially over or under value the business to the dismay of the workers or former owners respectively. Instead, such values should be based on the typical conditions witnessed prior to the announcement of the transition to worker ownership. The expiration of the bonds could occur at different times, so the firm is not required to repay the principle of every bond all at once.

So what becomes of the original owners during the transition period? If preferred, the workers could take an inclusive approach to transition, by declaring joint management with the original owners, with their influence receding over time. This of course will depend on who the original owners are. If they are individuals or a small group of shareholders who have been deeply integrated in the firm's day-to-day practices, this is likely to be more appropriate than in cases where shareholders have remained relatively distant from the company's operations. For firms with a multitude of shareholders, their elected board members could potentially become engaged with the process, as these individuals will likely have an intimate knowledge of the firm and will have previously been involved with the key decisions taken by the shareholders. Where a joint approach to management is chosen for the temporary transition period, the workers still hold ultimate control of the firm, and are able to prevent the type of asset stripping activities already mentioned. However, the original owners (or their representatives) still have a voice in the day-to-day managing of the firm, until they receive the full value of their shareholding and the debt is cleared. Although the original owners have joint responsibility of managing the firm, they do not have control over the distribution of the profits. Their advisory responsibilities are to ensure that the workers can be given bespoke guidance over the managing of the firm by those that have previously done so. It also benefits the existing owners, as quality guidance stemming from an abundance of experience will increase the likelihood of a successful transition, thereby protecting the value of future repayments. Alternatively, the workers may decide to manage the firm without the guidance of the original owners, relying instead on support from the DfED, specialist advisers, trade unions or some other kind of organisation.

Support from the Cooperative State

For transitioning firms with smaller profit margins, the central bank could enact a 'quantitative easing for the workers' program[100]. This would enable such firms to complete their transition process at a faster pace. Quantitative easing is a process whereby central banks electronically create money which is used to purchase financial assets such as bonds and shares. This policy was utilised in response to the Great Recession of 2008. The purpose of QE was to lower the financial returns on these instruments, to make physical investments more attractive compared to speculative investments, such as bonds and shares. For the purposes of a transition to worker ownership, the central bank, working alongside the DfED, should target state backed financing to particular firms in need of assistance. Ideally, these loans should be distributed through private sector banks and similar financial institutions, with a government guarantee to cover the losses of any loans which can no longer be repaid. Such losses would stem from the inevitable minority of companies who will cease trade during the transition period due to unrelated economic and financial factors.

Where a particularly large firm requires QE-backed support to finance a transition to employee ownership, the central bank could purchase shares held by the existing owners and transfer those shares to the workers in exchange for a debt obligation. This arrangement should be a cheaper option for the firm, as this would likely incur a lower rate of interest compared to any debt financing arranged privately with the previous company owners. Where the central bank does not purchase all tradable shares, the saving the company gains from the shares that have been purchased by the central bank will enable the firm to purchase any outstanding shares with greater ease. Alternatively, where shares have already been exchanged for bonds, the central bank could purchase these bonds from the previous company owners and then swap those bonds with the firm for a debt obligation with a lower rate of interest or perhaps a longer repayment period. This too will reduce the cost of transferring ownership, either by reducing debt interest or lengthening the repayment period to suit the financial situation of the firm in question. This approach will not be appropriate or practical for all companies undergoing the transition process, but it does give the cooperative state a means of targeting firms with an otherwise lengthy and costly transition period. If this policy is ever utilised, the central bank should be expected to maintain a stock of bonds or other debt instruments for a long period of time and should expect a lower overall return compared to other financial assets previously purchased using QE[101]. This should reflect the central bank's role as a facilitator in this process.

Evasion and Aversion

Not all business owners will be willing to accept the mandatory sale of their business to their workers. A minority may seek to evade or avoid this process. This could occur from the very beginning of the process. The first step of transition, as we have noted, is the creation of an employee board which will represent the workers during the transition period. Companies that fail to recognise or engage with their employee boards, or prohibit its creation altogether, should be penalised. The company owners could be threatened with judicial action, or in the worst cases see their property seized by the DfED which would then be donated to the workers. This would be the worst case scenario for the original owners, as they would see the transfer of ownership of their company to the workforce without receiving any remuneration. There could also be a bizarre situation where the workers do not wish to form and register an employee board, seeking to resist the transition to employee ownership. In this case, to avoid judicial repercussions, the company owners should form an employee board unilaterally, and appoint employees onto that board. Although appointed, the members of that board should still be democratically accountable to the remaining workforce, who are more likely to get involved once they see the process begin.

The next key step of the transition is the notification of all employing businesses to begin plans for the transition process. Each firm must then reply to the DfED with a plan accepted by the workforce which aims to deliver that process in the most appropriate fashion. The deadline for replying to the DfED with a proposal will again depend on the company and the complexity of the process, although for most firms one should not expect it to take longer than a year. The firm in question should then begin the actual process of transferring ownership very shortly after. Firms who cannot plan for this due to legitimate reasons should have the capability of applying for a temporary deferment, but this should only be the case for the most extraordinary cases. For those businesses who fail to prepare a plan, the DfED should step in and issue a plan on the company owner's behalf, in consultation with the workers. It is likely that an immediate transfer of ownership will take place, depriving the owners of all ownership and managerial responsibilities. As the DfED would set out a business case on the behalf of the original owners, it would be able to set a plan which is more favourable to the workers at the expense of the original owners. Again, this prospect should act as a coercive incentive against evading or avoiding the ownership transfer process. It is in the interest of both parties to ensure a collaborative and respectful partnership is established.

Another way for the original owners to disrupt worker ownership from being established and sustained would be to extract value from the business prior or during the transition process. Why would this occur? Although the firm is being sold to the workforce, either gradually or all at once, the original owners are likely to be remunerated for this sale over time, and are unlikely to receive the value of the company all at once. This may provoke the owners, who may wish to recoup the whole value of their investment immediately, to asset strip the firm and reinvest the proceeds elsewhere. This would leave the firm unable to effectively operate, potentially putting the entire future of the firm at risk. If this is attempted either before, during or after the transition process, it should be treated as a form of theft.

Whatever the firm loses from this practice must be regained. The first process, before the transition period has commenced, is to ensure that an employee board is established which has the necessary power to block or propose important company decisions. As such, asset stripping methods like this should not occur. If asset stripping occurs deliberately in the brief time before the board has been established, any income or capital lost by the firm should be calculated and the figure deducted from the total saleable value of the firm. Proceeds of the asset stripping could be seized by the DfED and repatriated to the firm. This should ensure that any asset stripping activities make the original business owners worse off rather than better off. The cooperative state should not just be on the lookout for asset stripping, but any kind of corporate raiding or tunnelling[102] that benefits the original owners at the expense of the worker-owners and the firm they now own and manage.

Managing the Transition on the Shop Floor

The workers need to be given adequate support to feel comfortable and confident with the transition process.

> At the time of buyout, employees in their new roles as owners can suffer from some of the same illusions about employee ownership as traditional economists do – such as the idea that every decision will have to be discussed by everybody. It takes leadership to make clear the practical rules.
>
> Erdal (2011:165)

Establishing an employee board, either unilaterally or in partnership with the company's original owners, is a key first step. This will give the whole workforce an opportunity to shape the transition process. It can give the most enthusiastic workers an opportunity to be elected onto the board, whilst those who are less keen to get involved can feel comfortable knowing that they will be consulted on the major issues but will not be involved in every decision. The board members will be given the opportunity to sit on the company's regular board of directors with voting powers related to the transition process and decisions which effect the future of the firm (during and after the transition process). For small businesses, where there may be one business owner/manager and a small handful of workers, the workers could elect one person to represent them, who will work alongside the business owner to develop the transition process. The firm may also decide to contract a consultant, or potentially even hire a new or existing employee to take direct charge of the transition process, what we could call a 'transition officer'. This individual would be responsible for engaging with both the existing owners and the employee board to ensure that the practical aspects of the transition are managed effectively. This means developing a timeframe, arranging the important legal agreements and taking that leadership role Erdal (2011) mentioned earlier. They would be responsible for drafting the 'practical rules' in which worker-owners would conduct themselves post-transition. This could take the shape of a company constitution, or a code of social statutes as Gamson and Levin (1984:227) have advocated. In the eyes of both parties, this individual (or team, for larger companies) should appear to be as neutral as practically possible. It is important that both parties are happy with the end result. As the power dynamics between the staff and original owners starts to alter, having a transition officer can be essential to ensuring the promise of worker ownership becomes a practical and effective reality.

Cornforth (1983:177) notes how workers in transition worker cooperatives often find it difficult to adapt into their new roles when pre-existing hierarchies remain in place. This is why the employee board is so important, as it establishes an immediate mechanism which challenges the total authority of the business owners. The workers themselves have the ability to choose which ownership transfer method is taken, it is then up to the firm's management or transition officer to develop a plan for transferring ownership with this taken into account, information which is then passed onto the DfED. These processes of collaboration and negotiation will prepare the employees for worker ownership in the long run, when debates and negotiations between the worker-owners arise in future. There is a potential role for trade unions to embrace here, assisting the workers with establishing an employee board and highlighting the most appropriate methods of transition. Of course, if unions were to take up this offer, they must represent all of the workers, not just those with union membership. The process of transition needs to be ran as smoothly as possible for all parties involved. The following suggestions for a transition process are outlined in the Nuttall Review, it suggests to:

- involve all concerned, as much as possible, perhaps through a joint working party;
- changes can make people anxious, and so employee ownership should be kept as simple as practicable and agreed with all concerned;
- prepare the way carefully with briefings to the owners, employees and management;
- document the proposals and, if possible, start with a trial initiative; and

- make arrangements for maintenance, monitoring and evaluation.

Nuttall (2012:44)

These points were discussed in relation to a non-mandatory transition, but all of these points remain relevant. Ensuring the transition process simple and accountable is paramount, as it provides all employees an opportunity to get involved and keep up to date. Maintenance, monitoring and evaluation is also imperative, as it allows issues to be weeded out and successes to be maintained. Although business management can eventually be introduced into the education system, training courses need to be introduced across the board for existing workers, preferably during the transition stage, so workers are equipped with the necessary skills for when they finally take control of the enterprise. Although we have already discussed how cooperative management should be included within the education system, there needs to be mechanisms in place for workers of conventional firms during this transition phase. Bringing them up to speed is essential if worker ownership is to succeed over the long run.

Movements of Capital

Time will not stand still during the transition process, all else will not stay equal. The firms in question must remain competitive, both domestically and internationally. This means new investment mechanisms must be established as soon as the transition period begins, to ensure firms have the means of remaining competitive in their respective markets. As outlined in the manifesto, a reformed bond market must be established, not just for those using bonds as a means of transition, but for those seeking to use bonds as a long term method of investment. As outlined in Chapter 7, there should be no real difference in the supply and demand of investment capital for a capitalist or cooperative economy. The same should be true during the transition from the former to the latter. The sudden intention to change the ownership of the vast majority of companies may temporarily spook investors, as the economy adjusts to a new unprecedented economic model. Although an investor may earn a lower percentage of the returns in a worker-owned firm to begin with, over the longer run they could potentially earn a higher income from the firm as the workers boost productivity, efficiency and innovation, increasing the incomes for both workers and investors. With that being said, the cooperative state must always be prepared for when the business cycle induces the next recession and investment dries up.

The difference [in investment] may be very small once investors have become accustomed to the new system, although during the period of transition, before workers' co-operatives had demonstrated that they have the same interest in appointing and the same capacity to recruit professional management which conventional enterprises have, suspicion of the new enterprises may create a larger temporary confidence gap.

Jay (1977:19)

A 'credit crunch' should not emerge if rational choices are made. What occurs in reality however, may be something far from the usual practice of reason. Investors could decide to transfer their capital to another country, depriving the economy of necessary investment. In this instance, the cooperative state should move to establish regional cooperative banks, with the capacity to facilitate small and large investments. An injection of 'quantitative easing for the workers' could be used to make up the shortfall of out-flowing capital and to provide 'loanable' funds for these new banks. Loans must be given on the rightful assumption that they can be paid back – these banks must not be used to prop-up or subsidise firms that cannot obtain investment through market providers. Once the transition has transpired and confidence has been restored, these regional banks can become self-sufficient without state funds, possibly based on the Italian model discussed in Chapter 7.

It should soon become apparent, from the beginning of the transition period, that investors are now guaranteed a more stable return, albeit without claims to ownership or the sovereignty to manage the firm. Long term investment with stable returns would appear to be in stark contrast to the more 'fast and loose' style of investing we have seen in recent times. The benefits derived effect both the firm and the investor.

As this change proceeded, owners of capital would gradually find it to their advantage, instead of maintaining the struggle of the old system with work-people of only the worst description, to lend their capital to the associations; to do this at a diminishing rate of interest, and at last, perhaps, even to exchange their capital for terminable annuities. In this or some such mode, the existing accumulations of capital might honestly, and by a kind of spontaneous process, become in the end the joint property of all who participate in their productive employment

Mill (1848:203)

For firms in the process of completing their transition process – particularly for those using bonds to replace former shares – investors may be reluctant to invest in a company with existing debts to the former owners. This could put such firms at a disadvantage over their competitors, who can receive the necessary investment to innovate and capture a greater share of the market. If such a situation were to unfold, this too would be a justification for setting up regional cooperative banks to lend over a longer periods where transition debts do not inhibit further investments to innovate. For example, the repayment process for these loans could begin once the ownership transition process has been completed. These too must be distributed according to the financial viability of the investment being considered. Business grants could be offered for as long as they are fiscally sustainable to the cooperative state and ensure that the firm being invested in has an adequate business case. All of these measures are built to ensure companies have the necessary investment capital required to remain competitive and sustainable throughout this period and beyond.

International Relations

Geopolitical pressures have a significant part to play in national economic affairs. A cooperative state embarking on a transition of this scale should expect to receive some form of political response from foreign governments, both supportive and critical. There could well be pressure put upon the cooperative state to allow the entry of foreign firms to establish themselves using the conventional investor-owned model. This could come from foreign governments, international institutions and creditors, or some other influential actor. There are multiple reasons why this may be the case. Foreign nations may be keen for their domestic companies to establish or sustain themselves in the cooperative economy. These companies may be owned by the foreign government or perhaps privately owned but supported by the foreign government for political reasons. There are also ideological reasons. A successfully functioning cooperative economy may put pressure on other governments to follow suit. For 'pro-business' governments of capitalist economies, this pressure to adopt worker ownership will be at odds with those who have a stake in the status quo. There is an interest in disproving the benefits of worker ownership for those who have something to lose from it. Using foreign policy and economic policy to artificially reduce the attractiveness of worker ownership could therefore be seen as a legitimate response by such actors.

The international relations of a cooperative state will depend on which country and how many countries decide to switch to the cooperative model. Throughout this research we have assumed that our hypothetical cooperative state will probably be a developed Western economy such as the UK. Smaller perhaps less developed countries may find it more difficult to sustain a cooperative economy in a world of influential corporate giants and oligarchs. Larger nations like the UK would face less pressure due to its economic weight and global influence. Whichever nation seeks to transition to worker ownership, it must be prepared to defend its principles and counter any potential foreign meddling. However, protection of one's distinct and unique economic model is no excuse for becoming insular and protectionist. A cooperative economy needs to be a globalised economy. As we have seen before, a cooperative economy must remain competitive if it is to sustain itself – this means being open and internationalist. Any cooperative state must be prepared to uphold the tenets and foundations of its economic model, especially from those with an ulterior motive to discredit or dismantle it. This means using its own foreign and economic policy to deter and counter any unjust and perverse measures foreign actors may take. Such meddling is much less likely to occur when this commitment to deter and counter is made clear and definitive from the outset.

The End of Transition

Although the beginning of each firm's transition will start at roughly the same time, the completion of the process will be different for every firm. It must also be understood that not every single firm will make it through this process. Those which were unprofitable to begin with may not recover, even once the workforce has had the opportunity to turn things around. For others, the process of transition itself may be enough to seal the fate of the firm, for example it could uncover structural weaknesses of the enterprise that were unbeknown beforehand. Firms without adequate support may not get through the process in one piece, workers may disagree, or the negotiations between workers and company owners may break down to the point where productions ceases. Although it is the primary purpose of the DfED to prevent this, it will not be prevented in each and every case. No transition is ever completely smooth and faultless. Lessons must be learnt when things go wrong, and pragmatic responses to unforeseen complications must be delivered effectively.

The purpose of the DfED must change once the transition period has been completed by the majority of firms. Its purpose must now be to sustain the new worker-owned firms and encourage the birth of new worker-owned firms moving forward. This means preventing instances where neocapitalist practices emerge and ensuring all firms have access to quality advice to the new and emerging issues they will inevitably face. Developing and encouraging the best democratic practices will help to ensure that the employees of all firms have the means of making their voices heard. As we have seen throughout this study, the worker-owned firms with the best mechanisms for employee engagement see the best results. The DfED must also observe how these firms develop over time, the unforeseen challenges they may face, the unique successes of the few that could be replicated by the many. New forms of procuring investment may be made available, new forms of democratic management, new ways of deliberating between employees. Having a known and neutral government department with a primary purpose in these matters will ensure the cooperative mould remains sustainable.

The opponents of worker ownership will no doubt gain momentum and popularity from time to time, especially at moments when the cooperative economy enters recession, as all economies do, or faces some other economic challenge. If opposition stems from a legitimate reason, change should indeed follow. No economic model lasts forever. However, if the opponents come to challenge worker ownership in order to reinstall investor-capitalist ownership and the dual-contradiction, this must be seen as a violation on par with those willing to strip us of our political freedoms and democracy. Economic democracy must be allowed to flourish. It is a form of democracy with practical relevant to the day-to-day lives of the working majority and will have a material impact on all those who engage with it. It is a principle that must be fought for, a principle that must be championed, nurtured and safeguarded.

Conclusion

The purpose of this study has been to reveal the capability of worker ownership to form the basis of a new economic system. This has been possible thanks to a vast collection of books and academic papers that have explored certain elements of worker ownership in one form or another. Indeed, little effort has been taken, up until now, to bring together all of this work to build a radical argument such as this. There have always been those who have understood worker ownership to be a plausible alternative to conventional capitalism, but there has never been a concerted effort to build a reasoned justification and method of bringing that alternative to life. Radical economic ideas come in and out of fashion as the wider economic climate changes, whilst others have been consigned to the dustbin of history. Economics seems to have lost a sense of radicalism that it enjoyed so prevalently in the previous century. Indeed, the 'dismal science' has never been so dismal. This needs to be corrected. There is clearly a demand for new ideas to resolve the fundamental economic challenges of our time, including old ideas which have never been truly explored and experimented. Accepting the status quo is reckless, it ignores the contradictions and limitations of the present system and ignores the possibility of a better alternative. Worker ownership, as we have seen, can be that better alternative.

Main Findings

The Dual-Contradiction Lives On

Capitalism is built on the assumption that workers are only employed if they create/enable more money for the business owner than what the business owner pays that worker. This inequality cannot be justified, whether we use the radical reasoning of Marx or the free market reasoning of the neoliberals. This inequality, by its very nature, ensures that work is not linked to reward. Workers are paid a fixed wage regardless of the effort they apply into their work. The dual-contradiction guarantees lower household incomes, lower productivity and lower employee welfare.

Most economic inequalities stem, in one way or another, from the dual-contradiction and its consequences. Solving it should be the ambition of any individual genuinely seeking to reverse the heightening levels of inequality we are currently witnessing. It is no surprise that as of 2017, "the lower half of global adults collectively owns less than 1% of global wealth, while the richest 10% of adults own 88% of all wealth and the top 1% account for half of all global assets." (Credit Suisse, 2017:11). If inequality is left to widen out of control, significant social and political disruption is likely to follow suit. Unless action is taken now we risk entering a new Belle Époque era, where inequality continues to widen up until the point where it can no longer be tolerated by the poorest. If left unchallenged, a period of peace and injustice is quickly superseded by a period of anguish and chaos. It has not been the purpose of this work to predict the future, nor give a harrowing interpretation of the injustices of today. There is plenty of literature exploring these subjects. Instead, our purpose has been one of hope and optimism, for an alternative that can begin to turn the tide back in the favour of those who produce wealth, rather than those who currently earn and own it.

Worker Ownership Works

Employee-owned firms already exist in the niches, spaces and margins of many capitalist economies. There is no denying that this form of business model can operate effectively and sustainably in a market economy. Further still, wherever they do operate, they function to boost household income, boost productivity and boost employee wellbeing. When employees own a share of the company they work for, they work more efficiently, more productivity, they bring forward a level of commitment not otherwise seen. This brings us to the principles we have developed throughout this work, which give a rational explanation of why worker-owned firms succeed and why they are superior to the conventional capitalist firm:

- The Incentive Dynamic: Workers need employment to maintain subsistence. With worker ownership there is a coercive incentive for workers to remain employed, a remunerative incentive to apply as much effort as possible to maximise income and a moral incentive to do right by their co-workers.
- The Market Dynamic: Under a market system, if there is demand for a particular commodity, a worker-owned enterprise will be incentivised to supply that demand. This allows the incentive dynamic to be realised.
- The Principal Balance: In order for that firm to continue supplying that demand, it must be competitive and disciplined in that particular marketplace. There needs to be a balance between market competitiveness and worker satisfaction/income.

Another principle which has featured throughout this work is the 'profit principle', the idea that worker-owned firms seek to maximise income per head rather than seeking to maximise total profit. As was revealed in Chapter 8, empirical studies have shown that creating new jobs and retaining existing employment is equally as important as maximising income per head. This finding conforms to the incentive dynamic, where both maximising income and maintaining employment are equally as crucial. When combining all of these principles, it reveals a theoretical explanation of why worker-owned firms can function effectively.

Labour, capital and output markets function slightly differently under worker ownership, but the end result should not be too dissimilar to what we find in conventional capitalist economies. The supply of workers should still meet demand. The supply of investment capital should still meet demand. The supply of output (goods and services) should still meet demand. Although ownership and control ultimately lies with the workers, the way in which worker ownership functions can differ greatly. Ownership can be held in a trust or held directly by individual workers. The way the firm is managed can be done so using direct democracy, most suitable for smaller firms, or through elected representatives, which is more appropriate for firms with a larger workforce. The worker ownership model is not static and inflexible, there is scope for experimentation and a democratic means of bringing about change when it is desired.

The Long Wait to Nowhere

Worker ownership will not transcend the niches, spaces and margins of capitalist economies to become the mainstream without the necessary mould to support it. The cooperative movement is founded on the principle that change should be bottom-up rather than top-down. This is commendable, but the necessary laws, institutions and support structures which cooperatives and worker-owned firms more generally rely upon require top-down assistance. An interstitial approach to cooperative development is insufficient, it requires a ruptural change from the state – a cooperative state.

Worker-owned firms have always been on the margins of society. We have seen spouts of worker ownership at particular points in time, only to be followed by a withering away of existing firms and a drought of new firms to take their place. The more these cycles have occurred the more lessons have been learnt. Indeed, it would not be controversial to conclude that there has never been a better time to start (or transition to) a worker-owned firm. Tailor-made services are emerging that can provide the sector with the necessary support, guidance and in some instances, capital investment. This is encouraging, but not sufficient. The long wait for worker ownership to become the economic mainstream could be a long wait to nowhere, especially if we descend into another trough of degeneration, underinvestment and a low growth of start-ups. Now is the opportunity to seize the moment and propel the worker ownership model into the mainstream, ending the perpetual peak and trough process we have observed historically. If achieved, this will seal the fate of the dual-contradiction once and for all.

Another World is Possible

Building a cooperative economy is one small step on the journey to reclaiming the wealth we all collectively create. A world where half of all wealth is owned by the richest 1 per cent is neither desirable nor stable. By resolving the inequalities of the workplace, we can begin to tackle other inequalities, both directly and indirectly. It is no surprise that worker ownership tends to lead to healthier and happier workers. We should also expect the workers of a cooperative economy to become more politically engaged. If democratic decision making is commonplace in the world of work, it is more likely that those workers will participate in the political process. Having a stake in the company you work for reduces the sense of injustice many workers of capitalist firms feel on a daily basis. Happier, more productive and more engaged workers will reduce social tensions rather than provoke them. This is essential at a time where our societies face great challenges ahead of us, from climate change, biodiversity loss and the unknown effects of technological advancements. Facing up to these challenges with high levels of inequality, a disengaged electorate and a feeling of injustice among the masses will not bode well. Worker ownership is no panacea, nor will it lead us to some kind of demo-utopia. What it can achieve is a strengthening of our economies and societies, preparing them for the next great struggles of our time. Another world is possible.

---

[99] A targeted ruptural approach to transition should focus on the core reforms of the cooperative manifesto. To avoid further short-term disruption, the additional reforms should be given a longer term priority, perhaps once the transition phase has concluded.

[100] In the UK, this could be used to replace the conventional QE program delivered by the Bank of England since 2009.

[101] This being largely irrelevant as the primary purpose of the QE program was not to generate an income but instead to lower interest rates and spur private sector investment

[102] This is the illegitimate transfer of assets and profits out of a firm for the benefit of those who control them.

Bibliography

Alessandrini, M. and Messori, M. (2013) 'Workers' Effort: A Comparison Between Capitalist and Cooperative Firms', Working Paper, *LUISS Guido Carli / Department of Political Science*, 2013:2.

Alperovitz, G. (2005) *America Beyond Capitalism: Reclaiming our Wealth, our Liberty, and our Democracy.* Hoboken, NJ: John Wiley & Sons, Inc.

Atkinson, A. B. (2015) *Inequality: What Can Be Done?* London: Harvard University Press.

BBC News. (2011) John Lewis to offer customers investment bond. Available at: http://www.bbc.co.uk/news/business-12659718

Bebchuk, L. and Fried, J. (2004) *Pay without Performance: The Unfulfilled Promise of Executive Compensation.* London: Harvard University Press.

BIS (2011) *A Guide to Mutual Ownership Models.* Available at: https://www.gov.uk/government/uploads/system/uploads/attachment_data/file/31678/11-1401-guide-mutual-ownership-models.pdf

Bonin, J. P., Jones, D. C. and Putterman, L. (1993) 'Theoretical and Empirical Studies or Produce Cooperatives: Will Ever the Twain Meet?, *Journal of Economic Literature*, Vol. 31:3, pp. 1290-1320.

Burdín, G. and Dean, A. (2009) 'New evidence on wages and employment in worker cooperatives compared with capitalist firms', *Journal of Comparative Economics*, 37, pp. 517-533.

Burns, P. (2006). *Good Business: The Employee Ownership Experience.* Employee Ownership Association. Available at: http://employeeownership.co.uk/wp-content/uploads/Good_Business___The_employee_ownership_experience.pdf

Callahan, D. (2004). *The Cheating Culture: Why More Americans are Doing Wrong to Get Ahead.* Orlando, FL: Harcourt.

Clayre, A. (1980) *The Political Economy of Co-operation and Participation: A Third Sector.* New York: Oxford University Press.

Cole. G. D. H. (1944) *A Century of Co-operation.* Oxford: George Allen & Unwin Ltd.

Cornforth, C. (1983) 'Some Factors Affecting the Success or Failure of Worker Co-operatives: A Review of Empirical Research in the United Kingdom', *Economic and Industrial Democracy*, 4:2, pp. 163-90.

Credit Suisse (2017) *Global Wealth Report 2017.* Available at: http://publications.credit-suisse.com/tasks/render/file/index.cfm?fileid=12DFFD63-07D1-EC63-A3D5F67356880EF3

Dalkir, K. (2005) *Knowledge Management in Theory and Practise*. Burlington, MA: Elsevier Butterworth–Heinemann.

Davies, W. (2011). *All of Our Business: Why Britain needs more private sector employee ownership*. Employee Ownership Association. Available at: http://employeeownership.co.uk/wp-content/uploads/All-Our-Business.pdf

Dickstein, C. (1991) 'The Promise and Problems of Worker Cooperatives: A Survey Article', *Journal of Planning Literature*, 6:1, pp. 16-33.

Doucouliagos, C. (1995) 'Worker Participation and Productivity in Labor-Managed and Participatory Capitalist Firms: A Meta-Analysis', *Industrial and Labor Relations Review*, 49:1, pp. 58-77.

Drèze, J. H. (1976) 'Some Theory of Labor Management and Participation', *Econometrica*, 44:6, pp. 1125-1139.

Einstein, A. (1949) 'Why Socialism?', *Monthly Review*, Issue. 1.

Elster, J. (1989) 'From Here to There; or, If Cooperative Ownership Is So Desirable, Why are There So Few Cooperatives?', *Social Philosophy and Policy*, 6:2, pp. 93-111.

Erdal, D. (2011) *Beyond the Corporation: Humanity Working*. London: The Bodley Head.

Erdal, D. (2012) 'Employee Ownership as a Form of Economic Democracy', Teorija in Praksa, 49:6, pp. 935-951.

Erdal, D. (2014) 'Employee Ownership and Health: an Initial Study', in Novkovic, S. and Webb, T. (2014) *Co-operatives in a Post-Growth Era: Creating Co-operative Economics*. London: Zed Books.

Fairbairn, B. (1994) *The Meaning of Rochdale: The Rochdale Pioneers and the Co-operative Principles*. Available at: https://ideas.repec.org/p/ags/uscoop/31778.html

Fakhfakh, F., Pérotin, V. and Gago, M. (2011) 'Productivity, Capital and Labor in Labor-Managed and Conventional Firms', Working Paper, *Travail, Emploi et Politiques Publiques*, 2011:8.

Fanning, C. M. and McCarthy, T. (1986) 'A survey of economic hypotheses concerning the nonviability of labour-directed firms in capitalist economies', Chapter 1, in Jansson, S. and Hellmark, A-B. *Labour-Owned Firms and Workers' Cooperatives*. Aldershot: Gower Publishing.

Flecha, R. and Ngai, P. (2014) 'The challenge for Mondragon: Searching for the cooperative values in times of internationalization', *Organization*, 21:5, pp. 666-682.

Gamson, Z. and Levin, H. (1984) 'Obstacles to the survival of democratic workplaces', Chapter 9, in Jackall, R. and Levin, H. *Worker Cooperatives in America*. London: University of California Press.

George, D. (2007) 'Workers' Savings and the Right to Manage', *Journal of Economic Surveys*, 21:3, pp. 534-552.

Harrison, J. F. C. (1969) *Robert Owen and the Owenites in Britain and America*. London: Routledge and Kegan Paul Ltd.

Harvey, D. (2014) *Seventeen Contradictions and the End of Capitalism*. London: Profile Books.

Hayek, F. A. (1944) *The Road to Serfdom*. London: Routledge.

Heras-Saizarbitoria, I. (2014) 'The ties that bind? Exploring the basic principles of worker-owned organizations in practice', *Organization*, 21:5, pp. 645-665.

Holyoake, G. J. (1875-9) *The History of Co-operation*. London: T. Fisher Unwin.

Ireland, N. J. and Law, P. J. (1982) *The Economic of Labour-Managed Enterprises*. London: Croom Helm.

Jay, P. (1977) 'A Co-operative Economy: The Workers' Co-operative Economy', Chapter 2, in Clayre, A. (1980) *The Political Economy of Co-operation and Participation: A Third Sector*. New York: Oxford University Press.

Jay, P. (1980) 'Summing Up: Peter Jay's Reply', Chapter 15, in Clayre, A. *The Political Economy of Co-operation and Participation: A Third Sector*. New York: Oxford University Press.

Jones, D. and Marinescu, I. (2018) 'The Labor Market Impacts of Universal and Permanent Cash Transfers: Evidence from the Alaska Permanent Fund', *Working Paper, NBER Working Paper No. 24312*.

Jossa, B. (2005) 'Marx, Marxism and the cooperative movement', *Cambridge Journal of Economics*, 29:1, pp. 3-18.

Jossa, B. (2015) 'A Few Reflections on the Reasons Why Cooperative Firms Have Failed to Gain a Firm Foothold', *Open Journal of Business and Management*, 3:3, pp. 265-280.

Kasmir, S. (1996) *The Myth of Mondragon: Cooperatives, Politics and Working-Class Life in a Basque Town*. Albany, NY: State University of New York Press.

Keynes, J. M. (1930) 'Economic Prospects for our Grandchildren', in Keynes, J. M. (1932) *Essays in Persuasion*. New York: Harcourt Brace. pp 358-373.

Laffont, J. J. and Martimort, D. (2001) *The Theory of Incentives: The Principle-Agent Model*. Princeton, NJ: Princeton University Press.

Lampel, J., Bhalla, A. and Jha, P. (2010) *Model Growth: Do employee-owned businesses deliver sustainable performance?* Project Report. Employee Ownership Association.

Lawrence, M. and Mason, N. (2017) *Capital Gains: Broadening company ownership in the UK economy*. (Policy paper). IPPR Commission on Economic Justice.

McCain, R. A. (1977) 'On the Optimum Financial Environment for Worker Cooperatives', *Zeitschrift für Nationalökonomie*, 37:3-4, pp. 355-384.

Mason, P. (2015) *PostCapitalism: A Guide to our Future.* London: Allen Lane.

Marshall, A. (1890) *Principles of Economics.* (1920 8th end.). London: Macmillan and Co.

Marx, K. (1847) *The Poverty of Philosophy.* (marxists.org edn.) Moscow: International Publishers.

Marx, K. (1857-61) *Grundrisse.* (1973 Penguin edn.). London: Pelican Books.

Marx, K. (1867) *Capital: A Critique of Political Economy, Volume I.* (1990 Penguin edn.). London: Pelican Books.

Marx, K. (1875) *Critique of the Gotha Programme.* (marxists.org edn.) Moscow: Progress Publishers.

Marx, K. (1894) *Capital: A Critique of Political Economy, Volume III.* (marxists.org edn.) New York: International Publishers.

Mayfield, C., Purnell, J. and Davies, W. (2012) ' Why aren't there more companies like John Lewis? The difficulties of breaking the stranglehold of shareholder capitalism', *Public Policy Research*, 18:4, pp. 216-221.

Meade, J. (1980) 'Labour Co-operatives, Participation, and Value-Added Sharing', Chapter 6, in Clayre, A. *The Political Economy of Co-operation and Participation: A Third Sector.* New York: Oxford University Press.

Mellor, M., Hannah, J. and Stirling, J. (1988) *Workers Cooperatives in Theory and Practise.* Milton Keynes: Open University Press.

Menger, C. (1871) *Principles of Economics.* (1976 Ludwig von Mises Institute edn.). Auburn: Ludwig von Mises Institute.

Mill, J. S. (1848) *Principles of Political Economy: With Some of Their Applications to Social Philosophy.* (2004 Hackett edn.). London: John Parker.

Miyazaki, H. and Neary, H. M. (1983) 'The Illyrian Firm Revisited', *The Bell Journal of Economics*, 14:1, pp. 259-270.

Morris, D. (1992) *The Mondragon System: Cooperation at Work.* Institute for Local Self-Reliance.

Nuttall, G. (2012) *Sharing Success: The Nuttall Review of Employee Ownership.* London: Department for Business, Innovation and Skills.

Oakeshott, R. (1980) 'A Co-operative Sector in a Mixed Economy: Piecemeal', Chapter 3, in Clayre, A. *The Political Economy of Co-operation and Participation: A Third Sector.* New York: Oxford University Press.

Pencavel, J. (2012) 'Worker Cooperatives and Democratic Governance', *Stanford Institute for Economic Policy Research*, Discussion Paper No. 12-003.

Pencavel, J., Pistaferri, L. and Schivardi, F. (2006) 'Wages, Employment, and Capital in Capitalist and Worker-Owned Firms', *Industrial and Labor Relations Review*, 60:1, pp. 23-44.

Pérotin, V. (2012) 'The performance of worker cooperatives', Chapter 8, in Battilani, P. and Schroeter, H. (2012) *The Cooperative Business Movement, 1950 to the Present.* New York: Cambridge University Press.

Pérotin, V. (2016) *What do we really know about worker co-operatives?* Co-operatives UK. Available at: https://www.uk.coop/sites/default/files/uploads/attachments/worker_co-op_report.pdf

Piketty, T. (2014) *Capital in the Twenty-First Century.* London: Harvard University Press.

Polanyi, Karl. (1944) *The Great Transformation: The Political and Economic Origins of Our Time.* Boston: Beacon Press.

Raworth, K. (2017) *Doughnut Economics: Seven Ways to Think Like a 21st-Century Economist.* London: Random House.

Ricardo, D. (1817) *On the Principles of Political Economy and Taxation.* London: John Murray.

Roberts, C. and Lawrence, M. (2017) *Wealth in the twenty-first century: Inequalities and drivers.* (Discussion paper). IPPR Commission on Economic Justice.

Standing, G. (2011) *The Precariat: A New Dangerous Class.* London: Bloomsbury Academic.

Smith, A. (1776) *The Wealth of Nations.* (2007 MetaLibri edn.). London: W. Strahan and T. Cadell.

Smith, S. C. (1984) 'Does employment matter to the labour-managed firm? Some theory and an empirical illustration', *Economic Analysis and Workers' Management*, 4:18, pp. 303-318.

Smith, S. C. (1994) 'Innovation and market strategy in Italian industrial cooperatives: Econometric evidence on organizational comparative advantage', *Journal of Economic Behavior and Organisation*, 23, pp. 303-320.

Smith, S. C. and Rothbaum, J. (2013) 'Cooperatives in a Global Economy: Key Economic Issues, Recent Trends, and Potential for Development', *Policy Paper No. 68.* Bonn: IZA (Institute for the Study of Labor).

Stiglitz, J. (2012) *The Price of Inequality: How Today's Divided Society Endangers Our Future.* New York: W.W. Norton & Company.

Summers, J., Timming, A. and Erdal, D. (2014) *Scotland's Economic Future Post-2014: Submission from Strengthening Democracy Programme.* Written submission for 'Scotland's Economic Future Post-2014 Inquiry'.

The Ownership Effect (2018) *The Ownership Dividend: The Economic Case for Employee Ownership*. London: LID Publishing

Thornley, J. (1981) *Workers' Co-operatives: Jobs and Dreams*. London: Heinemann Educational Books.

Tortia, E. C. (2007) 'Self-financing in Labor-managed Firms (LMFs): Individual Capital Accounts and Bonds', *Advances in the Economic Analysis of Participatory & Labor-Managed Firms*, 10, pp. 233-261.

Van Lerven, F., Hodgson, G. and Dyson, B. (2015) *Would there be enough credit in a sovereign money system?* London: Positive Money.

Vanek, J. (1969) 'Decentralization Under Workers' Management: A Theoretical Appraisal', Chapter 23, in Vanek, J. (1975) *Self-Management: Economic Liberation of Man*. Harmondsworth: Penguin Books.

Vanek, J. (1970) *The General Theory of Labour-Managed Market Economies*. London: Cornell University Press.

Vanek, J. (1971) *The Participatory Economy: An Evolutionary Hypothesis and a Strategy for Development*. London: Cornell University Press.

Vanek, J. (1975) *Self-Management: Economic Liberation of Man*. Harmondsworth: Penguin Books.

Vanek, J. (1977) *The Labor-Managed Economy: Essays*. London: Cornell University Press.

Voltaire, F. M. A. (1759) *Candide*. (1998 Electronic Scholarly Publishing Project edn.). Available at: http://www.esp.org/books/voltaire/candide.pdf

Webb, T. and Cheney, G. (2014) 'Worker-owned-and-governed co-operatives and the wider co-operative movement: Challenges and opportunities within and beyond the global economic crisis', Chapter 5, in Parker, M., Cheney, G., Fournier, V. and Land, C. *The Routledge Companion to Alternative Organization*. Abingdon: Routledge.

Westenholz, A. (1986) 'Democratic management and efficiency', Chapter 6, in Jansson, S. and Hellmark, A-B. *Labor-Owned Firms and Workers' Cooperatives*. Aldershot: Gower Publishing.

Wilkinson, R. and Pickett, K. (2009) *The Spirit Level: Why Greater Equality Makes Societies Stronger*. New York: Bloomsbury Press.

Wolff, R. (2012) *Democracy at Work: A Cure for Capitalism*. Chicago: Haymarket Books.

Wright, E. O. (2010) *Envisioning Real Utopia's*. London: Verso.